U2

SONGS + EXPERIENCE

THIS IS A CARLTON BOOK

Published by Carlton Books Ltd
20 Mortimer Street
London W1T 3JW

ISBN 978-1-78739-089-8

Editorial Director: Roland Hall
Editorial: Malcolm Croft, George Goodall
Art Editor: Russell Knowles
Design: Emma Wicks
Production: Yael Steinitz
Picture Research: Steve Behan

A CIP catalogue for this book is available from the British Library

Printed in Dubai

10 9 8 7 6 5 4 3 2 1

Some of the Material in this book was published as *Into the Heart* and *U2 Stories Behind the Songs*

ACKNOWLEDGEMENTS

Dedicated to Bill Graham, 1951–1996.

For this new book – a reinvention of *Into The Heart: The Stories Behind The Songs of U2* – the publishers, Carlton Books, proposed adding into the mix the text and illustrations from Brian Boyd's *U2 Experience*. It was a great idea, bringing Brian's pen pictures of the individual members of the band, and a whole lot more besides – along with lots of fresh photographs and brand-new material from your truly – into what I hope will be a tome that U2 fans will love and cherish...

It's hard to believe, but it is now almost 40 years since I first met Bono, Adam, Larry and The Edge, and they have never been less than utterly courteous and genuinely helpful and supportive in all our many encounters over that frighteningly long period. This book might have happened without their co-operation, but I certainly wouldn't want to have read it! Thank you.

A lot has been written about U2, some of it very good.

Researching early editions of this book, the insights to be gleaned from John Waters' *Race of Angels - The Genesis of U2*, Bill Flanagan's *U2 At The End Of The World* and Brian Eno's *A Year With Swollen Appendices* were particularly valuable. Carter Alan's *U2 Wide Awake in America* and Dave Bowler and Bryan Dray's *U2: A Conspiracy of Hope* were very useful sources of reference and information. Pimm Jal de la Parra's exhaustive *U2 Live: A Concert Documentary* is a remarkable labour of love! As is *U2: A Diary* by Matt McGee. And then, of course, there is *U2 On U2*, by U2 and Neil McCormick, a massive tome that tells the band's own story in brilliant documentary form.

Other reference points included Pete Williams and Steve Turner's *U2: Rattle And Hum*; *U2: The Rolling Stone Files* edited by Elysa Gartner; *The Penguin Book of Rock 'n' Roll Writing*, edited by Clinton Heylin; *The Unforgettable Fire* by Eamon Dunphy; *Faraway, So Close*, by B.P. Fallon; *The Greenpeace Book of The Nuclear Age*, edited by John May; *Cultural Icons* by James Patza; *Bono On Bono: Conversations With Michka Assayas*; a variety of interviews in newspapers and magazines, including producer Jolyon Thomas' intriguing natter with Murray Stassen of Audio Media International; and numerous editions of *Propaganda*, the U2 fan magazine, and U2 Collectormania. I don't think I have taken any undue liberties with any of this material but if I have – sorry!

Inevitably, I plundered the Hot Press files and in particular the material gathered in *The U2 File*, *U2: Three Chords* and *The Truth and U2: Northside Story* (books for which I also have to take final responsibility). Finally, in terms of critical writing about U2, there is still, I think, nothing to match Bill Graham's superb, early *The Complete Guide to The Music of U2*. Its existence made my job more difficult because so much of what Bill wrote hit the bullseye.

Very special thanks to agent-supreme, Marianne Gunn O'Connor, and to Kieran Kelly. A huge thanks also to Olaf Tyaransen, who undertook so much of the preparatory hard labour, on my behalf, for the original editions of this book. Others who helped enormously at different stages, were Ali Hewson (who loaned me her husband!), Gavin Friday, Nadine King, Candida Bottaci, Regine Moylett, Brídín Murphy Mitchell, Catriona Garde, Lindsey Holmes, Deirdre Crookes, Martin Wroe, Sebastian Clayton, Brian Celler, Paul McGuinness, Joe O'Herlihy, Steve Iredale, Flood, Neil Storey, Guggi, Dermot Stokes, Neil McCormick, Colm Henry, Steve Lillywhite, Howie B, Daniel Lanois, Mark Crossingham, David Harris and Dave Fanning. Special nods too to Matt McGee and everyone @ atu2.com, Gina Cloe, Annelies de Haan, Caroline van Oosten de Boer, Lars Nylin, Erik Timmerman, U2ft.com, U2interference.com, U2start.com, dreamoutloudfilm.com and David Barry.

At Hot Press, along the road, Liam Mackey, Stuart Clark, Róisín Dwyer, Valentina Magli, Colette Rooney, Ross Fitzsimons, Pat Carty, Mette Borgstrom, Chris Hackney, Paula Nolan and Mark Hogan helped greatly. Thanks a million to all – and to the current, fantastically hard-working, Hot Press crew. As MacPhisto might say, 'I'm baaaaaack'. My latest editor at Carlton Books, Roland Hall, was a model of patience throughout what must have been a strange trip through someone else's wires.

Finally, I want to salute Máirín Sheehy, Duan Stokes (along with Hilary Hughes and their lovely children, Siena and Aoibhe) and Rowan Stokes, who have supported me wonderfully down all the days. I love you.

ALSO BY THE AUTHOR

– *Philip Lynott: Still In Love With You* (Hot Press Books)
– *Covered In Glory: The Hot Press Covers Book* (Hot Press Books)
For more info, go to shop.hotpress.com

SONGS + EXPERIENCE

NIALL STOKES

CARLTON
BOOKS

CONTENTS

APOLLO
APOLLO
SIRIUSXM PRESENTS
U2
A SPECIAL SUBSCRIBER EVENT
SIRIUSXM PRESENTS
U2
A SPECIAL SUBSCRIBER EVENT
Cinderella EYEBROWS

INTRODUCTION

"A book is a mysterious object, I said, and once it floats around the world, anything can happen. All kinds of mischief can be caused, and there's not a damned thing you can do about it. For better or worse, it's completely out of your control." Paul Auster, *Leviathan*,1992

As with books, so with songs...

Writing a book about the stories behind U2's songs, it seemed necessary to live, sleep and eat the music. You keep looking for extra clues, something you might have missed. Some songs begin to grow, the more you listen. Others fade. But some just keep on growing till you know you're never going to get them out of your head. Ever. "*Take my hand,*" you sing, "*you know I'll be there if you can, I'll cross the sky for your love.*" And people look at you. You hadn't even realised you were singing.

It's one of the standard questions nearly every cub rock reporter asks, with all solemnity, as if it's never been asked before: how do you go about writing your songs? Bono calls it songwriting by accident and it describes the process pretty well. But, however the songs are written, more often than not over the past 40 years, the end results have been glorious. U2 have developed in every imaginable way. Boy was a brilliant, original, debut album, which had its share of insights, but no one could claim that the lyrics were its strongest suit. Travelling, within six years, from there to the maturity of *The Joshua Tree* was an extraordinary achievement. But even then, in an industry where so many artists who consider themselves to have arrived are content to rest on their laurels, U2 refused to allow themselves to stagnate.

Achtung Baby, released in 1991, was their second acknowledged masterpiece and also introduced a new phase for them aesthetically and intellectually. Broadly speaking, *The Joshua Tree* and *Rattle and Hum* had been direct, emotional and heartfelt. In contrast, *Achtung Baby* was oblique, coded and elusive, and the follow-up *Zooropa* continued in the same vein. There were reasons for this shift other than the ever-present desire to make great records. It had to do with the fact that, with *The Joshua Tree*, U2 became one of the most successful rock groups of all time. And with that success came a whole private jet-load of baggage. Suddenly U2 found that they were a target for the tabloids. *Rattle and Hum* was widely panned. And, in some quarters, their commitment in itself became a cause of ridicule. Against that backdrop, on the surface at least, *Achtung Baby* reflected a strategy to conceal rather than reveal. It was a deliberate attempt to step out of the mainstream, to challenge audiences and to confound critics. With *Achtung Baby*, with the Zoo TV tour that followed it, and with *Zooropa*, U2 became more playful and experimental. The group's sense of humour was discernible in their music for the first time. Sometimes misunderstood, *Pop* continued in the same vein. But for *All That You Can't Leave Behind* and *How To Dismantle An Atomic Bomb,* the band released themselves again from the need to run everything through the hip-ometer – and made music that was no less hip as a result. Having hit No.1 all over the world, 2009's *No Line On The Horizon* would, somewhat strangely, become regarded as a lesser U2 record, dismissed by Larry Mullen himself with its pithy re-titling as No Craic On The Horizon – but it spawned one of the truly great, awe-inspiring U2 songs in 'Moment of Surrender' and its companion 360° Tour became the highest-grossing in music history. An album too is a mysterious object.

As serious fans will know, the band's determination, every time they enter a studio, is to make the best U2 record ever. That bloody-minded commitment has not been diminished by either the trappings of success, or the cruel and irreparable ravages of time. The intention, then, was that *Songs of Innocence* and *Songs of Experience* would be a two-part magnum opus. The opening gambit, *Songs of Innocence*, released in 2014, came from the heart, with Bono delving into his own personal story to powerful effect. Life intervened. The world turned on its axis. A rough beast slouched towards Washington. The grim reaper shouted from across the hall. Running behind schedule, *Songs of Experience* became a different kind of beast. MacPhisto was back. All bets were off.

They say that in love there are no rules. Nor should there be in rock 'n' roll. One of the things that makes U2 great is their recognition that nothing is sacred in the pursuit of excellence.

It's a fine theory – until you attempt to put it into practice. That's where the sheer grinding hard work comes in. But since they first blazed a trail into our hearts towards the end of the 1970s, U2 have put in more of that than almost any other band on planet Earth, and they have the songs to prove it. And the scars.

Niall Stokes, Dublin, 2018

BEFORE THEY WERE U2

BY BRIAN BOYD

Drummer Seeks Musicians to Form Band." This was the note a 14-year-old Laurence Mullen posted on the bulletin board of his school in Dublin on 25 September 1976.

Auditions would take place in the kitchen of his parents' house. Mount Temple School on the north side of Dublin is known for being a progressive and liberal seat of learning. It attracted students who had been thrown out of other schools, which was why Adam Clayton ended up there. It also encouraged self-expression, which suited Paul Hewson (Bono), and it prioritized musical activity, which appealed to David Evans (The Edge). In their teens, Bono and his friends gave each other nicknames. Bono got his from the name of a Dublin hearing-aid shop. He didn't like it at first, but when he found out it was Latin for "good voice" he took to it. He dropped the "Vox" and just became "Bono". The Edge was so christened because he always seemed to be in between one world and another.

Larry Mullen had been playing drums since the age of nine. But drumming alone in his bedroom was beginning to bore him and so in September 1976, he posted his now famous note on the school's bulletin board.

Auditions for the Larry Mullen Band were held in Larry's parents' house in Artane, Dublin – not too far from Mount Temple School. As Larry set up his drum kit, in strolled David Evans and his older brother, Dik. Both could play a bit of guitar, but both were shy and preferred to stay in the background. Adam Clayton – the "bad boy of Mount Temple" – swanned in wearing an eye-catching Afghan coat. Adam could talk the talk and walk the walk and bluffed his way into becoming the band's manager as well as its bass guitarist. Enter Paul Hewson (Bono): a fidgety ball of energy, he was auditioning for the part of guitarist, but it soon became apparent he was an awful guitar player. Desperately trying to get him away from the guitar, but wanting to keep his presence in the band, Larry and Adam politely suggested he try doing vocals instead.

Mullen was happy with the response to the ad – he was now the leader of a five-piece band. "But the thing is we were only the Larry Mullen Band for about ten minutes," remembers the drummer of that first meeting. "Then Bono walked in and blew any chance I had of being in charge." Clayton, the most worldly and hippest member of the band, suggested they call themselves "Feedback". When he explained what this musical term meant, the other four members agreed, thinking it sounded good and technical.

Feedback began as a covers band and the first ever song they played together was Peter Frampton's 'Show Me the Way'. Songs by Thin Lizzy and the Eagles were also attempted but with the punk/New Wave scene hitting Dublin, Feedback knew they had to write their own material if they wanted to be taken seriously.

There was an early setback when The Edge's brother, Dik, left to join another band. The now four-piece decided to rename themselves "The Hype" and just 18 months into their fledgling career (and after rehearsing every weekend and after school as many times as they could), they entered into a talent show "to find

Baby faces: Determined to make a name for themselves, U2 strike a pose at an early gig in 1976.

> “This [contest] means we can solve our money problems in a big way, particularly with regard to equipment. Now we hope to be able to buy a van.” Bono

the most talented and entertaining pop group or showband". It was held in the city of Limerick on 18 March 1978.

Days before the show, they decided on another new band name. Clayton, still the manager, asked a well-known Dublin musician called Steve Averill for help. Adam said he was looking for a name that sounded a bit like "XTC". Averill came up with ten band name ideas – the last suggestion on the list, "U2", caught Clayton's eye.

U2 won the Limerick talent contest. The first prize was a very generous £500. In addition to the prize money, U2 were given free studio time to record their first demo. Manager Clayton began ringing every Irish music DJ and record company person in Dublin to talk up the talent-showwinning U2. Having been advised that the next step for the band was to secure a recording contract, Clayton decided U2 needed a "real" manager. A Dublin music journalist and early champion of the band, Bill Graham, told Clayton he knew the very man for the job: Paul McGuinness. McGuinness went to see U2 play two months after the talent show win at a gig in Dublin. Afterwards, he took the band to the pub next door – but the band members were too young to be served alcohol. McGuinness talked to them about the Beatles and the Rolling Stones, about songwriting credits and income distribution. The band members' eyes got wider as McGuinness started talking about what they should do with all the money that would be flowing in once their debut album went to Number 1. The band were keen but still a bit suspicious of this "old man" (McGuinness was all of 27 when they met) and his "posh" accent. But McGuinness had total belief in U2's potential. And unlike Adam, he seemed to know what he was talking about. A deal was struck. A career was born.

On fire: Bono and The Edge pose for press shots in Dublin's Trinity College.

Four piece: In the early days, sometimes Bono's best friend Guggi stood in for Larry Mullen for band photo shoots.

SOUND
021 745

> “There were bands who looked better than us, played better than us and wrote better songs than us. But nothing was ever going to stop me picking up a microphone and trying to say something through U2’s music.” Bono

The Dandelion Gigs

Just out of school and with no record label deal, U2 spent 1979 playing anywhere that would have them. Bono squeezed himself into a pair of too tight leather trousers, took mime classes, applied some eye-liner and borrowed some stage dance moves from Siouxsie and the Banshees. The venues: car parks, mainly.

By the end of the summer their plan had worked. CBS Records (now Sony) decided to release a 12-inch EP featuring three of the band's best songs for the Irish market. Such was the buzz for the release by this band from the Dando that a local DJ held a phone-in competition on his rock show so fans could vote for which of the three songs should go on the A side. Live favourite 'Out of Control' became the band's first-ever single release, backed by 'Stories for Boys' and 'Boy-Girl'. The band were thrilled when it made the Irish singles chart at Number 19. A Top 20 hit for their first single!

It was time for U2 to tour the United Kingdom. In advance of the London dates, Bono warned the *Record Mirror* music newspaper that U2 "wanted to take everything and break everything in the UK – I want people in London to see and hear the band. I want to replace the bands in the charts now because I think we're better."

Their first show at London's Hope and Anchor – where they were billed as "The U2s" – attracted a total of nine people. The Edge broke a string halfway through and the band sulked off early. However, the following night at Covent Garden's Rock Garden, they broke double figures. Paul McGuinness opened a bottle of champagne to celebrate. The band were dejected, but people from Island Records already had their eye on this weird new Irish band. Even back then Island saw the UK as the wrong fit for the band; imagine how American audiences would take to them ...

Vox pop: One of the earliest ever U2 promotional shots. This was taken in Dublin in 1978.
Stage mob: U2 at the Country Club in Cork, Ireland, on 4 February 1980. The city is home to most of their long-serving live touring crew.
Air guitar: U2 played one of their first-ever gigs outside Dublin in March 1980 at the Garden of Eden pub in Tullamore, County Offaly in the midlands of Ireland.

BOY

It was always going to be called *Boy*. "The album cover has been in the back of my mind for two years," Bono explained, just after its release. "There is a feel to it. Holding the cover and listening to the album is perfect."

The title was decided on long before this band began to record. It wasn't a concept album, but there was a strong linking thread running through the songs. U2 were still in their teens when they signed to Island, and *Boy* reflected it unashamedly.

"The songs are autobiographical," Bono stated. In an explosive burst of adolescent energy, they embraced the teenage themes of confusion, longing, faith, anger, loss and burgeoning love in a nakedly emotional way.

At the heart of the record was the frantic search for an identity in which all of the band were themselves still immersed.

Having played most of the songs for over two years, U2 probably believed that they knew them thoroughly. It still wasn't an easy album to make. A lot of tough, disciplined work went into getting the rhythm section tight, and Bono had to confront in earnest for the first time the need to finish definitively the band's songs.

Under Steve Lillywhite's sympathetic direction, *Boy* emerged bright and shiny, all glistening treble, shimmering guitar, exuberant drumming, breathless vocals and urgent bass. It was a lyrical, romantic, spiritual odyssey, which resonated with one particularly distinctive quality. Above all, *Boy* was an honest record.

I Will Follow

Iris Hewson died on 10 September, 1974, following a brain haemorrhage. It was a terrible twist of fate, coming as it did just after her own father's funeral at the Military Cemetery in Blackhorse Avenue, Dublin. Bono was 14 at the time, and the experience devastated him. Even now, he admits that he finds it difficult to remember what his mother looked like. It is impossible to imagine what he might have become if she had lived. What we can say is that he was plunged into a period of emotional turmoil, that he began running in 1974 and that he has scarcely stopped since – and that this restlessness has been a powerful motivating force in his work. Bono remembers his adolescence as a time of psychological violence and 'I Will Follow' captures some of the drama of that era, the four walls coming down on top of the song's narrator in an image that captures well the suburban claustrophobia that was returned to, almost obsessively, throughout the first album. But there is something else going on here: a sense of terror and confusion which runs deeper than the common crises of identity from which teenagers suffer.

His friends on Cedarwood Road remember Bono as a kind of stray

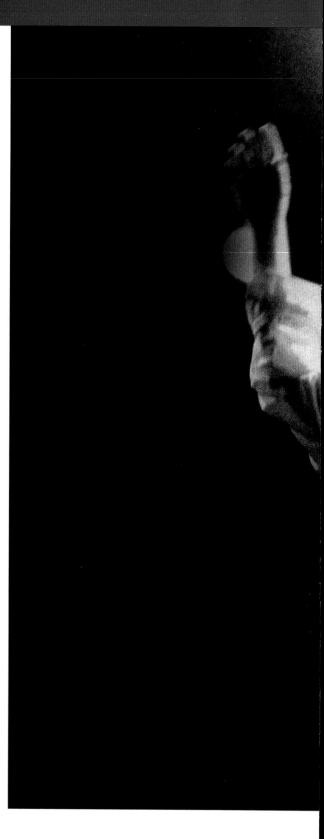

Spot light: By their later standards, the band's early live shows were rudimentary affairs.

Release date: October 1980
Catalogue number: ILPS 9646
Producer: Steve Lillywhite
Track listing: I Will Follow/Twilight/Into the Heart/Out of Control/Stories for Boys/The Ocean/A DayWithout Me/Another Time,Another Place/The Electric Co./Shadows and Tall Trees
Highest chart position: No. 52 (UK), 63 (US)

after his mother died. He'd turn up at Gavin Friday's house one night, and Derek Rowen's the next, just in time for tea. "He was calling around as much to be with my mother as he was to be with me, I have no doubt about that," Gavin recalls now. They fed him and minded him, but he had to return all the same, as twilight fell, to a house inhabited only by men – his father Bob, his brother Norman and himself.

In the past, Bono has talked about the song being a sketch about the unconditional love a mother has for a child, but it is clearly more than that. There is a palpable yearning in the lyrics that has much more to do with what a child feels when his mother walks – or is taken – away from him, and the suicidal urge to follow. "*A boy tries hard to be a man/His mother takes him by the hand*," Bono sings and immediately you know that this is not the stuff of which teenage pop is normally wrought. Opening *Boy*, 'I Will Follow' was a perfectly appropriate statement of intent, signalling that this was an album about teenage confusion and rites of passage, but also – and perhaps more crucially – that there was a restless spirit at work which could never be satisfied with conventional or clichéd answers. Looking back now, with the benefit of both hindsight and experience, it's a song of which Bono clearly remains proud.

"I think it's coming from a very dark place," he says. "Pop music at its best seems to have a duality. Whenever it's one thing or the other it's flat, but if it has two opposing ideas, pulling in different directions, it achieves a different kind of power. 'I Will Follow' has both anger, real anger, and an enormous sense of yearning."

The band's performance was suitably urgent, marking the track down as one that would inevitably be released as a single to coincide with the launch of the album. In particular, The Edge careens in on the kind of treble high that became his trademark. At the time a limited guitar player in conventional terms, he was an original stylist even then. "I knew more what I didn't want to sound like than what I

Back stage: The Edge and Bono take a break after given it their all for a show in Cork, Ireland, in 1979.

We had the chance to leave the country when we signed to Island, but we stayed here because the roots of the band are in Dublin. U2 is an Irish expression." Bono

wanted to sound like early on," he said later. "In some ways that's why my playing is so minimal. Play as few notes as you can, but find those notes that do the most work. If I could play one note for a whole song I would. 'I Will Follow' is almost that." It is, as a result, concentrated and hugely powerful. "Most of the early rehearsals were just rows," Bono recalls. "It was just one long argument. I remember picking up Edge's guitar and playing the two-stringed chord for 'I Will Follow' to show the others the aggression I wanted. It was his riff but I wanted it to have an edge to it." There is a hallucinogenic quality to the lyrics – "*Your eyes make a circle/I see you when I go in there*," Bono sings in the bridge, desperately trying to make sense out of feelings of separation and loss. 'I Will Follow', finally, is the love song it set out to be. But it is as much about a boy's confused love for his mother as it is about a mother's unconditional love for her child. The journey had begun. U2 were going in two different directions at once.

I Will Follow Written: U2 • Duration: 3' 36" • US singles chart position: 81

Twilight

"The subtext," Bono says, looking at the lyric sheet, "is everything. Isn't it?" He can't resist a wry chuckle, looking at the rough type from the inner sleeve of *Boy*. "Those lyrics are wrong," he says looking at the text of one track. "That's wrong," he repeats, scrawling the correct lyric to another. 'Twilight', he leaves untouched.

The song first surfaced on the B-side of their second single 'Another Day', released through CBS in Ireland. Legend has it that it was recorded in just five minutes and suffered as a consequence. But on *Boy* it comes through strongly, a small epic that's loaded with sexual ambiguities. No one in Ireland thought of the song as dealing with homosexuality, or the confusion of sexual identity that so many adolescents feel to one degree or another. And yet it's there in the lyrics, once you come at them from a certain angle. In Dublin, "the old man" was the common term for your father. But in Britain and the US, where gays expressed their identity in more overt ways, this song seemed to be for them. Bono sings: "The old man tried to walk me home, I thought he should have known." Who he was and what he should have known is never explicitly stated.

"It was curious," Adam Clayton reflects. "But we picked up a strong network of gay fans on the strength of *Boy*. We didn't have a clue what was going on."

"Then we did an interview with this guy, Adam Block," Bono continues, "who was gay, and he was saying that he'd always thought of us as a gay band. And I was like, 'Wow! you must be joking!' He made the point that within the gay community, people were excited about the fact that we were the first band to deal with sex outside machismo. Rock 'n' roll was always written from the point of view of men – or at least of boys pretending to be men – but we were doing something different."

Twilight Written: U2 • Duration: 4' 22"

An Cat Dubh / Into The Heart

When U2 formed in Mount Temple Comprehensive School on the north side of Dublin, Bono had already started the relationship with Ali Stewart that would result in marriage. But the path of true love didn't always run smoothly.

They split for a short time and Bono – as ever, restless and hungry for experience – had a short fling with another schoolmate.

"That one's about sex, definitely about sex," Gavin Friday says, without the slightest hesitation. "But I think you should ask him why 'An Cat Dubh'? Irish wasn't his thing. If that had been me, fine, because I was Fionán and that Irish thing was there in the background, but not in Bono's case. So why not just call it 'The Black Cat'? Where sex was concerned, Bono was very precocious as a teenager. He was a lot more knowledgeable than the rest of us in Lypton Village."

"It's definitely about sex, that," Bono agrees. "I think the title is in Irish because the girl it was about was a sort of 'as Gaeilge' type of person. What happened was that Ali and myself had split up for a minute and I just ran off with somebody and felt guilty about it.

"The image is of a cat and a bird. The cat kills the bird and shakes it – you know the way they do, they play with the dead prey – and then sleeps beside it. That's where the image comes from. It's like someone has taken you, thrown you around the place and then you sleep beside them. I think for the sake of the song I switched things around, but in reality I think I was the cat. I was the one who did the dirty. That lyric should read 'and when she is done/she sleeps beside the one'."

In fact, 'An Cat Dubh' was as important for its muted, evocative instrumental passages as for its – again – sexually ambiguous text. The lyrics may have been improvised, as Bono told Neil McCormick of *Hot Press* during 1981, but the music felt as if it had been thought

Double vision: U2 at an early photo shoot, just after the band had completed *Boy*.

through. The restraint in the instrumental passage leading from 'An Cat Dubh' into 'Into the Heart' is especially impressive, a performance from The Edge that anticipated the unique genius he would bring to contemporary rock guitar-playing. "We spent all our time on the music," Bono reflects now, "and on working out improvisations. We got hooked on guitar sounds, on bass lines, on drums. And then when we were doing that, we'd maybe seize a few minutes and I'd write the song down. Even though a lot of these songs were played live before we recorded them, I never learned the lyrics. Playing the Dandelion Market – or wherever – the lyrics would be changed. I think we can blame Iggy Pop for that. We'd read that he improvised his lyrics on the microphone and if it was good enough for Iggy, it was good enough for us. So it wasn't like I had worked out the lyrics and then had time to think about them. They were always changing."

The segue from 'An Cat Dubh' into 'Into the Heart' had more to do with the exigencies of performance than with theme. The sequence worked on stage, and therefore it made sense to do it that way on record. It remains a piece of shimmering, quiet beauty. The dynamics are beautifully controlled by producer Steve Lillywhite and the clear, ringing guitar has a haunting, ethereal quality. The lyrics of 'Into the Heart' beset the weakness that could inhabit songs that were being made up as the band went along. No doubt the intention is to mourn lost innocence and what the late Bill Graham of *Hot Press* called the destruction of the secret garden of youth – and that effect is evoked musically with great tenderness and feeling. But it wouldn't have taken much in the way of craft to hone lyrics that seem curiously selfcontradictory on paper to a stage where they had a level of internal coherence. Craft would come later.

"It's really a non-lyric period, in one sense," Bono reflects now. "Nobody talked about lyrics back then. It wasn't really on the agenda. I think it was only really after *Unforgettable Fire* that we started saying – or that I started saying – hold on a second, give me a bit of space here, to think about these things, to thrash these things out."

For now, to a large extent, it was down to where the group's instinct would take them. On balance, they weren't doing badly.

An Cat Dubh/Into The Heart Written: U2 • Duration: 6' 21"/1' 53"

Out of Control

U23 was U2's debut recording salvo. Released on CBS Ireland, it came in 7" and – almost unique in Ireland at that time – 12" formats. Jackie Hayden, then marketing manager of CBS , enlisted the assistance of Ian Wilson, the producer of the *Dave Fanning Rock Show* on 2FM, the pop channel attached to the State broadcaster, RTE. Listeners to Dave's show were invited to help pick the record's A-side from 'Out of Control', 'Stories for Boys' and 'Boy Girl', by voting for their favourite. They opted for the first, which went on to become one of U2's best-known anthems.

Compared to the original version, the *Boy* re-interpretation had an even greater power and clarity. In the neo-punk era "oh-oh-ohs" and "oh-e-ohe- ohs" were commonplace and the band indulged themselves here, but it scarcely diminished the energy and sense of compulsion which marked this song as something special from the start. It had been written on Bono's 18th birthday.

"'Out of Control' is about waking up on your 18th birthday and realising you're 18 years old and that the two most important decisions in your life have nothing to do with you – being born and dying," Bono told me in 1979, before the release of *Boy*. "The song is written from the child's point of view and it's about a vicious circle. He becomes a delinquent but the psychologist says, 'It's in his childhood'. No matter what he does, it can't be because he wants to – it's always because of what went before, and there's no decision in anything. Then again, that's [a] slightly spiritual [theme] – the question, what is happening if you've no freedom?" Remembering now in tranquillity, Bono places the song in the context of his own psychological traumas at the time. He recalls flipping out in school at the age of 16, turning over chairs and tables, and not knowing himself what switch had gone on – or off – to cause the explosion. It was a feeling that recurred: he was haunted by the sense that the whole crazy business of human life, and human reproduction in particular, was out of control. The song was an attempt to come to grips in an adolescent but nonetheless urgent way with the reality of existential angst as it gnaws away at the heart's core.

Nowadays he isn't inclined to take it too seriously. "That one was translated by the Japanese," he says. "It went out with the album and the Japanese version of the opening lines translated back into English as '*Monday morning/Knitting years of gold*,' which is a hell of a lot better than '*Monday morning/Eighteen years of dawning*'."

Out Of Control Written: U2 • Duration: 4' 13"

13 (There Is A Light)

But for an 18-year-old those feelings were utterly real, and the sense of impending disaster which accompanied any notion that you might simply replay the same old suburban dramas enacted by your parents was impossible to shake off.

"My father had lived through the '50s depression," Bono reflects, "and as a result he taught us not to expect too much in case we might feel let down. His attitude was: don't do anything that seems like you're aiming higher than your allotted station. All my mates were intent on going to college and on doing things. I'd always been bright in school – I never did a tap but I'd done well and the last thing I wanted was to stay stuck in any kind of rut.

"Joining the band was my emancipation from all this. At that age, it was my ticket to freedom. It was my way of attempting to change the circumstances of the world I was living in."

Again, the musical arrangement is significant. From Larry Mullen's thumping drum entry, the song powers along with the expected urgency. But where other bands of the era might have gone for overkill in a tortured guitar solo, U2 instead dissolve the focus to let Adam Clayton's quietly insistent bass line through. There's a languor to the instrumental break which suggests that U2 will refuse to go for the obvious.

Halo effect: At an early London show, Bono dispenses with the microphone. His exuberant stage actions were always a cause of concern for the other band members.

"We knew what sort of material we wanted," The Edge told *Hot Press* at the time, "so if you want a particular idea, you start picking instruments and amps and effects and what have you. When you start doing that, you start to develop a sound. Then, when you have a sound, you find certain things work better on that and you get into a certain vocabulary of music. And before you know what's happening, you're on the way to a style, a sound and to musicianship."

'Out of Control' was an important stepping stone along the way.

"Is this a record?" –

13 (There Is A Light) Written: U2 • Duration: 4' 19"

Stories For Boys

'Stories For Boys' was one of the band's earliest songs. A highlight of their live set, it was chosen for *U23*. At the time, Bono explained it in relatively conventional terms. "All the songs point to one thing – getting people to think for themselves," he told Hot Press. "There's also a reaction against heavy advertising and television images. I remember seeing heroes on TV – people like James Bond – and thinking, 'I'm not very good looking – I'm not going to get things like that,' and being unhappy about it."

But there were other things that they might have been qualified to comment on, too. The band's manager, Paul McGuinness, was always convinced that it was a song about masturbation. Gays too identified with it, reading a homo-erotic slant into the lines: "*Sometimes when a hero takes me/Sometimes I don't let go/Oh oh oh/Stories for boys*."

"This was it. For the gays in our audience, this was definitely a love song to a man," Bono smiles. "I thought of 'Stories For Boys' as just simple escapism. And it's not really. We were very conscious on one level but there was a whole subconscious thing going on too."

Bono has often spoken about the feeling that he is merely a conduit, the vehicle by which ideas, emotions and feelings, are delivered into the public realm. Now, he wonders if he and the band really knew what they were saying. "I never write lyrics until the last minute because they're constantly building as we work out the song. They build subconsciously, because I found that I can write exactly what I want to write subconsciously, better than sitting down and trying."

It's a very particular approach to the aesthetics of songwriting and sometimes it works. But at this early stage there was often a feeling that, in fact, the words to U2's songs were themselves out of control. Or maybe that was appropriate, after all.

Stories For Boys Written: U2 • Duration: 3' 02"

The Ocean

U2 grew up on Dublin's north side. Along the complicated shoreline of the county, a series of beaches run from Dollymount strand out to Sutton beach, on to Howth and then back into the Portmarnock inlet. Out further there's Portrane, Skerries and Rush – they were small towns, their economies built around the summer holidays, weekend breaks and day-trips that people from the north of the city used to take there. Bono's family, on his mother's side, had bought a former train carriage, located on a farmer's land, close to the sea in Rush. All of the family would go there at weekends and revel in the lure of the sea.

The farmer who owned the field died and his son took over. He told the family that there was no contract entitling them to keep their holiday home on his land and that he wanted the carriage removed. When it didn't happen, he had the site levelled, destroying the carriage in the process. They took him to court and won, but Rush didn't hold the same appeal any more and they moved their holidaying to a caravan in Skerries. The Irish sea was common to both places.

Dubliners are familiar with the sea, so there was no giant leap of the imagination required for Bono to picture himself wandering at its edge. "'The Ocean' is just a complete teenage thought," Bono said in 1981. "It is the thought of everybody in a band who thinks he can change the world. There is another verse which got left out on the record: *'When I looked around/The world couldn't be found/Just me by the sea'*, which is the resignation that no matter what, people are going to go their own way." The most crucial line, however, is in the first verse:

"*A picture in grey, Dorian Gray/Just me by the sea/And I felt like a star*." On one level, this is just teenage narcissism and self-indulgence. Musically, it achieves an appropriately lyrical and poetic quality – but Bono's response now is one of amusement. "That takes some fucking neck," he says. "We used to open the show with that. In a way it was so audacious. And it's nicely ironic. It's quite smart and a great opening gambit for a show. '*I thought the world could go far/If they listened to what I said.*' So many people feel that, but so few say it. That's great."

The Dorian Gray reference is to Oscar Wilde's character. Gavin Friday remembers it as being on the Leaving Certificate syllabus."I'd certainly read Wilde," Bono recalls. "I'd read Joyce. I'd read other Irish writers, as well as people like Baudelaire, because I thought they were arty or whatever." There was a poet on the premises. He was searching for a voice.

The Ocean Written: U2 • Duration: 1' 34"

A Day Without Me

The Edge had already begun to fashion a distinctive guitar style. There was very little of the blues in his playing. You'd never hear him plucking out a 12-bar walking rhythm on the bass strings. He seldom played solos. And he didn't torture his young musician's fingers by attempting to b-e-n-d the notes. Instead he used open strings to create a drone-like effect. There was a lot of treble in his playing, arpeggios and harmonics touched and left to hang. And against that cushion he'd play melody lines, often of crystalline purity. If he was already advancing along this alternative track, there's no doubt that getting hold of an echo unit confirmed his direction as a guitarist.

Bono remembers a developing interest in atmospherics within the band, referring to David Bowie's *Low* and to Joy Division among the influences that were coming on-stream at the time. From Tom Verlaine of Television, The Edge had learned that less is more, and had begun to develop an awareness of the architecture of sound: songs could be built. It was, as he later told John Waters, about judgement and your brain rather than your fingers. It was about ideas. Gavin Friday identifies the Jam, the Associates and the Skids as having made a huge impact on the way U2 saw themselves.

Bono claims that he acquired the Memory Man echo unit for the Edge, believing that it would take the band into another musical realm. The guitarist admits that it was Bono's idea. He remembers borrowing money from a friend and getting a really cheap unit. With it as inspiration, they wrote '11 O'Clock Tick Tock' and 'A Day Without Me'. Originally intended as an enhancement, it became an integral part of The Edge's guitar sound. 'A Day Without Me' resonates with its cheap but highly effective technological magic.

It was the first track that U2 recorded with Steve Lillywhite as producer. Released as a single in advance of *Boy*, it confirmed for both Lillywhite and the band that they could work together. As singles go, this was a song with a big theme – or series of themes – which were only sketchily executed. A guy Bono knew – "He was an acquaintance of a friend of mine, Sean d'Angelo" – had tried to commit suicide. "In fact I went up to the hospital with Sean to see this guy and they tried to keep Sean in! He went to find a bathroom and he was gone for half an hour. When he came back he had this strange look in his eye. He'd been walking around the pharmacy, looking for a toilet, when they stopped him. They thought he looked like an inmate. They were asking: 'Where are you going?' And he was telling them that he was just visiting. And they were taking him by the arm and saying 'Everything is going to be alright. Just come this way.' It was very funny. He had a hard job trying to convince them that he was just in to see his mate."

The suicide attempt played on Bono's imagination and emerged in 'A Day Without Me', with the protagonist looking back at the world he has "left behind" from the perspective of the grave – or more likely a vantage point somewhere above the graveyard, as he watches the funeral and takes note of those who haven't shown up. "I was fascinated by the thought: would it make any difference if you did commit suicide?" Bono recalls.

Typically, that is just an undercurrent. The song also touches on the theme of insanity, and on the collapse of the self, reflecting another common teenage insecurity. But Bono also sees in it continuity from 'The Ocean'.

Most teenagers wallow in the feeling that the world has reserved a special kind of misery for them. They want to run, and to keep on running. But in the midst of all that self-pity, the feeling that they are special inspires some with a belief that, given half a chance, they can do almost anything. This was true of Bono. But it was also true of the whole band, who never had any doubt about the fact that they were going to become huge. As early as 1981, Bono was comparing U2 to the Beatles and the Stones, as if they – rather than Echo & the Bunnymen – were U2's true peers. He's inclined to view 'A Day Without Me' against that kind of backdrop. "'I started a landslide in my ego'," he quotes.

"That's a great opening line. A lot of this stuff is awful but that's really ballsy. I think this is about our own megalomania, actually [laughs]. There was never any doubt in our minds, certainly in my mind, that the band had something special, and that we were going to go all the way. That was it. And so this is – this was writing about the future success of the band. It's so embarrassing [laughs]. It's actually writing about this as a given. And saying 'good luck' to everyone else! Against the background of what was going on in and around Ballymun, I think the band gave me a sense of 'we're off'. That's how it felt." And that's how it was.

A Day Without Me Written: U2 • Duration: 3' 14"

Another Time, Another Place

Happiness is always somewhere else. The tragic hero of teenage artifice is frequently forlorn and disillusioned. There was very little in the way of joy on *Boy*, if you looked at the lyrics. And yet in many ways it was a very "up" record: the joy was in the making, in the musicianship, in the mission. It was in Larry Mullen pounding the drums. It was in Adam finding the confidence to launch into a melodic bass run to fill the space between The Edge's angular, ringing guitar slashes. It was in Bono unleashing the demons inside, posing and pogoing around the stage, leaping into the crowd and being – sometimes literally – carried away. The joy was in the group's sense of abandonment – of the conventions and restrictions implicit in being four suburban Dublin boys in the bleak '70s.

'Another Time, Another Place' is one of those wistful, evocative titles which sounds like it came first, though Bono has no memory of the Bryan Ferry album of that name. "At that stage, because so little attention was paid to lyrics, most of the songs did begin with the titles. Usually, we'd work on the music first, in fact we still do. And then, as the music begins to feel a certain way, the first thing we do is to find a title that captures the feel of the music, and then you work back from that."

You can argue that 'Another Time, Another Place' is merely self-indulgent, romantic stuff. It sounds seriously under-worked. But there is in it – as there is throughout *Boy* – an admirable sensitivity to the plight of children, lost in the suburban jungle. Here, simply, because they're here, because they're here, because they're here...

"I actually think it's about sex in Dublin as a teenager," another acquaintance from the era suggests. "It's about finding a place where you can be with your girlfriend, which was a real problem at that time." 'Another Time, Another Place' certainly prefigures a theme that would dominate U2's later music. "In my sleep I discover the one," Bono asserts, but it is never clear whether he means the Loved One or the Supreme Being – or both. Possibly he didn't know, although the promise *"I'll be with you now/We lie on a cloud"* certainly suggests some sort of romantic intent, Ali working her muse on him already.

Another Time Another Place Written: U2 • Duration: 4' 34"

The Electric Co.

A quick glance at the lyrics and you'd scarcely get any sense of what 'The Electric Co.' was about. Within Lypton Village, a defining emphasis was on developing a private language that only insiders could understand. There was a desperate desire to communicate – but only to those you thought would be capable of understanding.

Within the village set, people may have known that 'The Electric Co.' was a reference to Electro Convulsive Therapy, but the lyrics only hint at the deep sense of disturbance that the song in its entirety explores.

Gavin Friday remembers it as a common feature of the neighbourhood. He pictures women walking the suburban streets in mid-afternoon in their nightdresses. "It'd be a case of 'Oh, there goes Mrs So-and-so again.' And a couple of days later you'd hear that she was back in hospital. And everyone would be whispering that she'd got 'the treatment'. They'd whack her with an electric shock and she'd be back a few weeks later and she'd be stable for a while. There were a few women like that. Today they'd give them Valium or Prozac but they were big into ECT at the time."

When Sean de Angelo's friend tried to kill himself, he went about it in a spectacular way, with a chainsaw. He ended up in St Brendan's psychiatric hospital, notorious in Dublin lore simply as Grangegorman, or "the 'Gorman". It was a foul institution in which those with long-term psychiatric problems were effectively incarcerated. Electric shock treatment was frequently used and so the prospects for de Angelo's friend were bleak. It was as a musical set-piece, however, that 'The Electric Co.' exploded with the power of its concealed intent. 'The Electric Co.' burned with anger at the injustice of it all – beginning with the reality of mental disturbance and insanity itself, but more particularly raging against the hubris of doctors who took on themselves the power to mess with people's brains. "ECT is nothing more than witchcraft," Bono commented bitterly at the time.

"'The Electric Co.' was about anger," he says now. "It used to be an incredible release on stage. This idea that rock 'n' roll is a kind of revenge – on society, and on the people you perceive as having done you down – is really true. When you're on stage, and going all out, certain songs do become vehicles or vectors for that. For me 'The Electric Co.' was a licence to get in touch with that desire. I've jumped off balconies, I've whacked people, I've been whacked doing that song live. There's a bit of an Alex, the main character from *A Clockwork Orange*, in there. But essentially it was an angry, cathartic experience every time we performed it."

The Electric Co. Written: U2 • Duration: 4' 48"

Shadows And Tall Trees

William Golding's *Lord of the Flies* was an important text around Lypton Village. Part of the driving force behind that community within a community involved the rejection of adulthood and the mind-numbing convention that seemed to accompany it. The purity and innocence of childhood seemed far more attractive than a life of never-ending compromise.

And so Bono, Gavin, Guggi and the other inhabitants of this imaginary place resolved to live like children, and to behave with a child-like honesty. "We got into this *Lord of the Flies* idea of not growing up," Bono told John Waters, later. "We said, 'we won't grow up. We'll stay as we are . . . nine!' Ahem, I guess we succeeded there! It was a little bit gauche and a little bit all over the place, but that's where it was coming from."

That belief in the purity of a child's-eye view of the world is important in understanding the entire ethos of *Boy*. It underscored the band's reliance on instinct in the way the lyrics were written. And it explains, in part at least, the nakedness of some of U2's emotional pleading.

The title 'Shadows and Tall Trees' was taken from the fourth chapter of *Lord of the Flies*. "When I came up with the title, I remember thinking, 'Wow! I can do this!' Again it was like a moment of realisation," Bono recalls. It was an early U2 song, the only one from their original demo session, recorded with Barry Devlin of Horslips as producer, which made it onto *Boy*. A ballad, it feels as if more attention was paid to the lyrics than on most of the tracks on the album. "Yeah," Bono laughs. "Look at that: *'Is life like a tightrope/Hanging on my ceiling?'*. Ouch! I guess I would have considered that to be quite writerly at the time. But then there are other parts of it that are quite beautiful. *'Do you feel in me, anything redeeming/ Any worthwhile feeling?'* – which I guess if you were listening to it as a song or at a concert would have to bring something out. It would have to hit you on an emotional level."

The shadows and tall trees of the title were a reference to the atmosphere around the pylons that towered over Cedarwood Road and environs. "I remember thinking about that comparison between Lord of the Flies and where we were in Cedarwood, between Ballymun and Finglas. It was a quiet little street in one sense but my memory of it, growing up, is of being stuck between cowboys and indians, rumbles between the top end of the street and the bottom end of the street, between bootboys and skinheads, and so on. That's the way it was. And I remember thinking the shadows and tall trees are different here – but it's the same story, isn't it? It's all about war. We're all stuck on this island of suburbia and we're turning on each other."

The Mrs Brown, whose washing turns up in the third verse, was in fact Mrs Byrne, Iris Hewson's best friend and near neighbour on Cedarwood Road. Inevitably, the Byrne kids recognized the fact that their dirty laundry was being washed – or watched! – by Bono in public. "They were happy enough about that," he laughs. And why wouldn't they be, with immortality? Of a sort.

Shadows and Tall Trees Duration: U2 • Length: 4' 36"

WIP 6656
U2
NEW SINGLE
· I WILL FOLLOW ·
PRODUCER · STEVE LILLYWHITE
TOUR DATES
NOVEMBER
7 · EXETER UNIVERSITY
8 · SOUTHAMPTON UNIVERSITY
9 · MOONLIGHT · WEST HAMPSTEAD
11 · CANTERBURY UNIVERSITY
12 · BRADFORD UNIVERSITY
13 · LIMIT CLUB · SHEFFIELD
14 · TOWN HALL · KIDDERMINSTER
15 · BRISTOL POLYTECHNIC
18 · READING UNIVERSITY
19 · WOLVERHAMPTON POLYTECHNIC
20 · BLACKPOOL POLYTECHNIC
21 · NITE CLUB · EDINBURGH
22 · BRADY'S CLUB · LIVERPOOL
26 · MARQUEE · LONDON
27 · MARQUEE · LONDON
24 · COVENTRY POLYTECHNIC
28 · ASTON UNIVERSITY · BIRMINGHAM
29 · KEELE UNIVERSITY · STOKE
30 · JENKINSON'S · BRIGHTON
ISLAND

Right: An advert for the 1980 Boy tour from *NME* magazine.

OCTOBER

Portland, Oregon. 22 March, 1981. Four Irish boys, wide-eyed and trusting. Three girls sashay backstage. Hey, these must be groupies. The Irish boys are happy just to talk. And they do for half-an-hour. "Oops," the girls say, "time to go." And they're gone. They seemed pretty cool, didn't they? Very cool. "Has anyone seen my case?" Bono asks. Shit. His case is gone. Three smart Portland girls opening the door to their apartment, carrying a case. Inside are $300 and a bunch of hand-written scrawls. Lyrics. Bono's lyrics. For the new record. All gone.

Four Irish boys searching high and low. For the lyrics. Gone. Three years to write *Boy*. Now, 12 months' worth of hard labour stolen – with only 12 weeks left to write the follow-up. Nervous breakdown time. Things were fraught. Bono, Larry, The Edge heavily into Shalom Christianity. Adam, isolated. Touring taking its toll. The band almost falling apart. Steve Lillywhite driving Bono: "You can write a song in five minutes. Do your job." Thought of calling the album Scarlet (the colour of Bono's face when he discovered the lyrics had been nicked?) Decided instead on *October*. A big theme hinting at our own insignificance? Or it was the month the album would be released in?

Gloria

Paul McGuinness may privately have raged about the possibility that the involvement of Bono, Edge and Larry in the Shalom group might derail a band which he instinctively knew could become enormously successful. But he always respected the fundamental impulse behind the trio's action. 'His attitude was always very cool," Bono recalls. "He'd say: 'Look I don't share your views but I do believe it's the most important question, and I do respect the fact that you're trying to come to terms with it.' The only thing that he found in his own religion that he could relate to was the music, so he gave us an album of Gregorian chants."

The opening lines of 'Gloria' crystallise the central dilemma with which the band were forced to grapple throughout the album: "*I try to sing this song/I, I try to stand up but I can't find my feet/I try, I try to speak up/But only in you I'm complete*." The song reflects a desire to find a voice, a way of expressing at once the faith that was at the heart of their conversion, and the terrible confusion it had plunged them into. Bono feels now that he may have been too embarrassed about the ideas that were beginning to flood his work as a lyricist to write them down. Instead he improvised, with the result that he is stuttering, barely achieving any kind of coherence.

On 'Gloria' he succeeds. From listening to the Gregorian chant album, the idea emerged of doing the chorus in Latin. Gavin Friday remembers Bono asking a mutual friend to do the initial translation. The final draft was completed by Albert Bradshaw, a teacher in Mount Temple.

Whether Mr Bradshaw would have been aware of the song's more heathen antecedents is uncertain. As an Irish band, U2 were certainly conscious of Van Morrison and his sexual paean to 'Gloria'. However, on Horses, an album which hugely influenced U2, Patti Smith had done a magnificently potent, erotic, lesbian version of Them's garage band classic. "It is a love song," Bono says. "In a sense it's an attempt to write about a woman in a spiritual sense and about God in a sexual sense. But there certainly is a strong sexual pulse in there."

"You could hear the desperation and confusion in some of the lyrics," The Edge told Bill Flanagan. "'Gloria' is really a lyric about not being able to express what's going on, not being able to put it down, not knowing where we are."

Not being able to express what's going on? Perhaps. But – in this instance at least – doing it very well, all the same.

Gloria Written: U2 • Duration: 4' 12" • UK singles chart position: 55

I Fall Down

"A really funny thing happened during the October tour," Bono recalls. "We were playing the Ritz in New York and this girl slipped onto the stage. I used to do this thing even then of dancing with someone from the audience. She said, 'I'm Julie.' I met her afterwards. She's a daughter of a wealthy lawyer in New York, who kind of spun out and ended up coming back here to Ireland and getting involved in the Shalom group. She ended up in a relationship with Pod, who was in our road crew at the time."

"I think that John in 'I Fall Down' was actually Pod, who was

Rock gods: The October tour hit San Francisco in November 1981. For three of the band, the tour was a struggle to reconcile their Christian beliefs with a rock 'n' roll lifestyle.

Release date: October 1981
Catalogue number: ILPS 9680
Producer: Steve Lillywhite
Track listing: Gloria/I Fall Down/I Threw A Brick Through a Window/Rejoice/Fire/Tomorrow/October/With A Shout/Stranger in a Strange Land/Scarlet/Is That All?
Highest chart position: No. 11 (UK), 104 (US)

originally the drummer with the Virgin Prunes," Gavin Friday recalls. "He was one of the staunchest Christians going. It got to the stage where Pod couldn't talk to me because I was a heathen. An atheist. There was a period of about a year and a half when myself, Guggi and Bono didn't see eye to eye over various things. People used to run when they saw me and I was saying, 'I'm not going to sacrifice animals on stage.' And so Pod left the Prunes and went to work with U2 on their American tour, as their main roadie." Gavin himself had been involved in the Shalom group. "That didn't last long," he laughs. "I was pushed into a corner. It was a case of 'Let's change the name to The Deuteronomy Prunes, Gavin. Let's stop wearing eyeliner,' and so on. So I just said no, no, no. I knew I didn't want to buy into all this. But after he'd left the Prunes, Pod fell in love with Julie, who is also mentioned in the song. I think Pod was almost like a religious prayer-master in the group at the time. And so when he got together with Julie, she became another ringleader of the Shalom group, along with Pod."

The song is experimental in a number of ways. Whether the influence of Elvis Costello, Joe Jackson and Squeeze was seeping through is a matter for conjecture, but the introduction of the Julie and John characters frees the band from the tyranny of the direct declarations of emotional intensity that Bono was prone to. The Edge's shimmering piano, tightly worked backing vocals and a superbly judged Steve Lillywhite production mark this as one of the band's most fully realised early cuts.

Bono wouldn't go so far as to suggest that 'I Fall Down' was written about Julie before he met her. "I don't really know," he says. "That's what she thinks. And who's to say?"It could, of course, merely be a case of life imitating art. But if so, surely Bono would know who he originally had in mind when he created the Julie character in the song. "There was really no one that I can think of," he admits. "I have no recollection about where the idea for the song came from."

I Fall Down Written: U2 • Duration: 3' 39"

I Threw A Brick Through A Window

Punk rock was crucial to U2's formation. "Bono was the first punk in school," a former classmate recalls. "He turned up one day with a new haircut, tight purple straights, a '60s jacket and a chain leading from his nose to his ear. He wanted to freak everyone out and he succeeded." Bono acknowledges the anger that gripped him as a teenager. But he never felt easy with the emotion. "The old cliché of rock 'n' roll rebellion is a joke," he said around the release of *Boy*. "I think rebellion starts within your heart. I think going out and getting pissed and dying your hair red is not necessarily any indication of menace at all."

Thematically, 'I Threw a Brick Through a Window' would have sat comfortably on *Boy*. Musically it was more spacious than most tracks on the band's debut with a hint that they had been listening to some of Island's huge reggae catalogue. Lyrically, it returns to suburban

Up front: The band in concert in 1981 shortly after the release of their underperforming second album, *October*.

claustrophobia. "Bono was always crashing, bikes, cars – everything broke down on him, he'd always be losing things," Gavin Friday recalls. "We were walking around the neighbourhood and suddenly it was like: 'They're on drugs', and 'Paul Hewson's gone mad on a motorbike.' Suddenly we were weirdos. Now we were in bands, we were no longer lovely boys. We were brats.

"Once Bono was going to a party and decided to splash out on a bottle of wine. There was this couple up the road called Mr and Mrs Curley, and Bono was driving this crock of a car and crashed into their gate. The wine spilt all over the car and the Gardaí thought he'd been drinking. And there were all these fucking neighbours standing in judgement. And it was, like, 'I have to get out of this fucking kip.'"

There is anger and confusion here but it is as much about the senseless violence that erupts between men confined together in a small space. "There was a row in the house," Bono recalls. "My father, my brother and myself didn't get along at the time. I remember throwing a carving knife at my brother and it sticking in the door. I missed – but that's what 'I Threw a Brick Through a Window' was about."

I Threw a Brick Through A Window Written: U2 • Duration: 4' 54"

Rejoice

Bono talks about an extraordinary renewal that took place in 1976. Amazing things happened in Mount Temple, with nearly half the school undergoing some kind of religious experience. One of the teachers had quite an effect on a lot of people. She was always on about the Scriptures, the thing took hold, and during a period of about two months there was an eruption of spiritual fervour.

One of the girls eventually blew it by going to the headmaster's office and asking him to announce over the intercom that the school now belonged to Jesus. It was a measure of how intense the collective feeling had become. "That was the first wave," Bono says, "and there was a kind of an echo of it around about 1981 or '82. Charismatic things started happening. That was when we became involved in the Shalom group. We were studying the Scriptures. When everyone else was figuring out how to get served and how to score, we were all completely wrapped up in this."

'Rejoice' is a celebration of that spiritual involvement. It is also quite explicitly a rejection of the pretentions of bands like The Clash who were coming on at the time as if punk rock were the key to the revolution. The Edge has commented that some of Bono's best lyric writing is done under pressure, on the mic, but that theory isn't borne out here. You can sense the bluster, feel the desperation. "And what am I to do?" he asks. "Just tell me what am I supposed to say." Improvised on the spot, the line almost certainly sparked a silent cynical rejoinder from Steve Lillywhite, who was finding Bono's apparent lack of preparation enormously trying. But the singer succeeded in coming up with some memorable lines even under pressure.

"Only last week I had some American come up to me and say, '*I can't change the world/But I can change the world in me.*' So naive!" he reflects. "But there was something real happening all the same. At that point we were so removed from the culture. Rock 'n' roll – that was just the day job. We used to get together every single night, meeting in people's houses, reading, studying Scriptures. The band was what we did during the day." The Edge remembers *October* as an album that suffered because of the lack of time U2 had to prepare it. He has a point, especially given that it was his superb, propulsive guitar-playing that rescued 'Rejoice'. But, overall, there was less to celebrate here than Bono felt at the time.

Rejoice Written: U2 • Duration: 3' 38"

Fire

I remember Bono taking me out to his car, parked outside Windmill Lane studios in Dublin, and playing me the band's new single. The implicit distinction was important in itself. At that stage, U2 were still thinking about putting stuff together that would crack the charts, and during a break in their American tour, they'd stopped off at Chris Blackwell's studios in Nassau, in the Bahamas, to increase their chances.

On an initial listen I was struck by the glistening guitar power, the suggestion of sabres rattling and the sun glinting off them. It was a small triumph at least: released in June 1981, in advance of *October*, it provided the band with their first British chart success.

With its roots in the Book of Revelations and the circumstances of the second coming, it is apocalyptic in tone. But if you weren't already aware of the band's interest in religion, there was nothing that explicitly signalled the underlying biblical frame of reference. At a push, 'Fire' could have been about some imagined nuclear-fuelled Armageddon. However it was read at the time, Bono dismisses it now as nonsense.

"As I recall, 'Fire' was our attempt at a single. God knows where our heads were at," he laughs. "There was something good about it – I just can't remember what it was."

He isn't entirely serious when he attributes the song's failure to the fact that they were recording, for the first time, in the lap of luxury. "That was an amazing trip," he says. "It was our first time going to the Caribbean and it just blew us all away. There is that thing when you're in a baby band, where you feel that you're on holidays all the time, and you can't believe that you haven't been found out. So when you're in a place like Nassau, you don't really want to go in and work, do you? And you realise why all these great groups make crap records when they go to record there! It's because they just don't feel like working when they're in the Bahamas." The whole debacle had its lighter side – in retrospect. "You know the story about *Top of the Pops* and 'Fire'?" asks Bono. "It was our first time on Top of the Pops and the record company were really thrilled because we were going to have a hit single. We went on and the single went down because we were so bad. The miming was all over the shop and it was operatic in a way that TV will never understand. I was dressed in this black military kind of sleeping bag shirt, with a bad haircut."

Fire Written: U2 • Duration: 3' 52" • UK singles chart position: 35

Head band: In June 1981, U2 played at one of their first festivals: the PinkPop Festival in the Netherlands.

Tomorrow

When Bono went to see Ridley Scott's chilling futuristic thriller *Blade Runner*, he was impressed. But there was a flaw. At first he couldn't figure out what it was. Then it dawned on him. It was the music. "I am a fan of Vangelis," he said, "but in the '90s, people won't be listening to electronic music. Who wants electronic music in an electronic age?"

Bono felt that modernism was about to be rejected, because in the era that *Blade Runner* represented, it was not technology that would be needed most in art and in music but those instruments that restored people's humanity. On Bruce Springsteen's magnificent, low-fi Nebraska, he identified a fragile quality to the music that had to do with the tones and textures of the acoustic guitar and the harmonica. Released a year earlier, 'Tomorrow' had explored the same terrain, utilising the timelessness and the power of Vinnie Kilduff's uileann pipes as its signature.

The choice of an instrument that was intimately associated with Irish traditional music was undoubtedly a reaction to touring and the band's initial experience of the rigours of American roadwork. Bono talked about waking up suddenly and realizing that he was Irish. The more attention you pay to the lyrics, the more poignant they become. There was a time when Bono used to talk about 'Tomorrow' as a song about what was happening in Northern Ireland at the beginning of the '80s. In an atmosphere of deepening sectarian conflict, a knock on the door increasingly became an invitation to accept a bullet in the head. No one knew for certain what was waiting for them when they opened the door, opened the door . . .

But Bono has been revisiting the song recently, and is in no doubt now about what had really been troubling him so deeply back then. 'Tomorrow' is a song about the death of his mother – no more and no less. "*Won't you come back tomorrow/Won't you be back tomorrow/ Can I sleep tonight?*" he pleads, and the sense of desolation and loss is palpable.

"There are things that have to be worked out, that are going to come out," he says. "They'll find holes. It's still amazing to me that I could have convinced myself that this was about anything else. It's amazing that you can be so completely out of touch with yourself and with feelings you're trying to express."

Tomorrow Written: U2 • Duration: 4' 39"

October

Bono was always ready with a theory. "U2 music is not urban music," he said in 1980. "It's more to do with hills, rivers and mountains." He might have been talking about the context that gave rise to the immensely troubled and still deeply moving 'October'.

The Edge remembers it as a song that could have gone places, but Bono was bereft of further lyrical inspiration and they didn't have the time to squeeze out whatever sparks might have been flickering. They decided to put it out as it was.

Explorers: Bono and The Edge at the Torhout Festival in Belgium, 1982. From a musical Welsh family, The Edge is a fine singer in his own right.

'October' is suffused with an other-worldly sadness that taps into the tangled emotions that were driving the band just then, and that risked driving them apart. On the run-up to recording 'October', Bono, The Edge and Larry were living out in Portrane, beside the beach on the north coast of Dublin, with the Shalom group. Bono was baptised in the sea and they were living in a caravan in a field. They were praying a lot and fasting. The three Christian members of the band had been under a lot of pressure from other members of the Shalom group to quit. It was on the beach in Portrane that The Edge broke the news to Bono that he might be leaving the band. If The Edge was going, Bono decided that he would too – that they'd break up the band. The Edge asked for two weeks, to give him time to go away and consider his position. When he came back he had decided that being a Christian in a rock 'n' roll band involved a contradiction alright – but one he could live with.

"'October' . . . it's an image," Bono said in 1981. "We've been through the '60s, a time when things were in full bloom. We had fridges and cars, we sent people to the Moon and everybody thought how great mankind was. And now, as we go through the '70s and '80s, it's a colder time of the year. It's after the harvest. The trees are stripped bare. So 'October' is an ominous word, but it's also quite lyrical."

As extrapolations, go it makes some kind of sense. The title came first: it was what Bono wanted to call the album. The Edge hadn't played the piano in years but he had a real feel for it and he began to pick out this pure melody. 'October' was the result, and its nakedness said much about the crises the band had been going through, both personal and creative. 'October' captures U2 in a moment of supreme vulnerability, and is all the more compelling as a result. There may indeed have been a bigger, more complete song there to be written. But sometimes, as U2 would find again and again, these things are best left to find a life of their own.

October Written: U2 • Duration: 2' 21"

With A Shout

There is an underlying tone of defiance that runs throughout *October*. U2's debut album had been made in a spirit of optimism. The culmination of almost four years of apprenticeship, *Boy* harboured a surfeit of bounce: you got the feeling that U2 were ready to take on the world. But touring the album had been draining. The more they got to know about the music industry, the more U2 were repelled by the cynicism of it.

Their idealism had taken a battering, hearing stories about how bands they'd respected and been inspired by, like the Clash and the Jam, treated their road crew, and seeing the inner workings of the record business for the first time. In a sense, they went into the recording of *October* with the attitude that if people didn't like it, it just might be better for everyone concerned. Rejection would make it easier to walk away.

It's hard to conceive of anything that could have been so terminally unhip as Bono exhorting the great unwashed to make tracks for Jerusalem, but that's precisely what he did on 'With a Shout'. "We don't want to be the band that talks about God," he had said during 1980, but the crucifixion imagery was unmistakable. You could interpret it as a logical conclusion of Bono, Larry and The Edge's belief in what they thought of as the spirit that moves all things. Equally, you might dismiss it as an effective abdication of the responsibility he had, both to the band and to their audiences. Whatever the cause, there is no mistaking the spirit of abandon with which Bono met the challenge of constructing the lyrics. On the one hand there was trust: I will rely on Him for inspiration. On the other there was doubt: No matter what I do, it is all meaningless. And finally, there was perhaps a core of self-belief: Fuck them. Why should we hide what we feel?

Bono had been reading the Psalms of David at the time. "Yeah, there's triumphalism there," Bono reflects. "But in an odd way the walls of Jerusalem, or the walls of Jericho, were a great image for punk music, and the idea that went with it, that music could shake the foundations. The Psalms are amazing about music. They're all about bang that drum, whack that cymbal and, you know, dead bones rising up. Music as a wake-up call for the spirit – that was what we were driving at." You could say that it was a brave failure. The imagery would be revisited, much more effectively, later.

With A Shout Written: U2 • Duration: 4' 02"

Stranger In A Strange Land

In the early days, David Bowie had been a significant influence on the band. You could see it in some of Bono's stage moves: there was a self-conscious theatrical Bowie-esque side to the band in their pre-*Boy* days, that disappeared for a long time, resurfacing only with Zoo TV. It's curious then that Bono doesn't recall seeing Nicolas Roeg's *The Man Who Fell to Earth*, in which Bowie made his screen debut. That film was based on a Robert Heinlein novel; Heinlein also wrote *Stranger in a Strange Land*, which gave Bono the title for one of *October*'s most effective lyrics. Touring was a time for reading. Books were consumed on the tour bus and in hotel rooms. Some images, ideas, titles, lingered. The experience could also provide its own moments of inspiration.

"You have to remember that the only travel we did as kids was to go over to Wales on camping holidays," a friend recalls. "Bono used to go over to Wales to see some girl he knew from camping when he was ten. "I remember we all went over and knocked on her hall door and she was going out with another guy and it was like 'Fuck off!' And we were left camping on this site and it was the middle of winter so we thought, 'Let's walk around town in our underpants.' And we had airguns and we were all arrested – they thought we were the IRA or something. That was a big adventure for us. We were very sheltered."

So when U2 began to tour, it was an eye-opener. Perhaps if Bono hadn't lost his lyrics, there'd have been more postcards from a tour bus on *October*. In the event, 'Stranger in a Strange Land' seems like an exception. "We were going to Berlin," Bono recalls. "We were all in the back of the van in our sleeping bags and we had to travel through the corridor between East Germany and West Berlin. And we were stopped by this border guard. The song was just a little portrait of him. He was our own age, with short hair, in a uniform and his life was pretty grim and he was seeing these guys in a rock 'n' roll band passing through."

The song had a quality that was scarce on *October*: empathy: "*We asked him to smile for a photograph/We waited around to see if we could*

We were all in the back of the van in our sleeping bags and we had to travel through the corridor between East Germany and West Berlin." Bono

make him laugh/The soldier asked for a cigarette/His smiling face I can't forget." "That's quite a good lyric," Bono says, looking at the song afresh. It's been speculated that the soldier could as easily have been a British Army squaddie in Northern Ireland but, at most, that's an undercurrent.

Stranger In A Strange Land Written: U2 • Duration: 3' 56"

Scarlet

There had been a lot of pressure on the band to use their music in the cause of Christianity, of Jesus, of Shalom. People within the tightly knit group thought that U2 should use the platform they'd won to proselytise. "I remember thinking: does God need salesmen?" Bono recalls. "Do we really have to reduce this to pulpit-thumping? By this stage I'd been to America and I'd seen the state of the evangelicals and the fundamentalists, and of religious broadcasting in America – the preachers with their hands reaching out of the television trying to steal your money. People would say, 'Are you embarrassed? Are you ashamed?' I'm not ashamed. I'm just not going to go around and flog it like a second-hand car salesman." And so, 'Scarlet' takes a minimalist line. It may originally have been an instrumental piece for which Bono failed to come up with a lyric, but it stands the test of time all the better for its simplicity. The Edge is at the piano again, Adam Clayton contributes a resonant, melodic bass part and Larry plays the role of percussionist with admirable restraint.

The influence of Paul McGuinness' album of Gregorian chants is discernible in the straight choral lines of Bono's delivery. And there is something healing rather than triumphalist about the effect when he sings the one word over and over: "Rejoice".

A prelude to '40', it identified a vein that would yield further, greater riches later.

Scarlet Written: U2 • Duration: 2' 53"

Is That All?

The album could have ended with 'Scarlet', but for some reason that no one can quite figure out now, they felt that it needed an end-piece. Patti Smith used to make her records by writing her titles first, sketching out the word-frame and then creating the music with those suggestions in mind. Or so U2 had read. An ambience was created, the music took shape and then the lyrics were written and improvised on the mc, coming together by a kind of process of trial and error. She may have had an end-piece on Horses and the band wanted to follow suit. Or it might just have been that someone had thought that it was a good title for a final track – and once the title had been invented, they had to deliver the "song".

A good title it may indeed have been, but the end result is a mess. The guitar riff is lifted from 'The Cry', an earlier song that was often incorporated into 'The Electric Co.' but never made it onto disc. Otherwise 'Is That All?' was written in the studio, and it shows. Larry's cracking snare and superb drumming notwithstanding, it is confused and incoherent, but unintentionally revealing nonetheless. "Is that all that you want from me?" Bono pleads, in a giveaway line that seems to acknowledge his own feelings of creative frustration and failure.

"I think after the album came out we thought, 'Uuh'," Bono shrugs. *October* has its moments of sheer beauty. For an album that was frequently dismissed, parts of it stand up surprisingly well. But even when it fails, it tells us much about the confused and perilous state of mind U2 were in at the time. Arguably, 'Is That All?' says more about that theme than any other track precisely because it says so little. They should have known better.

Is That All? Written: U2 • Duration: 3' 01"

WAR

For all its ringing assertions of faith, *October* had been conceived in an atmosphere of doubt. The involvement of Bono, Larry and The Edge in Shalom Christianity had temporarily undermined U2's conviction about their mission as a rock 'n' roll band. The album was recorded under a cloud, in a rush. It had moments of sweet inspiration but it felt unfinished.

The trio were under increasing pressure from within the Shalom group – about how they should dress, what they should look like, the way they should sound. They resented being crowded, dictated to. Looking around, they didn't like the nihilism into which punk had descended. The New Romantics were seen as irrelevant, peddling pop of the most self-regarding and vacuous variety. Everything was out of kilter.

As U2 toured *October* through '81 and '82 they became hardened by roadwork. They had regained their confidence as a rock 'n' roll band. Bono was driven by a need to bring all the pieces together. Now was the time to declare war on everything that was cynical, phoney, defeatist and limiting. Their third album would be a document of the times. There could be no shirking. Personally, politically and musically, U2 would declare their independence. Loud, angry and demanding, the *War* album and tour would see U2 triumph.

Sunday Bloody Sunday

The events which formed the backdrop to one of U2's most explicitly political songs are etched indelibly into the text of Ireland's troubled colonial history. The counter-intelligence unit of the original Irish Republican Army, under Michael Collins, identified 14 British undercover agents who had been responsible for the systematic killing of members of Sinn Féin over the previous months. On 21 November, 1921, they broke into their houses early in the morning and assassinated them in their beds.

In retaliation, armed forces – in the form of the Regular Royal Irish Constabulary and the notorious Black and Tans, a ruthless auxiliary police force used to crush nationalist opposition – went into the headquarters of the Gaelic Athletic Association in Croke Park. There they opened fire on the crowd attending a football match. In all, 12 people were shot dead and 60 others were wounded. That day became known as Bloody Sunday.

That horrific double incident was echoed in Derry in 1972. In an infamous attack, the elite Paratroop Regiment of the British Army opened fire during a civil rights demonstration and killed 14 unarmed people. Another 14 were badly wounded. The images of that day remain unforgettable. In particular, footage of the man who would become Catholic Bishop of Derry, Edward Daly, holding his...

<continues on page 38>

War boys: U2 performing on Channel 4's music programme *The Tube* in 1983.

Release date: March 1983
Catalogue number: ILPS 9733
Producer: Steve Lillywhite
Track listing: Sunday Bloody Sunday/ Seconds/New Year's Day/ Like A Song/Drowning Man/The Refugee/Two Hearts Beat As One/ Red Light/ Surrender/40
Highest chart position: No. 1 (UK), 12 (US)

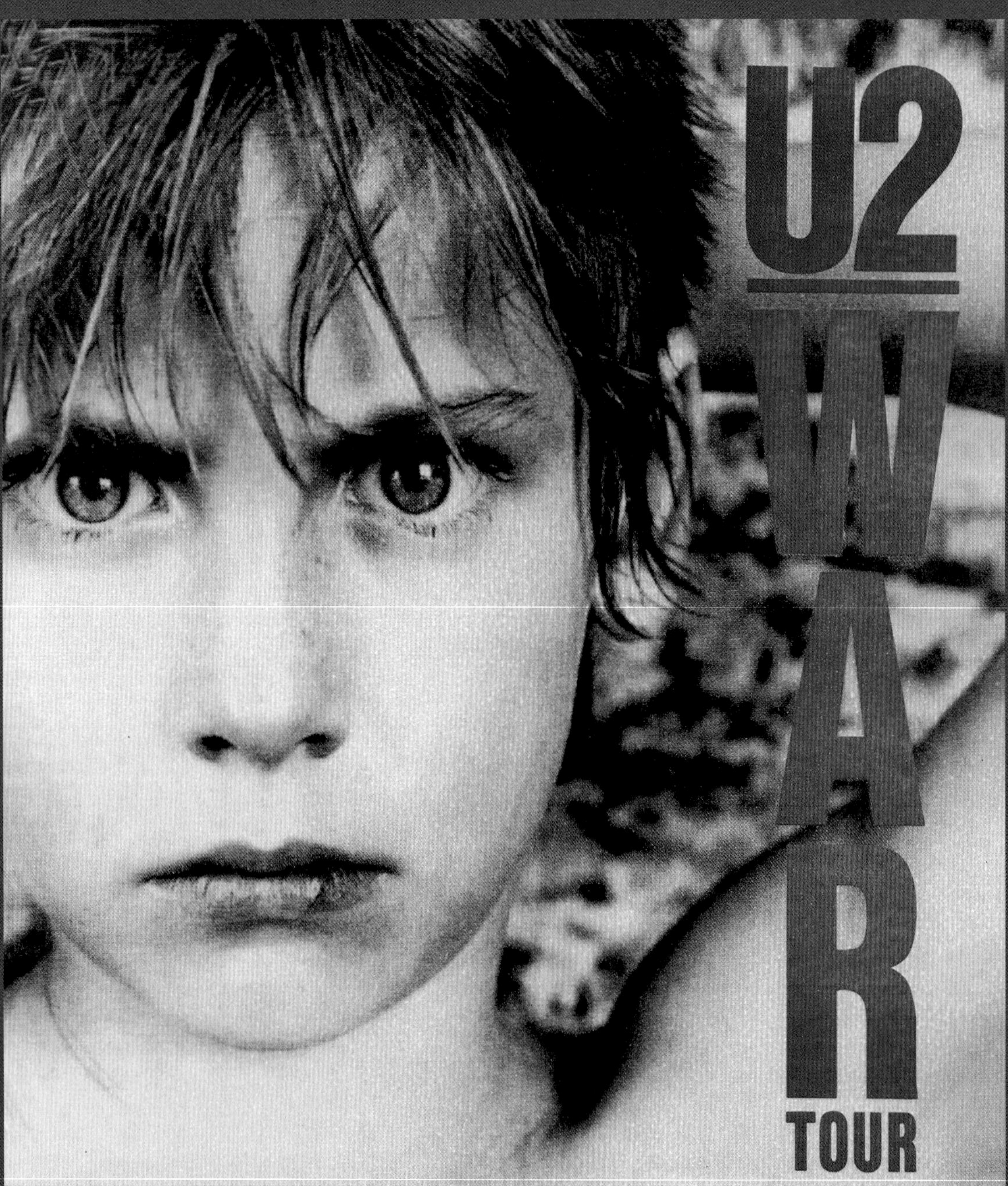

U2
WAR
TOUR
THURSDAY MAY 19TH 8 P.M.
CLEVELAND MUSIC HALL
WITH SPECIAL GUEST DREAM SYNDICATE
TICKETS: $9.50 ADVANCE $10.50 DAY OF SHOW
ALL SEATS RESERVED. ON SALE NOW AT PUBLIC HALL BOX OFFICE
AND ALL TICKETRON LOCATIONS
FOR FURTHER INFORMATION CALL 523-2229

War tour: Performing 19 songs – six from the new album, *War* – U2 rocked the Cleveland Music Hall on 19 May 1983. For the final song of the encore, '40 (How Long)', the audience continued singing several minutes after the band had left the stage.

THE MAKING OF WAR (1983)

BY BRIAN BOYD

When U2's third album was released, it knocked Michael Jackson's *Thriller* off the top of the UK charts. This was the big time. Just how big could this band get?

When U2 reconvened to record *War* in 1982, the band were under pressure. Their second album hadn't performed as well as expected, the early career plan to storm the US market had been torn up and the tensions between their religious faith and their commitment to the band's cause had only just been resolved.

But there was fire in the quartet's bellies when they began *War*. They knew they were up against the wall, some fans had been let down by *October* and the record company were getting anxious for a more commercial sounding record.

War began with Bono penning a love song to his long-time girlfriend, Alison Stewart (the two had been going out together since meeting at Mount Temple School). Married shortly after the *War* sessions began, Bono wrote 'New Year's Day' about his new bride – "*I want to be with you, be with you, night and day*." However, the song slowly changed and in the studio it became reshaped into an anthem of sorts for the Polish Solidarity Movement – who, at the time, were standing up to Russian-imposed Communist rule in their country.

'New Year's Day' was to prove significant for the band: as a single from the album, it became the band's first hit outside of Ireland and the UK and introduced the band, through massive radio play, to European audiences. It remains the fifth most played song ever on all the U2 tours.

While *Boy* was about adolescent dreams and *October* about spiritual questioning, *War* was in many ways U2's political album. 'Sunday Bloody Sunday' addressed the violence and political turmoil in Northern Ireland while other songs drew upon disturbing events in then apartheid South Africa and the continuing war in the Middle East.

As a complete piece of work, *War* sounded rougher and more urgent than anything they had recorded before. This was mainly due to The Edge using far fewer guitar effects (on previous albums he had drowned his guitar sound with delay and echo) and going for a more aggressive sound. Larry Mullen's military-style drumming added to the directness of the sound.

The cover of the album reflected the band's new musical approach. Peter Rowen, the six-year-old boy from the cover of the *Boy* album, returned as a stern-looking nine-year-old for *War*. As Bono explained: "Instead of putting guns and tanks on the cover, we've put a child's face. War can also be a mental thing, an emotional thing between lovers. It doesn't have to be a physical thing."

It was in fact a personal "war" between The Edge and his then girlfriend, Aislinn O'Sullivan (later his wife) that led to the album's stand-out moment. Following a row with Aislinn and still worried about the band's seemingly faltering career, Edge channelled all his frustrations into the guitar riff that held up 'Sunday Bloody Sunday'. There were still songs influenced by their religious faith. Both 'Drowning Man' and '40' have lyrics taken directly from the Bible. *War* also began the now sacred U2 album ritual of not finishing an album until literally the very last second. The final song to be recorded for the album was '40'. The song takes its title from the fact that it was written in ten minutes, then recorded in ten minutes, then mixed in ten minutes and then played back for ten minutes in the studio just as U2's recording time for *War* was up. For a song written so quickly, '40' became an important live moment for the band. It was used for years as the closing song at U2 concerts with the band walking off one by one until just the audience were left to continue singing the song's refrain – "How long to sing this song?"

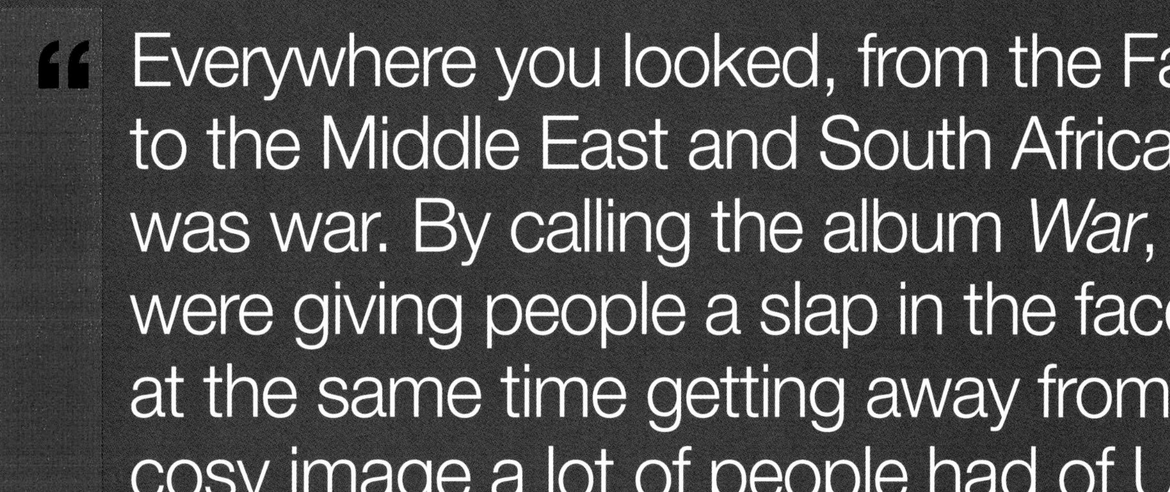

"Everywhere you looked, from the Falklands to the Middle East and South Africa, there was war. By calling the album *War*, we were giving people a slap in the face and at the same time getting away from the cosy image a lot of people had of U2." Bono

...handkerchief aloft as an improvised white flag, as he crawls on his hands and knees towards the lifeless silhouette of one of the victims of the slaughter, serves as an emblem of the innocence of those who had been slaughtered. Those two events formed the immediate political backdrop to the opening song on *War*...

"I can't believe the news today." It was an introductory line which crystallised the prevailing response to the series of outrages that devastated Northern Ireland throughout the '70s and early '80s. To a large extent those who lived in Dublin had been immune. But, in an increasingly politicised band, Bono had come around to the view that they could not simply wash their hands of the violence in the North, or of the injustices which had spawned it. "It was only when I realised that the troubles hadn't affected me that they began to affect me," he said at the time. "The bombs may not go off in Dublin but they're made here."

'Sunday Bloody Sunday' was not a partisan statement. Live, it was always prefaced with a disclaimer. "This is not a rebel song," Bono would declare. By that he meant that it was not to be taken as supporting the Republican cause. "What I was trying to say in the song is: there it is, in close-up," Bono explained. "I'm sick of it. How long must it go on? It's not even saying there's an answer." The important thing was at least to ask the right questions. It was The Edge's idea to explore the theme, and to link what was happening in Northern Ireland back to the original Christian blood sacrifice and subsequent resurrection on Easter Sunday. "Bono was away on his honeymoon," The Edge recalls. "I wrote the music and hit on an idea for the lyrics and presented it to the band when they got back." The song would articulate the band's own sense of bewilderment at the Northern conflict, but an incident at a US gig provided an immediate context for Bono. "I walked out of the backstage door in San Francisco," Bono explained, "and there were 30 or 40 people waiting for a chat and for autographs, and I was scrawling my name on bits of paper as they were handed to me. I got this one piece of paper and it was folded and when I opened it, it was a big dogma thing looking for signatures – I was about to sign my name on a petition to support some guy I'd never heard of, an Irish guy with Republican connections. And I got worried at that stage.

"As much as I'm a Republican, I'm not a territorial person. The whole idea of U2 using a white flag on stage was to get away from the green, white and orange. To get away from the Stars and Stripes. To get away from the Union Jack... I mean, I'd love to see a united Ireland but I don't believe you can put a gun to someone's head to make him see your way."

In that sense 'Sunday Bloody Sunday' was a protest song – not against any one act of violence but against a cycle of violence into which all of the protagonists in the Northern conflict seemed to be locked. Adam remembers that it was originally much more vitriolic, with an opening line that would have hung like an albatross around U2's collective neck for years to come: "Don't talk to me about the rights of the IRA." But better judgement prevailed. "The viewpoint became very humane and non-sectarian," Adam reflects, "which is the only responsible position." The urgency of the emotion did not, however, make it an easy song to produce. During the writing of *War*, Bono suffered from writer's block and one of his abiding memories

of making the album relates to how his wife, Ali, helped him through this traumatic period. "She was literally kicking me out of bed in the morning," Bono recalled. "She literally put the pen in my hand." During recording, considerable time was spent on the drum part. Larry Mullen Jnr. was exiled from the studio and located under the front staircase in Windmill Lane, the open spaces above lending his sound the natural reverb that producer Steve Lillywhite was looking for.

By chance, The Edge had bumped into Steve Wickham on the way home from a writing session and the violinist was brought into play, his fiddle colourations effectively stirring up some old ethnic ghosts and lending the song deeper Irish resonances. "Actually it starts as a folk song and ends up as one of those Salvation Army songs," Bono says now. "That was a good idea, but I don't think it came off, really."

A powerful song, it became a live staple, its anthemic quality lending itself to the stadium treatment towards which the band were inevitably being drawn. It resurfaced on the mini-album *Under a Blood Red Sky*, also released in 1983, but its apotheosis came during the Joshua Tree tour, which was being recorded for the *Rattle and Hum* album and film.

The version in the film was recorded on the day of the Enniskillen massacre, 8 November, 1987. This, too, was a horrific military operation, in this instance carried out by the IRA . A bomb was placed at the war memorial in the centre of Enniskillen town in Fermanagh. As a crowd gathered there to mark Remembrance Day, the bomb was detonated, killing 13 people. It was an action which was impossible to defend, and the ensuing wave of condemnation and revulsion shook the Republican movement to its core. Many would remember the Enniskillen bombing as the most appalling atrocity committed in the cause of Irish unity.

"Fuck the revolution," Bono declared on stage in Denver after the news had come through from Ireland, and the band proceeded to unleash a cathartic, emotional version of the song which reflected their anger – and that of so many Irish men and women – at another senseless, brutal act of violence, in which innocent people had been butchered. "It was the ultimate performance of the song," Bono confided in 1988. "It was almost like the song was made real for the day, in a way that it was never going to be again. Anything else would be less than that."

Sunday Bloody Sunday Written: U2 • Duration: 4' 39"

Seconds

The acoustic guitar that opens 'Seconds' and drives it was The Edge's idea. In fact, the song is a tour-de-force by the guitarist. For the first time, he sings lead vocals. It was The Edge's voice that U2 tended to double-track for harmonies. Bono figures his partner-in-crime's singing was under-rated: now that he was out in front, a lot of people failed to notice the difference and assumed it was Bono on vocals.

The track offered ample evidence that U2's canvas was broadening. There was musical irony in the juxtaposition of The Edge's jaunty acoustic pop confection with lyrics about the imminence of nuclear catastrophe. There's humour in the reference to a track by sland labelmates Troublefunk: *"They're doing the atomic bomb/Do they know*

Arena band: Bono on stage during the second date of the War tour in Manchester, 1982. Such was the album's success that they were playing in clubs at the start but finished, two years later, playing in arenas.

Rock stars: Bono gets the audience to sing along during a show early in the War tour.

High lights: Adam Clayton stands guard over Bono during the San Bernardino festival.

where the dance comes from?" And in a move that in many ways was ahead of its time, they lifted a sample from a 1982 TV documentary entitled *Soldier Girls*.

"The whole spectacle of these girls going through this incredible routine of training seemed perfect to slip in here," The Edge said in 1983. *"It's not obvious but if you listen close you can hear the refrain 'I want to be an airborne ranger/I want to live the life of danger'.* It's very disturbing." "I remember watching it in the Green Room in Windmill," Bono recalls. "It happened to be on and we made a recording of it. Sometimes things like that just fall into place." Overall, the track was curiously reminiscent of the Beatles – a positive recommendation at the worst of times. Not to be outdone, one close associate insists that the group were subconsciously influenced by the Human League, who had a track with the title 'Seconds' (about the assassination of John F. Kennedy) on their *Dare* album.

Meanwhile, in global political terms, during the early '80s, there was reason to believe that the lunatics had taken over the asylum. Under Margaret Thatcher's bellicose regime, American Pershing cruise missiles had been freshly installed in Britain. And in the USA, there was the scary picture of Ronald Reagan, a right-wing fundamentalist president who was quite clearly doddering and incompetent into the bargain. With his finger on the button, you got the impression that Armageddon might be unleashed at any time. Maybe even by accident.

"I've always felt physically ill at the concept of nuclear fall-out," Bono says. "We are the first generation of people to have to live with that possibility. It's all around us, it's in our heads. And it affects the way people feel about the world. I always saw it in apocalyptic terms. For the first time, it became possible – it is possible – to destroy everything."

Seconds Written: U2 • Duration: 3' 11"

New Year's Day

Adam had come up with the bass figure at a soundcheck. The Edge had developed the piece on the piano. Now, the band were five, maybe six tracks into recording *War* and Bono still hadn't got down the lyrics for 'New Year's Day'. "It was an unsettled time," Adam recalled later. "You looked around and there were conflicts everywhere. We saw a lot of unrest on TV and in the media. We focused on these."

In the end, Bono had to make up the lyrics on the spot. The singer had a set of images in his head that he felt would fit the mood of the piece. He began to describe them to the backdrop of the music. He was flying on a wing and a prayer and testing everyone's tolerance for the nth time in the process. But the opening line is beautifully arresting and what emerges is a haunting love song of considerable depth. It was the only real single on *War* and went straight into the UK Top 10 on release.

"I personally am bloody sick, every time I switch on the radio, of being blasted with this contrived crap," Bono said shortly afterwards. "It would be stupid to start drawing up battle lines but the fact that 'New Year's Day' made the Top 20 indicated a disillusionment among record buyers with the pop culture in the charts."

It does conform to the basic chart model in one respect at least, however. It is a love song, doubtless written by Bono with his new wife, Ali, in mind. But the impressionistic political backdrop connected with the mood of the time in an unexpected way. With the emergence of the Solidarity movement, from 1980 onwards the communist regime in Poland was being challenged for the first time since the Iron Curtain had been erected. Following a series of strikes, martial law had been imposed, in December 1981. Solidarity became a proscribed organisation and its leaders were arrested, among them Lech Walesa.

"Subconsciously I must have been thinking about Lech Walesa being interned and his wife not being allowed to see him," Bono commented. "Then, when we'd recorded the song, they announced that martial law would be lifted in Poland on New Year's Day. Incredible." Nothing changes on New Year's Day? You knew what he meant all the same.

New Year's Day
Written: U2 • Duration: 5' 35" • UK singles chart position: 10

Like A Song

Initially, U2 conceived of *War* as a knuckleduster in the face of the new pretty-boy pop that was flourishing in Britain in the early '80s. But it was also intended as a musical two-fingers to the self-styled cognoscenti who had been stepping up their attacks on U2 as being too worthy and sincere by far, not real rock 'n' rollers.

"I think 'Like A Song' was addressed to the critics who didn't get what we were about, who thought we weren't really punk enough," Bono recalls. "That's a subject that comes up again and again because people really do fall for this rebel thing. It's such a cliché."

"It made some kind of sense in the '50s and '60s. Against a conservative backdrop, that punk attitude had a real meaning. Now a lot of it is just dressing up."

Bono's anger isn't always well articulated in the song itself. "I don't think I got the tone of voice right," he observes. But he hits the bullseye once at least, in identifying the selfishness at the heart of most rock 'n' roll posturing. "*When others need your time/You say it's time to go*," he accuses. The band make a lot of thunderously impressive noise, but in the end 'Like A Song' remains just that. Like a song.

Like A Song Written: U2 • Duration: 4' 47"

Drowning Man

There aren't many songwriters who would attempt to get away with it. It remains inscrutable: there is no reference to a drowning man in there. It's to do with the way U2 constructed their songs at the time. "It was the title of a Sam Beckett-style play I'd started about a drowning man," Bono recalls. "I had a few scenes written. There was to be a guy in a chair with a blindfold and there was to be a little ballet thing."

In the build-up to recording *War*, The Edge remembers that it was a song they took for granted. Although most of the work still had to be done on it, they knew that there was the root of a very strong piece in there. When it came to putting it down, the song took flight,

Pop pilot: *War* – both the album and the tour – transformed U2's fortunes, taking them from New Wave misfits to serious chart contenders.

Sign of the times: Bumper sticker to promote the release of *War*.

Black and white: An early publicity shot of U2.

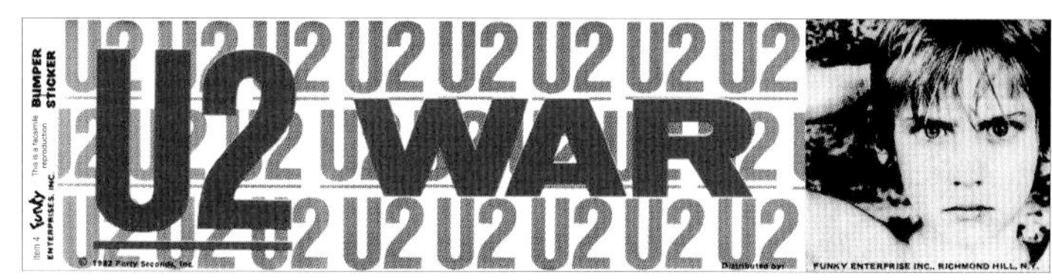

developing into one of the band's most sophisticated and successful artefacts. Rhythmically, Larry and Adam stitch it together beautifully, with more than a little help from The Edge on acoustic. Bono's singing is transcendant and there's a lovely eastern inflection to the counter-melody when Steve Wickham's violin lifts off towards the close.

"Whereas I know some of the songs on *War* could be re-recorded and improved," The Edge said in 1985, "with 'Drowning Man' it's perfection. It's one of the most successful pieces of recording we've ever done." I have a hunch that the phrase "drowning man" may have featured in the first draft of the lyrics, to be replaced as the song developed by the altogether more musical "take my hand". Whatever the truth in that, 'Drowning Man' has been interpreted as a love song in which the subject and object are deliberately merged, with Bono surrendering himself to a higher love, embracing both the sexual and the spiritual.

Looking back now at the reflection of his younger self in the mirror of the lyric sheet, Bono hesitantly describes it as a psalm. Mostly these are written from the point of view of David railing at God – but occasionally the perspective switches and what we read instead are God's words. At the height of his involvement in charismatic Christianity, Bono had been experimenting with the experience of speaking in tongues within the Shalom group. Bono would search for that higher state, improvising lyrics on the mic, allowing the words, the feeling – at its best, the ecstasy – to take hold. He remembers being up there recording 'Drowning Man'. It's a song written from the

perspective of a loving God. It may, in its way, be entirely presumptuous – but, far more importantly, its cup is overflowing with tenderness.

Drowning Man Written: U2 • Duration: 4' 14"

The Refugee

Steve Lillywhite had a rule that he would not do more than two albums with any one band or artist. It was time for U2, also, to move on to fresh alliances, and to use the opportunity to remodel their sound. They knew what they wanted: a harder, more urban, more rock 'n' roll feel than *October* had exhibited. Among those considered were Jimmy Destri, then of Blondie, Sandy Pearlman, who had worked with Blue Oyster Cult and The Clash, Roxy Music's Rhet Davies, and Jimmy Iovine, who had phoned repeatedly, insisting that he wanted to produce the band.

Along the way they'd considered the possibility of using an Irish producer. Bill Whelan had already formed a publishing alliance with the band's manager, Paul McGuinness, and they demoed one song at least with him. It turned up on *War*.

"I think when Bono went to America he became more politicised," one friend suggests. "He was hanging out with Cubans in San Francisco. In America, the blacks, the Italians and other immigrants have an amour for the Irish. Bono always got that kind of response, so he started to take an interest in what the Irish and the blacks and the Caribbeans had in common. I think that's where 'The Refugee' was coming from."

It was that, and more besides. The Irish film-maker Bob Quinn had been exploring the roots of Celtic culture. In an influential documentary, the Atlantean trilogy, he advanced the theory that the Celts had come to Ireland from Egypt and North Africa, taking their music and their art with them. Similarities had been detected between Irish traditional melodies and those of Middle Eastern folk and ethnic music. And in the same vein, art historians were beginning to identify unmistakable connections between Coptic art and the intricate and elaborate artwork hand-drawn by Irish monks in manuscripts like the Book of Kells.

That kind of discovery, and the debate it inspired, was hugely important in a country like Ireland, whose culture had been stultifyingly rigid and enclosed in the 50-plus years since independence had been declared in 1921. Among the younger post-'60s generation in particular, there was a growing awareness of the need to look outwards, and to learn from other cultures and other societies. This was now given fresh impetus by the recognition that our own roots and origins were far more complex – and far more interesting – than we'd traditionally been led to believe. Bono saw the Atlantean trilogy and later met Bob Quinn. It was almost inevitable that the curiosity which had thus been aroused would find an outlet in a song. "That was a passion at the time, that Irish music had to be re-invented or re-incarnated. At around the same time, I was trying to get in touch with John Lydon, to see if I could get him to record with The Chieftains. I had this idea that his voice sounded like bagpipes and I thought that

View from the top: U2 on the roof of Cork Country Club Hotel, Cork, Ireland, March 1980.

they'd be amazing together. Then we met Steve Wickham, who came in and played on 'Sunday Bloody Sunday'. I had spoken with Steve, over many nights, about how Irish music could be re-appropriated, because it was terribly unhip at the time. That became his project. He went off with that in mind and joined In Tua Nua. [He also later hooked up with The Waterboys.] So a lot of good came of all that."

The Troublefunk reference on 'Seconds' wasn't the only reason to suspect that someone had been doing some serious listening to black music. When *War* was being pieced together, Steve Lillywhite – who'd agreed to become involved one more time when all else had failed – took the Bill Whelan track and put the finishing touches to it. Larry Mullen's thumping tribal drums were mixed right up front and the band engaged in some suitably primitive chanting. The noise was impressive enough: it just didn't sound entirely as if U2 were wearing their own clothes, playing their own riffs, using their own voices.

"I haven't listened to that song in 10 years," Bono confesses, "but I think it's trying to be exciting and not quite pulling it off."

Curiously, Bill Whelan, who was credited with producing the track, found his own angle on the theme later in *Riverdance*. If reinvigorating Irish music, and in particular Irish dancing, was the objective, then Whelan achieved it spectacularly, with a successful musical that explored again the connections between Irish, American and – to a lesser extent – African music. In doing so, along with the show's producer Moya Doherty, Whelan succeeded in re-introducing an erotic dimension to an ethnic dance culture that had become sterile.

The Refugee Written: U2 • Duration: 3' 40"

Two Hearts Beat As One

Bono tied the knot with Ali Stewart on 21 August, 1982. The band were hugely in debt to Island Records at the time and the singer didn't have a whole lot of money to lavish on the occasion. Still, the Island connection had one distinct advantage: the owner of the label, Chris Blackwell, had extensive properties in Jamaica and the Bahamas. He loaned one of them, a house called Goldeneye which had once belonged to Ian Fleming, to Bono and Ali for their honeymoon. 'Two Hearts Beat As One' was one of two songs that Bono wrote there.

The second single to be released from *War* – and the band's second hit in Britain – it was another stab at fusing rock and funk and it was at least a partial success. Lyrically, Bono is still struggling to find a voice. "I don't know how to say what's got to be said," he confesses. But even more revealing, perhaps, is the undercurrent of desperation which the song announces. You can imagine Bono unable to bask in the comfort of his honeymoon house, his restless spirit inevitably contemplating with mounting horror the prospect of entering the studio again with a bunch of under-worked lyrical ideas and half-completed choruses scrawled on the back of cigarette papers and Air India sickbags. "*I can't stop to dance/This is my last chance*," he says, as if to excuse himself to Ali. And of course he may have been right: if U2 had not taken off with *War*, then it might well have been their last album, on Island at least. And if Island had dropped them, who knows what might have happened then?

"I didn't really write that many love songs in the straight sense because I think – does the world really need any more silly love songs?" Bono asserts. "But this is one. And in many ways I do think that it's beautiful. We're trying to make it groovy and we ain't quite pulled it off. I think if we'd tried it in a different key, we might have discovered a sexier groove and it might have worked better. But we never did that. Whatever the jam was in, I'd sing the song in that key. That's why there was a tightness in the vocals, which I find it hard to listen to now. I was screeching a lot of the time. But I think if a song like that had been delivered differently it would have more appeal to me now because it's a good song."

Two Hearts Beat As One Written: U2 • Duration: 4' 03" • UK singles chart position: 18

Red Light

An outsider visiting Ireland in the late '70s and early '80s might have been forgiven for concluding that the locals knew nothing about carnal delights, and had little interest in the pleasures of the flesh. The dominant ethos was still extremely conservative on sexual issues. The underlying reality was that the people had begun to move on, and the seeds of a more tolerant and liberal society were beginning to take root. But officially, it was a culture where condoms were still available from chemists only on prescription, homosexuality was illegal, and highly restrictive censorship laws ensured that erotic or pornographic books and magazines were almost completely unavailable.

It couldn't have been more different to New York, Hamburg or Amsterdam. Inevitably these somewhat exotic destinations held a particular allure for four young Irishmen in a rock 'n' roll band, enjoying the freedom of the cities they were visiting for the first time.

"I certainly remember a fascination with prostitution," Bono recalls. "We played Amsterdam and I remember seeing the girls for sale in the windows, lit in red. Thinking about it. Trying to figure out the reality of it, whether there was any or not. I was never judgmental about it." 'Red Light' is decidedly ambiguous. It's a love song, which could be addressed to one of the girls Bono had observed in the windows. Equally, it might be another somewhat parental, albeit affectionate homily directed at saving Adam's immortal soul. Or it could be written from the point of view of a prostitute, watching her clients come and go. Probably, in a way that was typical of U2's songs then, it is any or all of these things at once. Musically, the band make a stab at evoking an appropriately steamy cityscape. Kid Creole and the Coconuts, who were knocking on the door of stardom at the time, passed through town while U2 were recording the album, and the ensemble's trumpeter Kenny Fradley was hauled in to add a brassy bit. And then there were The Coconuts themselves.

"They came in," Bono recalls. "They wanted the lights turned down to do the recording and I think we had the studio lit in red, for effect. One of them started to take her top off. She wasn't undressing. She just took her top off, but we weren't used to that kind of thing. I remember the temperature in the studio was at an all-time high. Everyone was running around looking for cold water. We were that naive!"

Red Light Written: U2 • Duration: 3' 46"

TV stars: At the San Bernardino festival in 1983, U2 appeared to an audience of 125,000 people – at that point, their biggest yet. The festival was transmitted live from California on MTV.

Big rig: During their set, Bono distinguished himself by singing 'The Electric Co.' while scaling the stage's proscenium arch – all 30 metres (100 feet) of it.

Surrender

Bono was beginning to write songs. You can tell by the way he was

Off road: U2 in technicolor glory during a break from the War tour.

getting into using characters. And then there were the small poetic flourishes, lines that had a more finished feel to them. He was beginning to know his own strengths, to understand how to channel his creative energies more effectively. He was becoming a songwriter.

He'd met Sadie – not her real name – in New York. She was living on the street, hustling and doing whatever was necessary to keep body and soul together. Over 10 years on, she's still at the same game, only by now she's got a smack habit to feed. Back then, he was attracted to her and to the way in which she'd been able to let go of all the trappings of domesticity and respectability. He probably still is.

There's an ambivalence here that involves a huge leap forward from the biblical certainties of *October* and hints at the more complex world of *Achtung Baby* and *Zooropa*. The concept of surrender is a spiritual one, but it's rooted not in any conventional concept of virtue. It wasn't enough for Sadie to be a good wife, to raise a good family, to lead a good life. And so she took to the streets. "You've got to learn to let go in order to really live. That's what 'Surrender' is all about," Bono explains.

There's a reminder of the fascination with suicide on *Boy* when Sadie takes herself up to the 48th floor to find out, in the words of the song, what she's living for. "In one sense everyone's got to jump off. That's what it's all about – the idea that if I want to live, I've got to die to myself." The rest of the band provide the atmospherics, with The Edge enjoying himself playing a free role on slide guitar. But this is primarily Bono's track as he himself lets go, blissfully surrendering, fading, fading into the background.

Surrender Written: U2 • Duration: 5' 33"

The recording of *War* had been exhilarating, tense and finally draining. There were times during the course of their incarceration in Windmill when Steve Lillywhite had had to push Bono to the limits, forcing him to sing until his throat bled. Now, here they were, a track short and with their allotted studio time almost up. The band had enjoyed themselves in the past improvising B-sides and starting and finishing songs in an hour. The results were usually throwaway, but what the hell? They wanted to get '40' done. Steve Lillywhite said to go for it.

Adam was out of the studio and The Edge stood in, supplying a sweet, resonant melodic bass line that worked beautifully over the simple guitar strum. No point in changing it. At 6 o'clock in the morning, a belligerent bunch of musos in a local Dublin band arrived to begin the session they'd booked. They wanted U2 out. The band had to lock the door and mix the track while Bono was doing his final vocal take. His voice sounds ragged, 6 o'clock in the morning ragged. But whatever chemistry was at work as dawn crept in from the east over Dublin Bay, the band achieve a remarkable serenity. If this was what they'd been looking for throughout *War*, they'd found it in that final hour.

Partly it may be that they knew that their ordeal was over, that there was no point in trying too hard. Keep it simple. Get it down. It'll work out. '40' emerges as a lullaby, a hymn that's suffused with a deep feeling of peace and resignation. For the most part, the lyrics are lifted from Psalm 40, in the Psalms of David. But the desperate plea in the opening track, 'Sunday Bloody Sunday' – "*How long must we sing this song?*" – is revisited here as an incantation, a prayer.

'40' would become one of U2's best known tracks, chosen by the band to close their live shows throughout most of the '80s. The Edge called it a monument to U2, created in an instant.

"I really love that song," Bono says simply now. "I've seen some incredible scenes, I've seen some extraordinary sights, through it. I really love it."

40 Written: U2 • Duration: 2' 39"

Tour Legends: Under A Blood Red Sky

"U2 Declare War" read the tour poster. Over the course of the near worldwide War tour, the band moved up from clubs to halls to arenas. Along the way, there was a memorable show at the Red Rocks Amphitheater in Colorado.

The War tour began in Dundee on 26 February 1983 and ended in Tokyo on 30 November 1983. That sentence alone tells you all you need to know about the ground they travelled in less than a year. A series of pre-War tour dates in December 1982 – two months before the album came out – saw them getting to grips with the new songs live. The UK tour from February through to early April with shows almost every night left them tight and taut as a live band before the tour moved to the United States.

As they hit the big urban centres of Boston, New York and Chicago (all cities with sizeable Irish populations) in May 1983, they were playing out of their skins and receiving the best reviews of their career. The New York Times immediately singled out Bono as "a riveting public personality, leaping and crawling all over the stage and above it into the scaffolding" (which was almost word for word how Irish music journalists had reviewed his performance at the early Dandelion Market shows four years previously).

The success of the gigs meant that the *War* album stayed in and around the Top 20 album charts in the US for the duration of the tour. On 5 June the band played at the Red Rocks Amphitheater – a natural amphitheatre in the Rocky Mountains and a favourite of many a band. The show shouldn't have taken place – there was torrential rain on the day and flash flood warnings were issued. But a lot of money had been invested in culling a live album and live video film from the show and fans had walked through pouring rain to get to the venue, so the band persevered. It was so cold that evening that Edge could barely play his guitar and thankfully the large banks of mist concealed all the empty seats – many fans had just assumed the show had been called off because of the rain storms. Only half of the 9,000-odd seats were taken on the night.

The subsequent live album was called Under a Blood Red Sky (a line taken from 'New Year's Day'). The album cover – and film – is covered in crimson mist as a result of the rain and the lights illuminating the amphitheatre. Larry Mullen has always believed that the weather actually made the show.

Featuring old songs such as '11 O'Clock Tick Tock' and the singles from *War*, the album captured both the live passion and the skyscraping ambition of a band on the way up.

The live version of 'Sunday Bloody Sunday' has been cited as one of *Rolling Stone* magazine's "50 Moments That Changed the History of Rock and Roll", such was its dazzling impact on the night. The Red Rocks show is still regularly voted one of the gigs of the 1980s. Before the show and live album release (which was out a few months later) U2 were still a marginal, College Radio band in the US. But Red Rocks brought them to the attention of not just the MTV generation (the music channel regularly featured the full live video show) but also convinced many that the band were now ready to make the leap to arenas and stadia.

During the 1997 PopMart tour the band did consider returning to Red Rocks for a second show but were talked out of it as being a no win situation – the thinking being they could never re-capture that particular moment or the same rain storm.

In the summer months of 1983, U2 played their first big European festival dates and their biggest ever Dublin show at the Phoenix Park Racecourse in the city. They ended the eventful War tour with their first-ever shows in Hawaii and Japan.

The only worrying aspect of the War tour was the ever-present fear that Bono would harm himself while climbing up to the ceiling at almost every show. The Edge later confessed that Bono "scared the shit out of me" by climbing lighting rigs to display his white flag. But as the band already knew: it was too late to stop him now.

"We're not just another English fashion band passing through. We're an Irish band and we're here to stay." Bono

BONO

BY BRIAN BOYD

He applied for the job of guitarist but was pushed into becoming U2's singer. The frontman has been battered and bruised over the years due to his stage antics but is still coming back for more.

Paul David Hewson was born on 10 May 1960. He got the name Bono Vox from a hearing-aid shop of the same name in Dublin city centre. Bono and his teenage friends were in the habit of giving each other nicknames and before he was christened Bono he was known as "Steinvic von Huyseman". He soon dropped the Vox part of his new nickname (which is Latin for "good voice") and now everyone calls him Bono – even his family.

Never a singer growing up, he initially auditioned to be the guitarist in U2. Not being that great on the instrument, he was politely encouraged to put the guitar down and try out as the lead vocalist. Bono was as surprised as anybody that he could actually hold a note.

The death of his mother when he was just 14 traumatized him – and her image features in many a U2 song. He has frequently said that he turned to music to fill the gap her absence left.

His early work as the band's lyricist was abstract and a touch surreal but during the 1980s, when he found social and political themes to play with in the lyrics, he developed a more bombastic style. It wasn't until the *Achtung Baby* album that he started writing about his own personal experiences. But his most personal and confessional work appears on *Songs of Innocence* in which he literally "sings his life story".

As the band's frontman, Bono included mime routines in his early performances. He was always a loose cannon on stage – climbing up rigging, going walkabout in the audience or jumping off great heights. His improvised antics have been a cause of concern to the other members of the band. He has also badly injured himself on a number of occasions due to his stage behaviour.

During concert rehearsals in Munich in 2010, something Bono did to his back led to him needing emergency surgery which required months of rehabilitation. As a result, the band missed their planned Glastonbury Festival appearance and had to reschedule a whole leg of the 360° tour. His tenor voice has dramatically strengthened and improved in range over the years. His best ever-vocal delivery – according to the singer himself – is on 'Moment of Surrender' from the *No Line on the Horizon* album. He was never properly trained as a singer and he dislikes his vocals on the early U2 albums because he thinks he sings far too high on them. When the band began to play stadia in the mid to late 1980s, he was putting such a strain on his voice due to poor technique that he had to take singing lessons to learn the proper way of projecting his vocals.

Bono has recently revealed that the reason he wears sunglasses all the time is because he has glaucoma. His eyes have always been very sensitive to light – if somebody takes his photograph, he reports that

Strike a pose: Bono, aged 19. The photo remains a personal favourite.
Power chord: Playing guitar in Chicago.

he sees the flash for the rest of the day and his eyes swell up.

His on-stage performances have changed radically over the years. During the 1980s he was hectoring and humourless but as U2's music changed so did he and he now has a more playful side to his performances. Although a perfectionist and somewhat of a control freak when it comes to any representation of the band – whether on record or in concert – Bono has a self-mocking side that has grown over the years. He married Alison Stewart in 1982. The two had been going out together since they were at Mount Temple School at the same time. They have four grown-up children.

His time outside of U2 is spent on his work as an activist. He has a deep interest in the arts – primarily poetry and the visual arts. He cites Seamus Heaney as being his favourite poet.

Away from the band he has written (with The Edge) a Broadway musical called *Spider-Man: Turn Off the Dark*, which was not only the most expensive Broadway production ever but was marred by bad luck and injuries to the cast. The production closed in 2014. Previously he co-wrote the film *The Million Dollar Hotel* in 2000.

At the end of each U2 tour – such is the amount of energy and adrenaline that he puts into each performance – he needs to "decompress" for two weeks before returning to normality. Any precious time off is spent in his home in the south of France.

Bono the Activist

From the White House to G8 Summits, Bono has had an Access All Areas backstage pass to argue his case for economic justice for Africa. But his activism has caused strains within U2.

Whether it's to do with his teenage membership of a Christian prayer group, his sense of curiosity and adventure or the fact that his privileged lifestyle allows him to get involved in philanthropic works,

> “Hanging out with politicians and corporations is very unhip work. The band thought this [his activist work] would sink the ship ten years ago. I am not an idealist, never have been. I am just quite pragmatic about finding solutions. Preventing fires is cheaper than putting them out.” Bono

When in Rome: Performing in Rome, on the 360° tour, October 2010.

Bono has becoming a leading activist for causes relating to the African continent. It helps that his celebrity status opens doors for him and attracts the media to report on his work. It doesn't help – from his bandmates' point of view – that his commitment to his activism has at times reduced his role within U2.

Visiting Ethiopia with his wife, Ali, for six weeks after the Live Aid concert of 1985 sparked an attachment to the continent and a resolution to help, however he could. Bono primarily argues that the debt owed by African countries needs to be restructured to encourage their economic growth and that the developed world needs to work harder to help prevent the spread of HIV/AIDS on the continent. His advocacy work has seen him nominated three times for the Nobel Peace Prize and awarded a knighthood in the British honour lists in 2007. His early work at the end of the 1990s with Jubilee 2000, a lobby group calling for the cancellation of all debt owed by developing countries, led to work with the ONE campaign and the DATA group – both of which called for economic equality for African countries, the adjusting of international trade rules which militate against African countries and the elimination of curable diseases on the continent.

His work with these various groupings leads him to meet political leaders worldwide to argue his case and visit African countries to see for himself what is being done. These commitments sometimes clash with U2 recording sessions and although the rest of the band are supportive of his efforts, they do have concerns about how much time and energy he has left for U2.

His activist work is not without controversy. When he informed The Edge that he was meeting with President Bush in 2005 to discuss debt relief for Africa and there would be pictures of them together on the White House lawn shaking hands and smiling, The Edge tried to talk him out of the photo session, but to no avail. The Edge was anxious about U2 being seen to endorse a particular political leader. Bono's friendship with Britain's ex-Prime Minister Tony Blair (Bono has spoken at a Labour Party conference) does not sit easily with Larry Mullen. While Mullen does acknowledge that Bono “is prepared to use his weight as a celebrity at great cost to himself to help other people", the drummer has said he "cringes" when he sees the singer with Tony Blair and George Bush. Mullen regards both Bush and Blair as "war criminals".

Not known for doing anything by the half-measure, Bono is aware of the absurdity of a multi-millionaire rock star preaching about Third World debt and poverty but takes his commitment seriously. He prides himself on the fact that he can talk for more than an hour on HIPC conditionality – the terms under which the most highly indebted countries of the world are forgiven their loans – and has taken crash courses in economics, sociology and political theory so that he knows what he is talking about during meetings with the world's most influential political leaders.

"I've met people the band would rather I didn't meet," Bono has said of his activist work. "And there are some people I have to talk to, or appear in a photograph with, that in other circumstances I'd rather not."

Closer to home, it was Bono's idea to get two Northern Irish political leaders representing both sides of the divide to shake hands on stage at a show in Belfast just before a crucial referendum in 1998 about the political future of the country.

In 1999 Bono had an audience with the Pope to discuss Third World poverty. Noticing the Pope was interested in his trademark "Fly" sunglasses, the singer offered them to the pontiff, who promptly tried them on for size. The Vatican press office has never made the ensuing photograph available to the public.

Bono's main work now is with his PRODUCT(RED) campaign. Set up to encourage large companies who sell global brands to mark some of their range with the PRODUCT(RED) logo and to donate a percentage of the profit to benefit HIV/AIDS relief in Africa, the campaign has secured backing from many leading brands.

Pictured on the cover of *Time* magazine in 2002 for his activist work, the headline read: "Can Bono Save the World?". To his friends back in Dublin this was changed to "Can the World be Saved from Bono?"

THE UNFORGETTABLE FIRE

For their next studio album, it would help to find a new producer. They thought of Conny Plank. It didn't happen. And then in a flash of inspiration The Edge thought of Brian Eno. It is impossible to speculate what might have happened if Eno had said no. Instead he brought Daniel Lanois with him. They began the album in Slane Castle with the mobile. The sessions were open-ended, spacious, free. The band did a day's recording naked. "We got into gaffer art," Bono commented. Lanois, for one, lost some pubic hairs as a result.

But Danny was good on rhythms. Larry's playing became looser, funkier, more subtle. Adam's gained in confidence and poise. Gradually Bono learned to sing again. The relaxed, experimental feel of those initial sessions gave the record its fresh, exploratory tone. Not everything worked and, as the deadline approached, they opted to go back into Windmill. Bono was still agonising over lyrics. Less than two weeks before the band were due to go on tour, he announced that he couldn't do it.

He was given an ultimatum. Do it. The final ten days' recording were a nightmare. One or two tracks sound seriously undercooked. But on balance the exercise was thoroughly successful, producing U2's first album with a cohesive sound. With *The Unforgettable Fire*, U2 were reborn.

A Sort Of Homecoming

Bono had become a voracious reader. He was still interested in the Bible and in opening up its myriad secrets, but he was casting his net more widely now than ever before. He was immersing himself in fiction, philosophy, poetry. And the more poetry he read, the more he began to understand his songwriting mission as a poetic one.

He could occasionally be self-conscious about it. "I am a writer of words," he reflected in 'Dreams in a Box', a poem written during 1987. But there is no doubt that by the making of *The Unforgettable Fire*, he had begun to find his poetic voice.

Hats off: A photograph from 1985, which eerily resembles how they would be shot for *The Joshua Tree* two years later.

Release date: October 1984
Catalogue number: U25
Producer: Brian Eno/Daniel Lanois
Track listing: A Sort of Homecoming/ Pride/Wire/The Unforgettable Fire/Promenade/4th of July/Bad/Indian Summer Sky/Elvis Presley And America/MLK
Highest Chart position: No. 1 (UK), 12 (US)

The Unforgettable Fire-Tour

U2

LIVE

Special Guest ZERRA 1

NEW ALBUM The Unforgettable Fire
LP 206 530-620

Chromdioxid-MC 406 530-652

ISLAND

Im ARIOLA-Vertrieb

MAMA CONCERTS
THE CONCERT COMPANY

Montag, 8. Oktober 1984 · 20.00 Uhr

HAMBURG — CCH

Vorverkauf: Theaterkasse Central, Lilienstr. 24, Tel. 33 52 84 · Im Hamburg Tip, Tel. 32 43 12 · Theaterkasse Schumacher, Colonnaden 37, Tel. 34 30 44 · CCH-Konzertkasse Jungiusstraße 13, Telefon 34 20 25 und in allen bekannten Vorverkaufsstellen. · Veranstalter: Mama Concerts in Cooperation mit Konzertdirektion Karsten Jahnl

Bono had been reading the work of Paul Celan, a Jewish poet of mixed German and Romanian origin. Celan was an intensely spiritual writer, a mystic whose life and death were shrouded in ambiguities. His work posed a set of questions that were highly problematic for anyone of fixed religious convictions. Gradually, Bono, Larry and The Edge were leaving those certainties behind. But Celan opened up new avenues of spiritual doubt. "Poetry is a sort of homecoming," Celan had written, and it rang true for Bono. The phrase inspired a meditation that seemed to encompass in one impressionistic reverie many of Bono's familiar obsessions. It is written in a dreamy, cinematic style, the camera briefly capturing vivid images which then dissolve one into the next, a constant sense of movement propelling the song along. "She will die and live again, tonight," Bono sings, and sex and spirituality intermingle, in an unmistakable allusion to the little death and the (little) resurrection.

But while there is a sense in the lyrics that things are falling apart and the centre cannot hold, the extent to which the narrator seems in control of the words, of the ideas, of the poetry, is in itself reassuring. It's as if Bono is re-affirming his commitment to a life devoted to the search for poetic truth. While it might seem like a veiled reference to 'I Will Follow', the chant *"O come away/O come away/O come away/O come away say I"* is more likely an unconscious allusion to WB Yeats' 'The Human Child', and it was towards influences of that ilk that he was now drawn. "A lot of rock 'n' roll is banal ideas well executed," Bono reflects.

"Whereas I think a lot of what we do is really very interesting ideas, badly executed." 'A Sort of Homecoming' involved a lot of very interesting ideas well executed. It was a powerful opening to the album.

A Sort Of Homecoming Written: U2 • Duration: 5' 28"

Fire starters: Poster for The Unforgettable Fire tour date in Hamburg, Germany.

Positive negative: Contact sheet of Bono getting the crowd fired up on tour.

Pride (In The Name Of Love)

On the road, U2 are constantly working informally on new ideas. Rehearsals and sound-checks are recorded. From a musical point of view, this is how a substantial number of songs began. The band played Hawaii during the War tour, in November 1983. Live engineer Joe O'Herlihy was recording the sound-check. The Edge led the way into a series of chord changes. There was a mistake, and the band picked up on it: someone's slip had given a new twist to the piece. Joe recorded the incident in his mind: by now he'd learned to recognise these special moments. When the time came to record *The Unforgettable Fire*, he remembered precisely where the roots of 'Pride' were to be found.

Bono was working on something about Ronald Reagan. He had the title 'Pride' in mind for it, thinking a bout the kind that comes before a fall, thinking of the hubris which was the dominant characteristic of America's foreign policy during the Reagan era. But it wasn't working, and he began to get the feeling he was going to have to switch tack. The band had been to the Chicago Peace Museum and were impressed by the exhibit there dedicated to the black civil rights leader Martin Luther King. Shifting emphasis to the kind of pride that King had inspired in black people, Bono sensed that there was an entirely different song to be written.

At the centre of the song is a series of images that have the grainy feel of wire photos sent back from the front-line of resistance: *"One man caught on a barbed wire fence/One man he resist/One man washed up on an empty beach/One man betrayed by a kiss."* There is no sense that Bono had abandoned his religious beliefs, but the references are more subtle.

Recording 'Pride (In the Name of Love)' was extraordinarily difficult. U2 had done a backing track in Slane, but when they moved across to Windmill Lane it didn't feel right. With time ticking away, they decided to ditch what they'd done in Slane and re-record the track from scratch. It worked. Almost immediately they knew that 'Pride' was a killer. Chrissie Hynde of The Pretenders was in town and she dropped into the studio to assist with the backing vocals, though the sleeve credits refer to Mrs Christine Kerr. Not surprisingly, it became the first single from *The Unforgettable Fire*.

Pride (In The Name Of Love)
Written: U2 • Duration: 3' 49" • US singles chart position: 33

Wire

"When I started writing I didn't even know what a couplet was," Bono recalls. But by *The Unforgettable Fire* he had developed a much stronger sense of what the conventions were. When he got it right, then a song lifted and soared: 'A Sort of Homecoming' was a case in point, a tremendously visual, poetic, emotional word-festival. Things didn't always work out so well, however.

Whereas Steve Lillywhite had been highly rigorous and exacting in his attitude to songs, Eno was far more indulgent. Bono tended to come at his themes obliquely. Eno let him get away with it even when he ended up saying very little.

Bono was aware of the heroin that had begun to flood Dublin. He knew a couple of friends who'd become involved. Now he wanted to write a song that captured his own ambivalence to the drug. "I'm probably an addictive kind of person myself," Bono admits. And so that was what he wanted to convey lyrically.

There's an openness and sparkle to the music on 'Wire', which skips along on a light funk groove courtesy of an in-form Larry Mullen. The hand of Eno and Lanois is in evidence here, as the band veer in a direction already sign-posted by Talking Heads, whom Eno had also produced. But while the noise is impressive, the lyrics never get beyond mere sketchwork. "There is the fascination of death and of flirting with death that's part of heroin use," Bono reflected later. But none of that is conveyed here. There are moments of sardonic rhetoric that almost work – "*Such a nice day/To throw your life away*" – and the song ends in a kind of a nagging rap. But 'Wire' is an example of how flat a song improvised on the mic can be. "*Is this time, the time to win or lose?*" he asks, "*Is this the time, the time to choose?*" Bono knew what a couplet was now, alright. But that didn't mean he was William Shakespeare.

Wire Written: U2 • Duration: 4' 19"

The Unforgettable Fire

When the Americans dropped the atomic bomb on Hiroshima and Nagasaki, it was one of the final and most barbarous acts of World War Two. These two Japanese cities were utterly destroyed, and in human terms the toll was even more horrific.

A total of 67,000 people died immediately as a direct result, and thousands more were scarred, injured and maimed. But it was a catastrophe truly like no other in terms of its psychic impact: the effects of radiation from the bombs would last for generations, producing genetic mutations of the most chilling kind, and causing widespread leukaemia and cancer. The final death toll is almost impossible to calculate, though 200,000 is probably a conservative estimate. It was as close as we had ever come to Armageddon, a terrible spectacle of such frightening immensity that anyone who was close to it could never, ever forget – the whole world, it seemed, transformed into a gigantic charnel house.

Iwakichi Kobayashi was a survivor of the holocaust that had engulfed Hiroshima and Nagasaki. He drew a picture to illustrate his memory of what had happened. Japanese television picked up on the theme and invited other survivors to submit their own paintings. It became a kind of exorcism, a therapeutic outpouring of grief and horror at the atrocity which had been visited on innocent people.

The Japanese created an exhibition of the paintings and drawings from survivors of the holocaust, entitled The Unforgettable Fire, and it was housed within the Hiroshima Peace Memorial. During the early '80s, some 60 of the pictures had been taken on tour; they went on display at the Chicago Peace Museum, and U2 saw them there. "Painting was part of the therapy to help these people purge themselves of their internalised emotions," The Edge said at the time. "The image of that purging quality, coupled with the insight it gave into the horror of nuclear holocaust, stuck in Bono's mind. Later we found the title fit the new record in many ways, especially in reflecting its multi-coloured textures."

It was Bono's magpie instinct at work again. In a reversal of the norm that would be typical of the band, Bono thought of *The Unforgettable Fire* as the name of the album first. It was too good a title not to use it for a song as well – though what Bono produced by way of a lyric had little or no connection with the original source of the title.

"It was a soundtrack piece I'd been messing around with on the piano at home," The Edge reflected later. "It was a beautiful piece of music but I couldn't see how one could approach it lyrically or vocally. It was knocking around for quite a while, and myself and Bono were out in his house doing work on material for the record and I found this cassette of the piano piece and we decided to mess around with it. Within an hour, we'd written a verse section with Bono playing bass, and we virtually wrote the song there. Obviously it changed with drums and bass in the studio, but it was the first 20 minutes in Bono's house that counted."

Bono was still in a state of semi-permanent writer's block. "Writing songs scares the living daylights out of me," he said at the time. "It's been a huge problem and I just ran away." Even in a situation where they had the melody and the music, he was finding it hard to get a fix on the lyrics. "I see the rhythm of words as being important," he reasoned afterwards.

"They build up slowly and often I don't think it's ready yet – though everyone else may think it is, I can't let it go. That's why a lot of the songs tend to be sketches. 'The Unforgettable Fire', it's a sketch: '*Carnival/wheels fly and colours spin/face to face/in a dry and waterless place.*' It builds up a picture, but it's only a sketch." Some sketches, however, work better than others. This is an emotional travelogue, images shuffled through the memory to underscore the song's sense of yearning. It is a love song that links thematically back to 'A Sort of Homecoming', but it's imbued with a sense of foreboding that seems to anticipate the end of a relationship.

"It's classical, almost," The Edge said in 1985. "I see it as a music piece rather than as a song. Bono, in a very unconventional way, explores numerous melodies over sections. Instead of repeating melodies – you know, verses and choruses, which is what everyone does – we've got three chorus melodies and two

Fired up: In Rotterdam on 30 October 1984 as The Unforgettable Fire tour hits Europe.

Look right: In the hills outside Dublin during a break in the recording of *The Unforgettable Fire* in 1984.

verse melodies. It has a certain symphonic feel for me because there are so many intertwining themes. We could have recorded it better but for all its flaws, I just see it as a great piece of music."

The Unforgettable Fire Written: U2 • Duration: 4' 56" UK singles chart position: 6

Promenade

Van Morrison's legend looms large in Irish music. From U2's perspective, he was crucial. Following a period in seclusion, he had re-emerged in the late '70s and, the man's reputation as an abrasive genius notwithstanding, his music reflected a renewed sense of inner contentment. His interest in language, and in squeezing out new meanings from it, was undiminished. Van Morrison stretched words, broke them down, created new ones, and – occasionally in despair at the limits which this discipline imposed – plunged into a kind of primal articulation, letting the inner self rise to the surface and express itself. But guiding this search for descriptive, expressive resources beyond language was a profound interest in spirituality.

U2 could never merely follow the Morrison model, but it was reassuring to them, nonetheless, that he had managed to infuse his work with such a powerful sense of spiritual mission. It was inevitable that Bono would listen to and be inspired by his music, and on 'Promenade' that influence is unmistakable. Words are used for their sound as much as their sense, which was not new for Bono – but here there is a poetic surefootedness in the writing that marks a significant step forward.

After the War tour, Bono had spoken about the need for U2 to re-invent themselves. "Today was the last U2 gig," Bono said on the evening the tour finished. "But I'm not talking about the end of U2. This is the end of a cycle. We must develop new areas now. U2 is just beginning."

"I find it very difficult to listen to *War* now," Bono admits. "There is so much anger and the effect of that is to tighten up the voice, so that it becomes higher and more shrill. But on *The Unforgettable Fire* I learned to relax again. I learned to sing again."

Bono and Ali had moved from one side of Dublin Bay, in Howth, across to Bray. He was living in the Martello Tower, which he'd had re-designed. A spiral staircase led from the living room up to the bedroom. Above the bed was a glass roof, opening up a spectacular view of the night sky. The tower overlooked the Carlisle Grounds, where Bray Wanderers played their League of Ireland football games. All along the promenade are amusement parlours, snooker halls, fast-food outlets, restaurants and guest houses.

That background is evoked in impressionistic strokes, but 'Promenade' is unmistakably a love song that celebrates the spiritual dimensions of sexual desire. "*Turn me around tonight/up through the spiral staircase/to the higher ground.*"

Promenade Written: U2 • Duration: 2' 34"

Guitar star: The Edge on stage in Sydney, Australia in September 1984 during The Unforgettable Fire tour. Songs that sounded "unfinished" on the album came into their own when played live.

4th of July

One of Brian Eno's rules is that there are no rules. Sometimes, if you work too hard at something you kill it.

Occasionally when you're doodling, something emerges which is transcendent. Inspiration can strike in the most unexpected situations. You can frame the maxims in different ways. You can hone them till they're razor sharp. You can even develop them, as Eno did, into a set of Oblique Strategies. "The first I wrote was 'Honour thy error as a hidden intention', a reminder not to have too fixed a view about what was appropriate in a given piece," Eno explained to David Gan, "to accept the possibility that sometimes the things one doesn't intend are the seeds for a more interesting future than the one one had envisaged."

It is impossible to speculate about what Adam might have intended when he began to amuse himself with a sliding bass figure, in a break during recording, after U2 had put down a version of 'Bad' in Windmill Lane. Musicians do this kind of thing all the time and more often than not the germ of an idea is lost once somebody walks in with a cup of coffee.

"I started playing along with Adam, totally unaware that Brian was listening in the other room," The Edge recalled. "He happened to have some treatments set up for the vocal Bono had been doing and he applied those to the guitar. He thought it was really nice, so without bothering to put it on multi-track, which is the 24-track tape machine, he just recorded it straight down to stereo tape. It was very much a live performance. There was no way we could mix it or re-do any of the instruments." There was probably a temptation to get Bono to stick a vocal on top, but the singer must have been relieved when that option was dismissed. One less lyric to write. Whew!

The track is pensive and exploratory. In no way an attempt to celebrate Independence Day, it should be taken rather as a kind of musical diaryentry. Eno captured the moment for posterity. That was a vital part of his genius.

4th of July Written: U2 • Duration: 2' 14"

Bad

For the second time on *The Unforgettable Fire*, we are given to understand that Bono is addressing a heroin addict. There is a sense throughout 'Bad' that he doesn't know what he wants to say, and that he doesn't know what he's saying either. But, in a way, he says it eloquently anyway.

To begin with there's an empathy in 'Bad' which gives the song resonance. "If I could," Bono sings, "*Yes I would/If I could/I would let it go/Surrender, dislocate.*" It's an honest admission of his own vulnerability to the temptation that drugs like heroin represent. "It relates to what I was trying to do, much more overtly on Zoo TV," he states. "With those characters, I wanted to admit to those things, those sides of yourself, that want to run away from responsibility, and that find people who have run away attractive. I've always had a real respect for responsible people but I also have a real respect for irresponsible people."

'Bad' begins on a kind of drone, but it's the light, shuffling rhythm track, with Adam throwing in a dub-influenced bass part, that gives the track its addictive propulsion. "I think the experience of working with Brian and Daniel Lanois was a revelation to Larry," The Edge says. "Instead of his goal being technique or drumming ability, he became aware of new approaches to rhythm. He became aware of percussion."

Bono, meanwhile, was engaging in his own inarticulate speech of the heart. Like 'Wire', there's nothing in the night-lit world of 'Bad' that makes it clear this song has to do with junk. But there is a restlessness that speaks volumes. You begin to imagine the narrator prowling his room in the darkest hour before dawn, wrestling with the temptation to take the plunge. There is a desire to go over the edge, to experience whatever the other side might throw at him. The feeling is so intense that he can't express it clearly. His thoughts emerge in disconnected fragments. He repeats himself. If you wanted to get tough about it, you'd argue that 'Bad' says nothing. But it's a trip – a tense, nervy, intoxicating, exhilarating trip. "Comprehension had never been particularly important to me," says Adam. "It's much more important how the lyrics feel. If it doesn't sound right, then I'll consult Bono and try and figure out what's going on. But it's an instinctive thing. I find that it's only after six months of touring it and talking to different people that you get to the inner truths of the song."

Desperation, dislocation, separation, condemnation, revelation. All of those qualities are there in Bono's performance, except one. The time for condemnation was over. For now.

Bad Written: U2 • Duration: 6' 08"

"Writing songs scares the living daylights out of me. It's been a huge problem and I just ran away." Bono

Indian Summer Sky

Sometime in New York City – probably when the War tour hit Manhattan – Bono wrote the bones of 'Indian Summer Sky'. "Most of the writing was cinematic and very fast," Bono says. "It had a sense of wanting to break through a city to an open place."

A friend of Bono's had spent some time in Toronto. He felt troubled by a city that was "cool" and "shiny". "There had been a lot of massacres of Red Indian people in that area," Bono reports, "and he felt in some way as if there were troubled spirits still there. What I was trying to get across in 'Indian Summer Sky' was a sense of spirit trapped in a concrete jungle."

The song is imbued with an epic quality: on the one hand wind, ocean, sky and earth, on the other heart and soul. At one point, it anticipates 'With Or Without You' on *The Joshua Tree* as Bono sings, "*You give yourself to this the longest day/You give yourself you give it all away*." It's possible that the chorus – "*So wind go through to my heart/ So wind blow through my soul*" – sounds as much like Talking Heads simply because of Brian Eno's involvement. He had, after all, produced *Remain In Light*. The influence seems unmistakable, but there's nothing forced or unnatural here.

"In many ways," Bono reflected later, "*The Unforgettable Fire* was a contrast between bricks and mortar and music with the sky over its head."

He was beginning to move to the rhythms of nature. Now you could move your hips to U2. Now you could dance. And it felt good.

Indian Summer Sky Written: U2 • Duration: 4' 19"

Elvis Presley And America

The difference between the production styles of Steve Lillywhite and Brian Eno could not be more starkly expressed than by this track. Lillywhite was prepared to experiment, but Eno went much further.

He saw a piece that had been recorded as utterly malleable. You could open it up, slow it down, stand it on its head, reverse it – anything that might work was worth a shot. And so on an experimental day, when Daniel Lanois and he were fishing around for ideas, they slowed down the backing track from 'A Sort of Homecoming' and played it for Bono without telling him what it was. Eno encouraged the singer to improvise over it.

"It was partly a reaction to the Albert Goldman book, which tried to portray Elvis as the archetypal rock 'n' roll idiot," Bono explains. "But the way he held the mic, the way he sang into the mic – this was his genius. But his decline just tore at me, and when I picked up the mic it was a completely off the wall thing and I just began to sing." Bono approached the track like a jazzman, letting his voice take the song and following it, improvising the lyrics as he went along. Bono saw it as a dry run. The lyrical ideas could be sifted through and refined later. But Eno had other plans.

"He forced Bono to change his approach to recording," The Edge remembers. "Whereas previously with Steve, seven or eight different tracks would be collaged into a single vocal, Brian started insisting, whenever it was practical, on doing one take."

It still came as a shock to Bono when Eno told him that the cut was finished. It was one of Eno's oblique strategies in action: overtly resist change. And another: emphasize the flaws. "It was such an inspired performance," The Edge said flatteringly, "that we decided to leave it as it was." Not everyone would be so complimentary. Some of the band's most supportive critics hated the song. It wasn't what Bono was apparently trying to say about Elvis that rankled, it was the fact that 'Elvis Presley And America' so obviously sounded like a work-in-progress.

"I think that it does evoke that decline, the stupor, the period when he forgets his words and fumbles," Bono argued at the time. It wasn't a bad shot at post-rationalisation, but one thing's for sure: it may have been a useful harbinger for the journey to the heartland of rock 'n' roll that *Rattle and Hum* would involve, but 'Elvis Presley And America' would never be regarded as a U2 classic.

Elvis Presley And America Written: U2 • Duration: 6' 22"

MLK

The Unforgettable Fire had been coined as a phrase to describe the terror of the holocaust. However, U2 had seen another meaning in it. Just as 'Pride' could be conceived as a song about Ronald Reagan and written about Martin Luther King, it was possible to ascribe another sense to a phrase that played on Bono's imagination.

Fire, passion, belief – these were things that U2 had written about, things that they had dedicated their music to. Elvis Presley had lit a fire that was burning still. So too had Martin Luther King. With 'MLK', he became the hero of *The Unforgettable Fire*, the man whose memory was evoked in the end to soothe the anxieties which had riddled the album and which had crept up on U2 increasingly as the recording had progressed.

It was becoming a trademark. '40' had ended *War* – as 'Scarlet' should have ended *October* – on a healing note. Now that *The Unforgettable Fire* was done, it was time for a spiritual, and 'MLK' provided it. It was a lullaby, a song of reassurance and reconciliation. A song of hope. "*Sleep, sleep tonight/And may your dreams/be realised*," Bono sang, and it was made to be sung by thousands joined together in a gesture of communion. "Those people who were fighting for civil rights," Bono remarks, "they understood that music better than they understood 'Pride', which was rock 'n' roll music. They understood the tribute." Let it rain, rain on he.

MLK Written: U2 • Duration: 2' 32"

THE JOSHUA TREE

July 13, 1985. Live Aid. In front of the biggest television audience for a live music event ever, U2 stole the show. Sales of *The Unforgettable Fire* soared. Suddenly U2 were not just a big band. They were one of the biggest in the world.

It gave them some breathing space. The Edge wrote the soundtrack for Paul Mayerberg's film *Captive*. Bono went travelling, listened to the blues. Did 'Silver and Gold' for the Sun City album project with Keith Richards and Ronnie Wood, recorded with Clannad. The whole band did two tracks with Robbie Robertson.

In '86, they emerged in fits. For TV Gaga. The Conspiracy of Hope tour in the US. Self Aid in Ireland. A different band! They did dirty, loud, noisy cover versions of Eddie Cochran and Bob Dylan. They'd travelled a long, long way from the cultivated European atmospherics of *The Unforgettable Fire*. Bono was listening to roots music, folk, the blues. He was thinking about songs, reading about the deep south. The Edge had looked east on *Captive*. The band moved west with *The Joshua Tree*, into the arms of America. Bono's songwriting had more focus now. Greater depth. He was dragging himself up there alongside Dylan, Morrison, Lou Reed. "It's our most literate record yet," he said. That was an understatement. It went straight to No.1 in the U.S. and the U.K. In America it became the fastest-selling album of all time. It also delivered the first platinum-selling CD.

In the arid wasteland of the Nevada desert, the Joshua Tree survives despite the dirt, bone-dry sand and stone in which it is embedded. Somewhere down there is water. Somewhere down there is the source of life. Somewhere down there is hope. The challenge is to find it.

Where The Streets Have No Name

Sometimes you can hear it in your head first. A slow, dramatic, swelling keyboard drone.

A jangling rhythm part on guitar coming in over it. It sounds good – in your head. It feels like the start of something – an intro. But now you have to get it down on tape. Already there's some slippage. The first few steps you take never seem to capture the full glory of what you could hear, but if you come any way close, the momentum will carry you forward. The Edge, in his house in Monkstown, fooling around on a four-track Tascam home recording studio. Sticking down the keyboard on his own. Listening back to it. It'll do. Rewind. Then the guitar. The rhythm holds good. Try some variations on the chord. Little flicks off the major. Now you can see the bigger picture again. Imagine a bass. The drums coming in. It does feel good. The beginning of a song...

<continues on page 68>

Stadium rock: Bono stretches out at the De Kuip stadium in Rotterdam in July 1987. Such was the band's appeal at this time that they were regularly playing to audiences of 50,000-plus each night.

Release date: March 1987
Catalogue number: U26
Producer: Daniel Lanois/Brian Eno
Track listing: Where the Streets Have No Name/I Still Haven't Found What I'm Looking For/With or Without You/Bullet the Blue Sky/Running to Stand Still/Red Hill Mining Town/In God's Country/ Trip Through Your Wires/One Tree Hill/Exit/Mothers of the Disappeared
Highest Chart position: No. 1 (UK & US)

U2
WHERE THE STREETS HAVE NO NAME
THE NEW SINGLE
Released August 24th, 1987
7″ INCLUDES TWO NEW TRACKS · IS 340
12″ INCLUDES THREE NEW TRACKS · 12 IS 340
LIMITED EDITION 4 TRACK CASSETTE SINGLE · CIS 340

Hit single: 1987 poster to promote the release of 'Where The Streets Have No Name'.

THE MAKING OF THE JOSHUA TREE (1987)

BY BRIAN BOYD

With each of the four previous U2 albums very different to the one before, expectations were running high for their fifth release. But those expectations didn't allow for the fact that the band were about to record one of the best-selling rock albums of all time.

The Joshua Tree began in Ethiopia. A few weeks after Live Aid, Bono and Ali travelled to the African country for six weeks to see for themselves the impact of the devastating famine. Unable to sleep one night, Bono sat up in his tent, reached for an airsickness bag (the only thing he could find to write on) and wrote: "*I want to run, I want to hide, I want to tear down the walls that hold me inside.*" When The Edge later came up with the music to accompany these lyrics they had the album's centre point – 'Where the Streets Have No Name'.

With Brian Eno and Daniel Lanois invited back to produce the album, the band reassembled in a big Georgian house on the outskirts of Dublin in January 1986 to start work. It was called Danesmoate House, and Adam Clayton took such a shine to the place that he bought it later on – and still lives there today. It was the "non-studio" atmosphere of the house which led to some very relaxed sessions. Co-producer Daniel Lanois felt he was getting a particular sound from the rooms in the house and everyone – for once on a U2 album – seemed happy.

They knew they wanted tighter songs than were on *The Unforgettable Fire*. If many of those songs were deliberately left openended, here the focus was on conventional structures. The recording sessions were marked by the band emphasizing the primary colours of rock music – guitar, bass and drums.

Bono wanted the album to be about the United States – a country that they had spent more time in than in Ireland over the previous few years due to incessant coast-to-coast touring. The album was to be called The Two Americas and would deal with "hot button" themes from the foreign news headlines of the day. It was determined early on that this would be the band's first double album. Given the broadness of the subject matter there were enough songs there and the band felt on this, their fifth LP, the timing was right for a double album.

Two key events helped shape the songwriting. The band broke off recording to take part in the Amnesty International Conspiracy of Hope tour in the summer of 1986 in the US, which gave them political material that would find its way into the songs. And just as Bono and Ali had travelled to Ethiopia previously to see what was going on with their own eyes, this time the couple travelled to Nicaragua and El Salvador to witness the effects of US military intervention in these countries.

It was a love/hate album. The band had a deep appreciation of all aspects of US culture and admired the country's dramatic geographical spaces but were appalled by the Ronald Reagan years and particularly by US military intervention in Central America. The latter sentiment informed the songs 'Bullet the Blue Sky' and 'Mothers of the Disappeared'. But in there too was an acknowledgement of what the country was to many generations of Irish emigrants and how it was the US and not the UK who really put the band on a pedestal. 'With Or Without You' was Bono's love letter to his wife, Ali. Despite being newlyweds, the couple didn't see that much of each other due to the band's touring demands and Bono articulated his frustration through the song.

The album has rootsy/blues touches for the very reason that the band had realized that their musical education began and ended with the New Wave music scene that first fired them up as teenagers in Dublin. With U2 now under so much of a media spotlight, they were frightened by how little they knew about popular music's history, and songs such as 'I Still Haven't Found What I'm Looking For' even found the band incorporating elements of Gospel music into their sound. The song is notable for Bono expressing his doubts about religion.

'I Still Haven't Found ...' is Larry Mullen's song. He came up with a very original beat which allowed the band to go walkabout musically and the result was the most non-U2-sounding song to date. Bono sings at the very top of his range over the beat and by nailing something so different early on the song anchored the album and gave the band the confidence to explore a more rootsy style.

"The idea we had for the album was simply: let's actually write songs. We wanted the record to be less vague, atmospheric and impressionistic than *The Unforgettable Fire* – to make it more straightforward, focused and concise." The Edge on *The Joshua Tree*

Where the Streets Have No Name (continued)

...is one of those ones that seemed as if it didn't want to be born. "The way we write, we sometimes feel that the song is written," The Edge told John Waters, "the song is already there, if you could just put it into words, put it into notes. We have it, but it's not realised yet.

"If you saw us working in the studio sometimes, you'd be scratching your head trying to figure out what we were doing. Mostly, if we get the feeling that we're onto something good, we eventually do get there. And 'Where the Streets Have No Name' is a great example, because that took weeks of work to arrive at."

It nearly drove Brian Eno mad in the process. The more the band worked on the song, the more he resented it. At one stage he became so frustrated at the amount of time being devoted to 'Where the Streets Have No Name' that he wanted to erase the multi-track. "That's right," The Edge recalls. "We weren't in the studio at the time and he asked the assistant engineer to leave the room. He'd actually decided to do it. But the assistant engineer wouldn't go. He stood in front of the tape machine, saying, 'Brian, you can't do this'. And so he didn't. But it was close."

In the end it was Steve Lillywhite rather than Eno who mixed the finished product. "It took forever to get that track," Daniel Lanois told Rolling Stone. "We had this giant blackboard with the arrangement written on it. I felt like a science professor, conducting them. To get the rise and fall, the song's dynamic, took a long time." Rise and fall? That makes it sound almost sexual – a thought that mightn't be too far from the truth.

Bono certainly sounds restless and agitated as he launches into a confession: "*I want to run/I want to hide/I want to tear down the walls/*

Slide away: Bono looks on as Edge plays slide guitar on 12 June 1987 – their first time back at Wembley Stadium, London, since their Live Aid appearance.

that hold me inside/I want to reach out/And touch the flame/Where the streets have no name."

"It's been a theme all the way through the group's music," he says, "this sense of wanting to run, wanting to give in to the urge of the hunter. I always think there's two modes – hunter and protector. Or for me there is anyway. If I gave in to one I'd be an animal. And if I gave in to the other, I'd be completely domesticated. Somewhere between the two is where I live."

We all feel the crushing burden of domesticity to one degree or another at different times. 'Where the Streets Have No Name' expresses the corresponding desire to cut and run. But it also captures the desperate need for anonymity that someone in Bono's position frequently feels: where the streets have no name, neither do the stars.

The title undoubtedly draws on the time Bono and his wife Ali spent in Ethiopia during 1985. They'd gone there as volunteers, working with aid agencies on the ground, distributing food and assisting with health and educational initiatives. Bono came home to Ireland, to the Western world, with a profound sense of the vacuum at the heart of contemporary living. "The spirit of the people I met in Ethiopia was very strong," Bono says. "There's no doubt that, even in poverty, they had something that we didn't have. When I got back, I realized the extent to which people in the West were like spoiled children."

One of the strengths of the song is that it is never quite clear where the streets with no name are, or precisely what the phrase is intended to mean. He could be talking about Heaven. Maybe even offering us a glimpse into some kind of private hell.

"I can look at it now," Bono says, "and recognize that 'Where the Streets Have No Name' has one of the most banal couplets in the history of pop music. But it also contains some of the biggest ideas. In a curious way, that seems to work. If you get any way heavy about these things, you don't communicate. But if you're flip or throwaway about it, then you do. That's one of the paradoxes I've had to come to terms with."

Where the Streets Have No Name Written: U2 • Duration: 5' 37" • UK singles chart position: 4 • US singles chart position: 13

I Still Haven't Found What I'm Looking For

Some things stick in the memory. The Edge held a party in his newly reconstructed house in Monkstown on the south coast of Dublin, on New Year's Eve, 1986. By this stage the bulk of the work on *The Joshua Tree* was done and the band were relaxing. But Bono couldn't quite let go.

One of his most attractive qualities is the naked enthusiasm he shows for the band's own music. And so he explained to me that this was an album of songs, that U2 had finally learned what the word meant, and that he was convinced that they had just made by far their best album to date as a result. "There's one in particular," he explained, "that's amazing." And then he started to sing it to me. "It goes like this: '*I have climbed/the highest mountain/I have run/through the fields/only to be with you/only to be with you*.' And it's got this refrain," he expanded and sang on till he came to it. "'*But I still haven't found what I'm looking for*'."

The bass drum of some thumping dance track was whacking away next door, and the hubbub of party voices reigned all around – and yet I'll swear that I could hum the song the next day. It was that catchy. A perfect piece of pop music, it went to No. 1 in the US when it was released there as a single, and no one could have been in the least bit surprised. From the start, Bono clearly knew that he was onto a winner.

The song had entered the world under another title, 'Under The Weather'. It also had a different melody. But once The Edge had come up with the title and the theme of spiritual doubt had crystallised in Bono's imagination, then the momentum became inescapable. Dermot Stokes, who was writing more extensively for Hot Press at the time, had given him a tape of blues and gospel music, including tracks by The Swan Silvertones, The Staple Singers and Blind Willie Johnson. Eno, who had listened to a lot of gospel, further stimulated his enthusiasm. Now Bono knew that 'I Still Haven't Found What I'm Looking For' had to have its roots in gospel. But he also sensed that the theme was big enough to allow him to go for broke, to write an anthem.

'I Still Haven't Found What I'm Looking For' is beautifully written and elegantly constructed. The band trip lightly along on a groove that's a model of restraint, with an acoustic rhythm guitar break from The Edge where others might have preferred an instrumental solo. Bono's singing is soulful and heartfelt. No one puts a foot wrong.

"I used to think that writing words was old-fashioned," Bono confessed. "So I sketched. I wrote words on the microphone. For *The Joshua Tree*, I felt that the time had come to write words that meant something, out of my own experience."

You could sense it straightaway. 'I Still Haven't Found What I'm Looking For' was the real thing – though not everyone seemed to agree with that. In 1991, Negativland, an underground band based in San Francisco, released a record entitled 'U2'. It was a piece of attention-seeking pop larceny: they had re-mixed and re-modelled 'I Still Haven't Found What I'm Looking For', interspersing it with excerpts of an interview conversation between Bono and an American DJ, Casey Kasem. That it was a scam, both creatively and commercially, was underlined by the fact that U2's logo dominated the cover. One automatic reaction was that their fans might be conned into buying something under false pretences.

Island Records stepped in and took out an injunction to prevent further sale or distribution of the record. From the start it was a no-win situation for the U2 organisation. Negativland pleaded that there was no breach of copyright because 'U2' was a parody. And they argued that U2 were defining themselves as corporate rock animals by crushing what was essentially a subversive artistic statement. Which is all very well. But could U2 – or their record company – risk giving any and every scam merchant in the USA carte blanche to use and abuse their logo and their recordings on any pretence whatsoever?

"What was scary to me was that people who were criticising us weren't really listening to the records," Bono told David Fricke of Rolling Stone. "The records were not propagating any kind of 'men of stone' thing. *The Joshua Tree* is a very uncertain record. 'I Still Haven't Found What I'm Looking For' is an anthem of doubt more than faith."

I Still Haven't Found What I'm Looking For Written: U2 • Duration: 4' 37" • UK singles chart position: 6 • US singles chart position: 1

Group portrait: An official promotional photograph from *the Joshua Tree* album sessions.

Phone home: Promotional images for *The Joshua Tree* even made it on to Japanese telephone cards.

With Or Without You

Before recording *The Joshua Tree*, the band rehearsed in Danesmote, a period house in Rathfarnham on the outskirts of Dublin. The room they occupied was beautiful, with high windows and natural light flooding in. The rehearsals went so well that they decided to do the album there.

"We had experimented a lot in the making of *The Unforgettable Fire*," The Edge recalls. "We had done quite revolutionary things like 'Elvis Presley and America' and '4th of July'. So we felt, going into *The Joshua Tree*, that maybe options were not a good thing, that limitations might be positive. And so we decided to work within the limitations of the song as a starting point. We thought: let's actually write songs. We wanted the record to be more straightforward, focused and concise."

There are few better examples than 'With Or Without You'. It is that rare thing in the U2 canon – a love song – and it works, capturing an emotion that most people in serious relationships must have felt at one time or another when Bono sings, "*I can't live/with or without you.*" But the more you delve, the more you become aware that beneath its surface restraint lies a tangled web of complex anxieties. There is a spiritual dimension to the song as erotic love and agape love converge again in Bono's personal mythology, and he returns to the theme of self-surrender and ego-loss. But what does he mean by "*My hands are torn/my body bruised/She's got me with/nothing left to win/ and nothing left to lose*"? And who is "she"?

Bono doesn't like being specific about personal songs of this kind. Never did. "In 'With or Without You', when it says, '*And you give yourself away/ And you give yourself away*', everybody in the group knows what it means," he said in 1987. "It's about how I feel in U2 at times – exposed. I know that the group feel that I give myself away. I think if I do any damage to U2 it's that I'm too open. For instance, in an interview, I don't hold the cards there, and play the right one because I either have to do it or not do it." "The thing is to challenge radio," Adam told *Rolling Stone*. "To get 'With or Without You' on the radio is pretty good. You don't expect to hear it there. Maybe in a church."

What's more, U2 got it to No. 1 in the singles charts. "Paul McGuinness didn't want to release it as a single," Gavin Friday reveals. "But I told Bono that it was a certain No. 1. It was one of the biggest arguments I ever had with Paul, and in the end Bono sided with me. In fairness to Paul he did come up to me afterwards and apologise. He said 'You were right'. And of course I was."

With Or Without You Written: U2 • Duration: 4' 56" • UK singles chart position: 4 • US singles chart position: 1

Bullet the Blue Sky

In the sabbatical he took during 1985, Bono travelled extensively. With Ali, he went to Central America, under the auspices of Amnesty International, to observe and spent time in both El Salvador and Nicaragua. On the streets, Bono saw terrible poverty, a direct result of the American economic blockade and US support for the civil war being waged by the Contras.

"The spirit of the people in Nicaragua is being beaten down," he said at the time. "They've no food and no supplies. I was at a rally of Daniel Ortega's and you can tell from the look in people's eyes that they wanted so much to believe in their revolution. But people think with their pockets a lot of the time and you can't blame them for it. It's just sad to see the stranglehold the US has on Central America."

The US had been good to U2. But the things that were being done by Americans in Central America, ostensibly in the name of freedom and justice, were appalling. And U2 felt compelled to react.

'Bullet the Blue Sky' howls with anger and with fear. In El Salvador, Bono had seen government fighter jets flying overhead in a mission. He had heard the bark of guns in the distance that followed. That's the reality someone else wakens up to every day.

"I still believe in Americans," Bono said. "I think they're a very open people. It's their openness which leads them to trust a man as dangerous as Ronald Reagan. They want to believe he's a good guy. They want to believe he's in the cavalry, coming to rescue America's reputation after the '70s. But he was only an actor. It was only a movie. I think the picture's ended now and Americans are leaving the cinema a little down in the mouth."

'Bullet the Blue Sky' made one other connection, linking the disastrous US foreign policy under Reagan to his own religious fundamentalism and that of the Christian tele-evangelists. The Edge talked of Jerry Falwell: "He preaches that God is white, speaks in a Southern accent and has a wife and children. How does that relate to a Chinese peasant? It doesn't at all."

Or to a Southern black? The song contrasts the burning crosses of the Ku Klux Klan with the liberating sound of John Coltrane's saxophone. America: everything that's great about the world, and everything that's repulsive about it.

Bullet the Blue Sky Written: U2 • Duration: 4' 32"

Running To Stand Still

You couldn't escape the shadow of heroin in Dublin in the 1980. 'Wire' had dealt with this theme. So had 'Bad'. Now U2 returned to the theme, in a song clearly inspired by Lou Reed's towering 'Walk on the Wild Side'. 'Running to Stand Still' has an early lyrical reference to the seven imposing blocks of flats that scar the urban landscape of North Dublin and distinguish Ballymun, where Bono had grown up, from the rest of the city:"*I see seven towers/but I see only one way out*."

"I don't come from the viewpoint of someone who is completely unsympathetic to drug users," he said. Numerous friends, acquaintances and fellow musicians in Ireland had found themselves in thrall to heroin. Christy Dignam, lead singer with Aslan had endured a very public flirtation with the drug. And then in January 1986, Philip Lynott of Thin Lizzy had died of liver failure brought about by heroin addiction. When it comes that close to home, that there is no point in being judgemental.

"For two years, myself and Ali lived in Howth, on the same road as Phil," Bono confided, "and I would see him everywhere else but on that street. Every time I saw him he'd say, 'Why don't you come down for dinner? You know, you have to come down for a bite.' And I would say, 'You know, you have to come up for a bite. You have to drop up.' Every single time. And I never did call down and he never did call up."

The song is imbued with a real tenderness and compassion. But it isn't directed solely at those who are victims of heroin addiction. Bono goes further, empathsing with the central character.

"I heard about a couple," Bono explained, "and both were addicted, and such was their addiction that they had no money, so the guy risked everything on a run. He went and smuggled into Dublin a serious quantity of heroin, strapped to his body, so that on the one hand there was life imprisonment, on the other hand, riches. Apart from the morality of that, what interested me was what put him in that position."

Musically, 'Running to Stand Still' was improvised almost to tape using 'Walk on the Wild Side' and Elton John's 'Candle in the Wind' as a launching pad, but lyrically it was finely honed. It became one of the most important songs on *The Joshua Tree*. In its lack of moral certainty and its refusal to judge its subjects harshly, it looked ahead to the chaotic landscapes of *Achtung Baby* and *Zooropa*, in which the only certainty is uncertainty itself. That made it one of the band's most mature creations to date, a haunting, challenging piece of pop poetry that still resonates with lyrical truth.

Running To Stand Still Written: U2 • Duration: 4' 18"

Red Hill Mining Town

In '80s Britain, under the direction of Margaret Thatcher and its chairman Ian McGregor, the National Coal Board began to close what were deemed to be uneconomic mines. A miners' strike followed, with the National Union of Miners fighting the pit closures tooth and nail. It was one of the most bitter industrial disputes in recent history in Britain.

During the summer of 1984, Bob Dylan had played Slane Castle, just outside Dublin, and invited Bono on stage to join in an encore of 'Blowin' in the Wind'. Thrown a verse to sing by Dylan, Bono realised that while he recognised the song, he didn't know the words: he was forced to wing it.

In some ways that unplanned live collaboration saw Bono cross the great divide in musical terms. It confirmed for him just how much he still had to learn about the great tradition of singing, songwriting and musicianship. A friendship developed which saw him delving into Dylan's back catalogue and retracing the connections between the Irish and American folk traditions. This growing awareness of the power of the folk tradition was reflected in the band's participation in an Irish TV tribute to folk veterans the Dubliners. U2 chose a Peggy Seeger song and performed it with impressive authority. 'Springhill Mining Disaster' tells the story of how greed and exploitation in a coal mine in Nova Scotia ended in catastrophe. Bono delivered the song with passion and conviction.

All of these strands came together in 'Red Hill Mining Town'. It was criticised in some quarters for not being politically specific enough, but there is no doubt about where Bono's sympathies lie. "'Red Hill Mining Town' is a song about the miners' strike and the only reference to Ian McGregor is "*Through hand of steel and heart of stone/Our labour day is come and gone*"", he said. "People beat me with a stick for that but what I'm interested in is seeing in the newspapers or on television that another thousand people had lost their jobs.

"Now what you don't read about is that those people go home and they have families and they're trying to bring up children. And, in many instances, those relationships broke up under the pressure of the miners' strike. '*The glass is cut, the bottle runs dry/Our love runs cold in the caverns in the night/We're wounded by fear, injured in doubt/I can lose myself but I can't live without/'Cos you keep me holding on.*' I feel other people are more qualified to comment on the miners' strike. That enraged me – but I feel more qualified to write about relationships because I understand them more than what it's like to work in a pit."

Red Hill Mining Town Written: U2 • Duration: 4' 52"

In God's Country

Bono was trying to find ways of communicating his increasing sense of unease about the USA. 'Bullet the Blue Sky' had come spitting out in a spirit of anger. 'In God's Country' was more measured; it had an air of resignation. The image of the desert was at the heart of *The Joshua Tree*. "It has a spiritual aspect," The Edge reasoned, "which the record has, and also a great deal of mystery, which I like."

Adam went further: "The desert was immensely inspirational to us as a mental image for this record. Most people would take the desert on face value and think it's some kind of barren place, which of course is true. But in the right frame of mind, it's also a very positive image, because you can actually do something with blank canvas, which is effectively what the desert is."

That's the kind of thinking that informs 'In God's Country'. It sounds a bit like U2 playing U2 until The Edge drops in an Ennio Morricone-style guitar figure in the break. Bono, meanwhile, is restrained. Coming to him in a dream, the USA is characterised as a desert rose, a siren whose dress is torn in ribbons and in bows. "We need new dreams tonight," Bono sings. He's thinking about the dearth of new political ideas. "Except in Nicaragua," he says looking back. "That's why the revolution there was so important." "It's not your first reason for being on stage, to effect change in the political climate of a country," Bono said at the time. "I don't know what the first reason is, but that's not the first reason. But I like to think that U2 have already contributed to a turnaround in thinking."

Maybe 'In God's Country' would turn a few more heads around. Then again maybe not. You could argue that the chorus was too radio-friendly for that.

In God's Country Written: U2 • Duration: 2' 57" • UK singles chart position: 48 (as import) • US singles chart position: 44

Trip Through Your Wires

U2 didn't need to rush a new album so they took some time out. Individually and sometimes collectively, they went in search of fresh stimuli. Bono was searching for new musical roots, listening to folk, blues and country. And that search was reflected in the way he was thinking and how he looked.

It also connected with the musical changes that Ireland was going through in the mid-'80s. Mike Scott had relocated to Dublin with The Waterboys and had become obsessed not just with Bob Dylan and Van Morrison but also with the Irish folk tradition. The Hothouse Flowers were also in the ascendant, and making similar links. Both tended to turn up for spontaneous sessions in the strangest of places, so that Dublin became a city of buskers. It was against that backdrop that 'Trip Through Your Wires' was conceived.

U2 were to appear on a new Irish television programme, TV Gaga. On the night, the band trooped on looking like extras from some B-movie remake of Easy Rider. They performed 'Womanfish' – a song which subsequently disappeared without a trace – and 'Trip Through Your Wires'. There wasn't an echo effect in sight. Instead, we witnessed The Edge getting down 'n' dirty in a bar room bluesy romp, a drinking song that featured Bono wailing away crudely on a Dylan-esque harp solo.

"It was a hootenanny, a big yahoo," Bono said. "We kind of made it up at the moment and I just blew into the harp. The thing about Lanois and Eno in the studio is they're very supportive of the idea of a session. They get carried away with it and we get carried away with them getting carried away with it. It's just a vicious cycle in the right sense of the word." Lyrically it's relatively throwaway. It can be seen as another paean to the contradictory charms of America, personified as a woman. It could be about an unconventional sexual encounter and the attendant feelings of confusion and guilt. Or it can be read simply as an exercise in Dylan-esque personal myth-making: the singer broken down by the ravages of living the hard life being put back together by the love of a good woman.

Sex 'n' drink 'n' rock 'n' roll? It might have been Bono's own personal basement tape.

Trip Through Your Wires Written: U2 • Duration: 3' 32"

One Tree Hill

When U2 were on tour in New Zealand in 1985 they met Greg Carroll. A Maori, he worked doing front-of-house for the promoter on the band's Kiwi dates, beginning in Auckland. "There are five volcanic islands which make up Auckland," Bono explained, "and the tallest is One Tree Hill. Greg took me there on my first night in New Zealand."

Carroll was a bundle of energy, a live wire. "Paul McGuinness thought this guy's so smart we can't leave him here. Let's take him with us to Australia," Bono explained. Within a short time, Greg Carroll had become a valued member of the organisation.

Their world tour over, the band returned to Dublin. Greg Carroll came too. He worked as Bono's assistant and, in the few months he spent in Dublin, became like a brother to the singer. He was well loved and widely respected by those who knew him both within and outside the U2 camp. What happened was horrific. On the run-up to recording *The Joshua Tree*, he took Bono's Harley Davidson on a courier run. It was a bleak, rainy night. A car pulled out in front of him and Greg, going full tilt, ploughed into it. He was killed instantly.

"It was a devastating blow," Bono reflected. "He was doing me a favour. He was taking my bike home. Greg used to look after Ali. They used to go out dancing together. He was a best friend. I've already had it once with my mother. Now I've had it twice."

Even six months later, Bono found it hard to talk about, choking back tears in an interview. "The emphasis," he reflected, "among family and friends when we had a No. 1 record and were a big band was on how much you'd got – and not how much you've lost. The sense of loss came home through losing Greg Carroll."

The imagery of 'One Tree Hill' superbly evoked the seafaring heritage of Carroll's Maori ancestors. A spiritual tour de force, it is a hymn of praise and celebration which describes the traditional Maori burial of their friend on One Tree Hill and links it poetically with themes of renewal and redemption, with the river running, running down to the sea.

"Greg Carroll's funeral was beyond belief," Bono said. "He was buried in his tribal homeland, as a Maori, by the chiefs and elders. And there was a three-day and three-night wake and your head would be completely turned around. And ours were, again and again."

One Tree Hill Written: U2 • Duration: 5' 23"

Exit

Bono had gone west in his reading. He was interested in Flannery O'Connor, Raymond Carver, Norman Mailer. Looking for insights into the people of the vast place that had embraced them. Ways of understanding the ordinary stock first and then the outsiders, the driftwood – those on the fringes of the promised land, cut off from the American dream. He read *The Executioner's Song*, Norman Mailer's superb account of the life of Gary Gilmore. 'Exit' wasn't about Gilmore. It wasn't about Charles Manson either. But it trawls the area occupied by either or both, getting inside the head of a protagonist who's careening into psychosis.

Musically 'Exit' is like nothing U2 had ever done before. The antithesis of their bright, ringing, optimistic, inspirational selves, it was dirty, angry, loud, discordant, repetitive, noisy, black. If the intention was to invoke a sense of evil abroad, then it was effective, with Larry's blistering drum attack and Adam's low-down insistent muddy bass creating a powerful sense of being inside someone's skin, of feeling their palpitations en route to some unspeakable denouement.

"You could say that this is forbidden ground for U2 because we're the 'optimistic' group," Bono confided at the time. "But to be an optimist you mustn't be blind or deaf to the world around you. 'Exit' – I don't even know what the act is in that song. Some see it as a murder, others suicide – and I don't mind. But the rhythm of the words is nearly as important in conveying the state of mind."

That was the point of 'Exit': to convey the state of mind of someone driven, by whatever powerful urges, to the very brink of desperation. The undercurrent of religious imagery reflected a new awareness of the dangers of fanaticism implicit in faith. But there was no other message in 'Exit'. Except this is how it is out there: deal with it. And in a way, it was a method of purging the band's own demons, their own anger and fury at the vicissitudes fate had thrust upon them. It was a way of coming to terms with death and with grief. It was an exorcism.

High notes: Bono sings his heart out at a show in Las Cruces, Mexico, April 1987.

Live Aid: Bono joins George Michael, Freddie Mercury and others to sing 'Do They Know It's Christmas?'.

Wembley walkabout: Almost 75,000 people enjoyed U2's performance, which included Bono's dramatic onstage, and off-stage, antics.

As such, it was not without its own psychic cost. In the USA , a man accused of murdering Rebecca Shaeffer, a TV actress, claimed that he was inspired by listening to 'Exit'. It may have been no more than a smart defence lawyer coming up with a half-plausible plea of mitigation, but it wasn't the kind of accusation you wanted hanging over you, however spurious. But then, there was a whole list of positive lessons to be learned from *The Joshua Tree* too.

Exit Written: U2 • Duration: 4' 13"

Mothers Of The Disappeared

During 1986, U2 had agreed to participate in the Conspiracy of Hope tour in the USA with Sting, Lou Reed, Bryan Adams, Peter Gabriel and Joan Baez, among others. The tour was both a money-raising and a consciousness-raising expedition, undertaken on behalf of Amnesty International. The band had developed a close relationship with that organisation through Jack Healey, an Irish-American former priest, who put together the Conspiracy tour. He had helped in making connections for Bono in Nicaragua and El Salvador. Now, in a variety of shapes and guises, Amnesty concerns were resurfacing on *The Joshua Tree*.

Bono was struck by the accounts he'd heard of murder squads operating under the Argentinian military junta through the '70s and '80s. Those bleak decades precipitated a return to democracy during which hundreds of student opponents of the military regime had been arrested and were never seen again, dead or alive. In Argentina they became known as "the disappeared", and an organisation called Mothers of the Disappeared had been formed to campaign for full disclosure of what had happened to those who had been lifted.

'Mothers of the Disappeared' continues the tradition of '40' and 'MLK' – but it is less a celebration than a lament. It enters with disturbing sound effects and it never loses its ominous quality – The Edge's guitar is barbed wire, and Bono sounds like Dylan's man of constant sorrow, his yodel a high, lonesome sound. The song is an act of witness but there is no optimistic note of reassurance. Too much evil in the world. Some things just can't be explained. Even Bono was prepared to acknowledge that now.

Mothers Of The Disappeared Written: U2 • Duration: 5' 14"

LIVE AID AND U2 BY BRIAN BOYD

Simple really: two billion people are watching the Live Aid show, U2 are to play three songs including their new single 'Pride'. This is their most important show ever.

When Bob Geldof was organizing the giant Live Aid music concert at Wembley Stadium in July 1985, he was determined to have U2 on the bill – even if their then status didn't actually warrant an appearance. As a fellow Dubliner, Geldof loved U2 and Bono had flown across the Atlantic at a minute's notice to help out with vocals on the 'Do They Know It's Christmas' single from the previous December, which Geldof and Midge Ure had written to raise funds for Ethiopian famine relief. U2 are control freaks when it comes to their live appearances.

They don't like ceding control to anyone other than their immediate tried and trusted light and sound personnel. When informed there would be no time for a soundcheck, the band panicked but resolved to perform their three-song set to the best of their ability.

Opening song 'Sunday Bloody Sunday' worked well – clearly Bono was feeding off the energy of the 75,000-plus Wembley audience. "We're a band from Dublin. Like all cities it has its good and it has its bad – this is a song called 'Bad'," says Bono, introducing their second song. Six minutes in, when the band should be getting ready to start thinking about going into 'Pride', Bono has a rush of blood to the head. Leaping down off the stage, he gestures to a girl in the audience to climb over the security barrier and join him on stage. Trying to help her, he jumps further down so he's on ground level – way out of sight of the band on stage – and continues trying to extract various audience members from beyond the security barrier.

On stage, The Edge, Adam and Larry don't know what is going on. Worried glances are exchanged as they keep on playing the song. Had Bono decided to cut the set short and was now back in the dressing room? What were the band to do in front of their biggest-ever television audience?

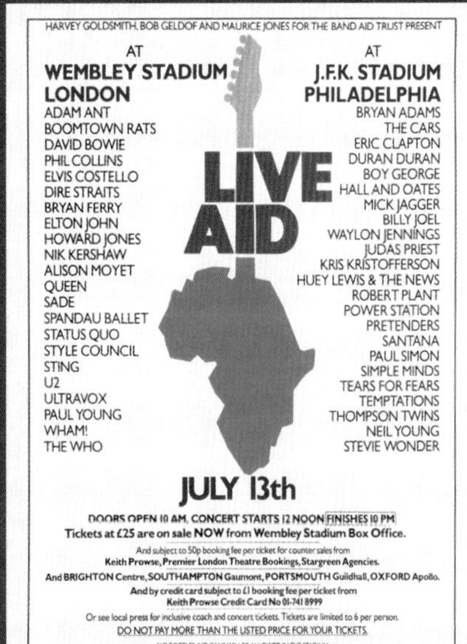

HARVEY GOLDSMITH, BOB GELDOF AND MAURICE JONES FOR THE BAND AID TRUST PRESENT
AT
WEMBLEY STADIUM
LONDON
ADAM ANT
BOOMTOWN RATS
DAVID BOWIE
PHIL COLLINS
ELVIS COSTELLO
DIRE STRAITS
BRYAN FERRY
ELTON JOHN
HOWARD JONES
NIK KERSHAW
ALISON MOYET
QUEEN
SADE
SPANDAU BALLET
STATUS QUO
STYLE COUNCIL
STING
U2
ULTRAVOX
PAUL YOUNG
WHAM!
THE WHO
AT
J.F.K. STADIUM
PHILADELPHIA
BRYAN ADAMS
THE CARS
ERIC CLAPTON
DURAN DURAN
BOY GEORGE
HALL AND OATES
MICK JAGGER
BILLY JOEL
WAYLON JENNINGS
JUDAS PRIEST
KRIS KRISTOFFERSON
HUEY LEWIS & THE NEWS
ROBERT PLANT
POWER STATION
PRETENDERS
SANTANA
PAUL SIMON
SIMPLE MINDS
TEARS FOR FEARS
TEMPTATIONS
THOMPSON TWINS
NEIL YOUNG
STEVIE WONDER
LIVE AID
JULY 13th
DOORS OPEN 10 AM, CONCERT STARTS 12 NOON FINISHES 10 PM
Tickets at £25 are on sale NOW from Wembley Stadium Box Office.
And subject to 50p booking fee per ticket for counter sales from
Keith Prowse, Premier London Theatre Bookings, Stargreen Agencies.
And BRIGHTON Centre, SOUTHAMPTON Gaumont, PORTSMOUTH Guildhall, OXFORD Apollo.
And by credit card subject to £1 booking fee per ticket from
Keith Prowse Credit Card No 01-741 8999
Or see local press for inclusive coach and concert tickets. Tickets are limited to 6 per person.
DO NOT PAY MORE THAN THE LISTED PRICE FOR YOUR TICKETS.
NO BOTTLES, NO CANS WILL BE ALLOWED IN THE STADIUM.
ANY DONATIONS WILL BE GRATEFULLY RECEIVED TO 'BAND AID TRUST'
c/o STOY HAYWARD 8 BAKER STREET, LONDON W1M 1DJ.

Larry Mullen remembers the experience as "excruciating", saying "We didn't know whether we should stop, we didn't know where he was; we didn't know if he had fallen." The band were well used to Bono climbing up scaffolding and going into the audience from as far back as their Dandelion Market days, but this was different – he was out of their visual range and nothing was coming through on his microphone.

Eventually Bono reappeared. There was still a few minutes left to play 'Pride' but instead the singer chose to continue with 'Bad', adding in improvised lyrical excerpts from the Rolling Stones' 'Ruby Tuesday' and Lou Reed's 'Satellite of Love'. When Bono realized their allotted time is up, he left the stage without making eye contact with any of the band.

In the dressing room afterwards, there is a furious row. Bono's antics had meant they hadn't played 'Pride', an important song to them at the time and his self-indulgence had ruined U2's big global moment. Bono was to claim later that the band were so incandescent with rage they wanted to sack him.

Back in Ireland, a distraught Bono got into his car and drove deep into the Irish countryside, feeling he had let everyone down – U2 most of all. He made sure he was out of touch because he didn't want to face another band interrogation about why he had ruined the performance. But as the days went by, it transpired that everyone was talking about the band's performance in a positive and enthusiastic way. By straying off script, Bono (still not that well-known at this stage) had become a hot topic. Outside Queen's performance later that evening, U2's set became the Live Aid moment – the one people still remember best.

Not for the first time, U2 had forged triumph out of apparent failure. That afternoon at Wembley Stadium was the moment U2 became a truly global band.

ACHTUNG BABY

Selina Scott in Central Park, New York. A mic stuck in Bono's face. She is flattering Bono, talking about his interest in social justice, his trip to Ethiopia, his involvement in the Sun City anti-apartheid project.

The Giants' stadium, later that evening. Selina is there again. So is Lou Reed. Lou can be curt. When he doesn't like Selina's questions he tells her where to get off. "Man, you got a lot of shit to deal with," he says to Bono. Maybe Lou misunderstood, but Selina seemed to be casting aspersions on U2 being interested in social justice. Bono's face flushed. Then the anger hit. She had seemed so – sweet.

He saw a line about U2 marketing idealism. And he thought, We've got to get rid of this baggage. It doesn't matter how sincere you are. Perceptions are more important than truth. You're a rock 'n' roll star. Your job is riddled with contradictions. Time to put them on the agenda. Enter *Achtung Baby*. Enter Zoo TV. And then U2's whole world started to fall apart.

Zoo Station

Wartime Germany. The Allies are wreaking havoc. Cities being bombed. In the midst of chaos, surreal humour. The walls of Berlin Zoo are knocked down and the animals escape. The citizens emerge from their bunkers in the morning. There are rhinos, pelicans, flamingos in the streets *Achtung Baby* was a nightmare to record. It nearly killed everyone in the band. There was a lot of tension in the air. On one of the darker days, Bono decided that a trip to the zoo would be in order. U2 bought ice-creams and walked round the zoo like school kids.

Bono was interested in the zoo. He'd read a novel about setting free the animals, a kind of introduction to Dadaism. Going right back to Lypton Village and the Virgin Prunes, that was his world. He began to feel that things were coming full circle, that maybe it was time to re-introduce characters like the Fool. They'd been moving in the direction of the literal.

Now, they needed to become Dadaist again. He was interested in the zoo as a metaphor. So there was a certain surge of recognition when they landed in Berlin to record the album. This place was like a fucking zoo alright. Even the train station was called Zoo Bahnhof. Zoo Station. The point was that the song would open the album with a statement of intent. Forget the previous reference points. You are about to embark on a journey into the unknown. So are we.

The first verse reads as if it could have been written from the point of view of a child about to be born: *"(I'm) ready to say I'm glad to be alive/ I'm ready, ready for the push."* And that suspicion lingers throughout, as if Bono is drawing inspiration from having watched his own first child struggling to find her bearings in an unfamiliar and sometimes hostile world. *"In the cool of the night/in the warmth of the breeze,"* he sings, *"I'll be crawling around/on my hands and knees."*

Bono was unhappy with his vocal performances when the band began to record *Achtung Baby*. He and engineer Flood distorted his voice. It gave Bono a different sound, and also a new persona to play with. The band sounded different too. The drums were hard, insistent, industrial. There were moments of sunlight, as the train emerged from the underground, flashes of openness captured on The Edge's guitar. But this was the beginning of a journey into the dark underbelly of human experience and the suggestion of a child's-eye view only made it more poignant.

Zoo Station Written: U2 • Duration: 4' 36" • US singles chart position: 10

Even Better Than The Real Thing

It had been bugging Bono for a long, long time. You switch on the radio and hear a soulful voice bellowing out something that sounds almost spiritual. It turns out to be a promo for a bank. You flick on the television. There's this incredible piece of footage that could be straight out of Vanishing Point, only it looks richer, denser, more expensive. It's a car ad.

It was around the time of the release of *Rattle and Hum*. "You can't tell the difference between the ads and the records any more," Bono said to me, clearly rattled by the way in which music was being co-opted and manipulated to serve the needs of commerce. And yet wasn't rock 'n' roll itself about commerce, about selling records? That thought was there as an undercurrent in 'Desire', a song about turning people on, that had Bono stuttering about *"Money, money, money, money, money, money"*.

'Desire' had been recorded with Paul Barrett and Robbie Adams handling engineering duties in STS studios in Dublin. Another song, started in the same session and then put to one side, had been called 'The Real Thing'. They took the multi-track of that to Germany and tried to work on it in Hansa Studios. But the atmosphere was so overloaded with melancholy that nothing happened. They couldn't crack it.

The Fly: A leather-clad egomaniac created by Bono for the album *Achtung Baby*, 'The Fly' was a parody of rock stardom. Here he is on stage in Rotterdam, July 1992.

Release date: November 1991
Catalogue number: U28
Producer: Daniel Lanois, with special thanks to Brian Eno
Track listing: Zoo Station/Even Better than the Real Thing/One/Until the End of the World/Who's Gonna Ride Your Wild Horses?/So Cruel/The Fly/Mysterious Ways/Tryin' To Throw Your Arms Around The World/Ultraviolet (Light My Way)/Acrobat/Love Is Blindness.
Highest Chart position: No. 2 (UK), 1 (US)

Zoo TV: U2's infamous Zoo TV tour rewrote the rulebook for live rock performance. Note the Trabant car hanging from the lighting system.

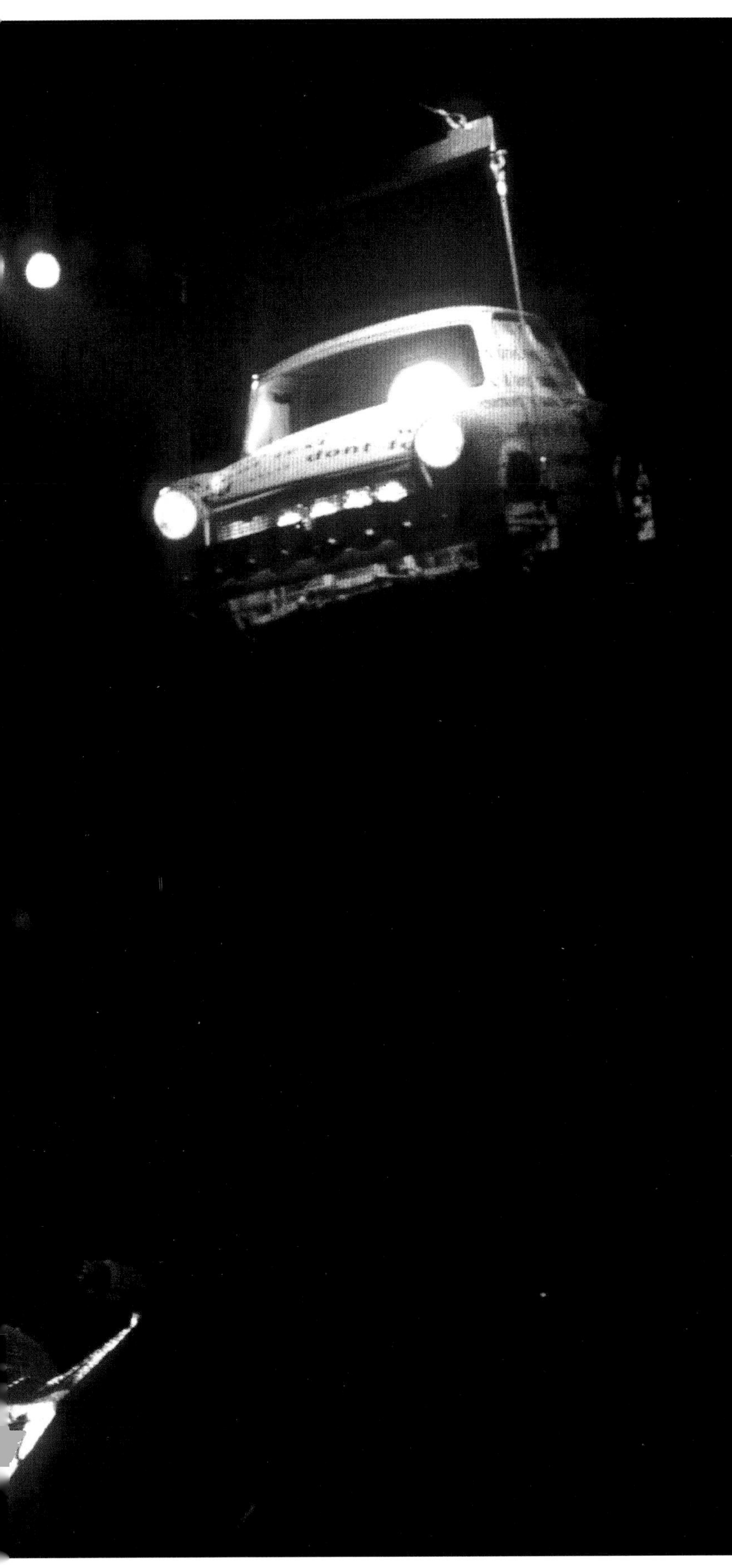

Back in Dublin, they set up in Elsinore, a mansion on the Dalkey coastline, near where Bono and The Edge live, to which the band give the name Dog Town.. It was there that *Achtung Baby* began to come together. The Berlin session had been racked by a mixture of creative divisions, personal tensions and an abiding sense of dislocation. Gradually these were overcome in the more relaxed, informal atmosphere of the new surroundings. The spirit of Berlin hung over the record, but now the darkness and claustrophobia could be turned to creative effect. By the time it came to finishing 'Even Better than the Real Thing', the band had rediscovered their sense of fun, tarting it up à la Marc Bolan in a tribute to the kind of glam rock that was on Top of the Pops when they were hitting their own teens.

"It had been called 'The Real Thing', which is a really dumb title for a song," Bono reflects. "So with these new eyes that we had, we thought 'Even Better Than the Real Thing' is actually where people live right now. People are no longer after experiences of truth. They are looking for true experiences, for the moment. People are no longer obsessed with the question 'What is the truth?' They want to know 'What is the point?' And the point is the moment. That's where we live right now, in this rave culture. Interesting things come out of that because living in the present, in the now – and not looking to what's around the corner – is very dangerous politically, ecologically, in relationships, to the family. But that's where people are at right now."

U2's interest in dance had been stimulated by their own plans to open a club, The Kitchen in the Clarence Hotel. Besides, there was an imperative always to be at the cutting edge of youth culture, to know what was going on, to absorb whatever lessons might need to be learned and to apply them smartly to the evolving band gestalt. 'Even Better Than the Real Thing' was evidence enough that Larry and Adam could mix it with the best of the new Manchester dance groups in the rhythm department but there was more than a hint of irony in U2's appropriation of the old Sly Stone gospel routine, the backing vocals pleading "Take me higher", before Bono delivers the chorus with what amounts to serene detachment.

The intention was to indulge the voyeuristic emphasis on appearance, to slide knowingly down the surface of things. The infatuation with the moment is superbly captured in the clubbers' heroic self-projection: "*We're free to fly the crimson sky/The sun won't melt our wings tonight.*" But underlying these erotic chimerae is something tragic. What else but the sound of a relationship cracking up could explain the lines "*Well, my heart is where it's always been/My head is somewhere in between/Give me one more chance/Let me be your lover tonight*"?

Meanwhile, the joke was on Coca-Cola, who had been using "The real thing" as their advertising slogan for years. It almost came full circle when Richard Branson approached the band, seeking permission to use 'Even Better Than the Real Thing' for his campaign to launch Virgin Cola. But that would have been one irony too far. The band refused.

Even Better Than The Real Thing Written: U2 • Duration: 3' 41" • UK singles chart position: 8 • US singles chart position: 32

One

Sometimes it can seem as if you're digging a hole. Another day, another recording session. Nothing seems to be coming right. You flounder around for six hours, and at the end of it you know that inspiration has gone on an extended holiday. But now that you're into the process there's no option but to keep going. And so you flounder some more. And then suddenly: BANG! U2 were in Berlin for three months and they delivered two songs. And one of them happened by accident. They were in the throes of working on 'Mysterious Ways' and looking for a middle eight. The Edge came up with two alternatives. Bono heard one of them and he thought "Massive new song!" He improvised a melody over the chords and it sounded good. "The Edge put the other middle eight on at the end of it and that just became the song. The melody, the structure – the whole thing was done in 15 minutes," Bono recalls.

Naturally, the band were excited. It was one of those happy accidents, those moments when the log-jam of ideas breaks and a song comes flooding through. Tapes of the work-in-progress were being delivered to Eno, who was coming back with comments and responses; in due course, he got this first, inspired draft of 'One'. The next time he showed up in Hansa Studios he was in buoyant mood.

"Brian arrived and he said that he liked all the material we had," Bono recalls. "We were surprised because everyone was freaked out about it. Then he said 'There's just one song I really despise, and that's 'One'." Bono laughs. "He felt it needed some serious deconstruction. So we went about that, and that's why it works. Because you can play it on acoustic guitar now and it works, but if you had heard it on acoustic guitar first, it wouldn't have had the same feeling."

Flood remembers the session well. It was one of those special occasions alright. "It was very, very quick," he says. "Bono sang 90 per cent of the melody and a lot of the lyrical ideas off the top of his head. It just came together. There was a moment and we caught it."

It is extraordinary to think just how close 'One' came to not happening. Given the shambolic way in which U2 operate in the studio, there's always a sense that songs are written by accident, but this was a particularly extreme case. And yet it emerges as one of their finest creations, a ballad of great depth and beauty that's open to a multiplicity of interpretations. "I think it was based loosely on the position I was in regarding my last girlfriend and my wife," Bono's old Lypton Village associate, Guggi, reflects, offering one interpretation. "I was with my last girlfriend, Linda, for 14 years. And then I got a little studio down in the City Arts Centre. I was working there and then I heard that this German painter was coming over for six months, to work, and it turned out to be Sybil. We started painting together and it sort of went from there. And I was very close, physically close, to Bono at the time because he was around and we were spending a lot of time together. And I think a lot of that is captured in the song." 'One' is a song about relationships. The implication of guilt, felt by someone who has just walked out on a long-term love, is there alright when Bono asks, "*Have you come here for forgiveness/Have you come to raise the dead/Have you come here to play Jesus/To the lepers in your head?*" But the song is also a meditation on the extent to which their Berlin sojourn was testing the band's own sense of unity. "That's an extraordinary thing about songwriting," Bono relates. "What something is in essence, you don't have to play to it. In fact if you play against it, you often get much more.

"'One', of course, is about the band," he adds. "It was after Adam flipped out in Sydney, and we'd had to do a show without him. We had just two nights to film, and the first was gone because he wasn't there. So we had one night to get it. But he looks amazing in the film and there's a real boldness to his playing. I don't know how he kept it together.

"We thought that was going to be the end, to be honest with you. We didn't know if we wanted to go on if somebody was that unhappy. And that performance of 'One' suddenly becomes what it is about that night. It does have that quality as a song. Going around Europe, when the stuff was going on in Bosnia, sometimes 200 miles from where we were playing, you'd get a similar kind of feeling – that that was what it was about."

Three videos were made for 'One', each drawing on a different interpretation of the song. One, directed by Mark Pellington and built around an image of buffalo being herded over the side of a cliff, was based on the work of the artist David Wojnarowicz, who died of an AIDS -related illness in 1992. It led to speculation that 'One' was a song about AIDS and that the lyric was a conversation between a father and his HIV-positive gay son. It always seemed like a somewhat liberal interpretation to me.

"It was part of one of the layers of the story," Bono argues. "If a song deals with any kind of sexual or erotic subject matter, then the spectre of AIDS has to be present. But it's not the only threat to relationships. Everything out there is against the idea of couples. The concept of fidelity is constantly undermined in every ad, every TV programme, every film, every novel you read. Sex is used to sell commodities. It has become a commodity itself. In fact, it's always been a commodity.

"If sex is even close to the centre of our lives, how come we've relegated the subject to where it's the property of the dullest of minds, to pornographers and the like? I still think it's virgin territory because you're prone to juvenalia in it, the 23 positions in a one-night stand type of boast, but there's much more out there than that."

With the Berlin session in the bag, the tape of 'One' was taken back to Dublin. What they had was a good foundation but it still needed what The Edge calls "foreground". That was when Eno came in and, with razor-sharp instinct, did a mix based on his personal prejudices, ruthlessly throwing out what he didn't like. It was the breakthrough they needed. They got a picture of an arrangement that would work.

Flood remained unconvinced. "I was the nagging doubter," he recalls. "I always felt it was a bit straight, until we did the final mix. It was all hands on deck. Bono didn't like a line in the vocal and we basically spent the whole day re-doing it. From that, we went into mix mode and it was me, Eno, Lanois and Bono sitting at the back, all doing different moves, getting the mix to be quite emotional.

"There's a point in the process when the technology gets lost and you can actually use the desk as an instrument. It started to happen on that mix. We got to just after the 'Love is a temple' section at the end and The Edge said, 'I've got this great idea for a guitar riff'. So on

Lounge lizard: Also appearing on the Zoo TV tour – Bono's other alter-ego, 'MacPhisto'.

the mix, there were three of us on the desk, the rest of the band vibing around and The Edge at the back of the studio, playing the guitar part live to the half-inch. "Personally, I feel that the song has such a strong emotional content – and we managed to completely honour and improve on that, the way we mixed it."

One Written: U2 • Length: 4' 36" • UK singles chart position: 7

Until the End of the World

What are the themes of *Achtung Baby*? You could put the same question to ten people and get ten different answers. The Edge said: betrayal, love, morality, spirituality and faith. Betrayal came first.

It was in the air. The Edge's marriage was falling apart. So was Guggi's. There was tension in the band. Now that they were working with rhythm loops, Larry wasn't even sure what his place was anymore. There was that morning where the others had succeeded in leaving him stranded. Larry had spent hours languishing in his East German hotel. When he got in to Hansa, in the end, he was furious and he let everyone know it. Betrayal.

Bono had been reading Brendan Kennelly's *Book of Judas*. Judas Iscariot was a remarkable character. The more you thought about him the more enigmatic he became. The redemption couldn't have happened without him. So was he the ultimate insider? It was interesting how he betrayed Jesus: with a kiss! What had been going on between them anyway? Written for Wim Wenders, 'Until the End of the World' is about an encounter in which sex is high on the agenda. There's a hint that only men were involved. There's also a strong suggestion of prostitution. And there is an unmistakable reference to oral sex: "*Surrounding me, going down on me/spilling over the brim*." But it doesn't stop there. "*In waves of regret, waves of joy*," Bono sings, "*I reached out for the one I tried to destroy*."

And you know that he must be thinking of an orgasm that's drenched in feelings of guilt. All of these elements are in there, of course, but the song is about betrayal and it's written from the point of view of Judas Iscariot. The line "*In the garden I was playing the tart/I kissed your lips and broke your heart*" refers to the scene in the Garden of Gethsemane, and there's no mistaking the implication of a homoerotic bond between Jesus and Judas.

On the other hand, there's a sense that Bono is writing about himself and his own capacity for betrayal. Or could it be about someone Bono felt had betrayed him? In truth it is about all the betrayals that were so central to U2 at the time.

Until the End of the World Written: U2 • Duration: 4' 39"

So Cruel

You could listen to *Achtung Baby* every which way. You could turn it upside down. You could look at it from a dozen different angles. It doesn't matter. No matter what way you come at it, there is blood on the tracks. And nowhere is this more evident than in the ballad 'So Cruel'.

Shine a light: Bono and Adam at McNichols Arena in Denver, Colorado in April 1987.

To describe it as bittersweet would be an understatement. 'So Cruel' is the desolate complaint of a lover who has been spurned but who remains in love with his tormentor. As a statement about marital infidelity, the sense of betrayal that accompanies it and the rage that almost inevitably follows, it would be hard to surpass. Bono is clearly drawing on the experiences of those close to him, and particularly on the emotional turmoil that The Edge and Aislinn had been going through.

"That's in there, but it's unfair to lump it all on The Edge and Aislinn splitting up," he explains. "That was one of the saddest things. I was their best man, and we all went through that. But that was only one part of it. There were lots of other things going on internally within the band and outside it. People are desperately trying to hold onto each other in a time when that's very difficult. Looking around, you see how unprepared for it all people are, and the deals they make."

Looked at from another angle, 'So Cruel' deals with possessiveness, jealousy and obsession – that part of the brain where sex and power are connected in a heady and addictive cocktail. Scott Walker was an acknowledged influence on the song. So, too, was Roy Orbison, for whom Bono and The Edge had written 'Mystery Girl'. The arrangement is something Flood takes credit for, highlighting a subtle piece of studio chicanery that transforms the song.

"If you haven't got a song there in the first place, none of this would make a blind bit of difference," he says, "but I think the way we shifted around the rhythm was very important. It was put down as a very straightfeeling backing track. The bass is played, but in the studio we doctored it to change the emphasis of where the bass line lay. That turned it into something that had a more unique feel about it, meshed against the song. That was one track where the technology available to us was crucial to the end product."

But in the end it is the poetry that makes it memorable. "Her skin is pale like God's only dove/Screams like an angel for your love/Then she makes you watch her from above/And you need her like a drug."

So Cruel Written: U2 • Duration: 5' 49"

The Fly

Blame it on the wardrobe man. Fintan Fitzgerald, who handles that end of the U2 operation, bought Bono the mad goggles. In the dark days in Berlin, Bono would stick on the fly shades and look at the world through the eyes of a character who was only barely forming in his imagination. It was childish, playful. Slowly but surely 'The Fly' was born.

The band had been hammering away at a piece with the working title of 'Ultraviolet'. Back in Dublin, the piece schismed into two parts. One became 'Light My Way'. The other was 'The Fly'. Fintan Fitzgerald also gave Bono a book of Jenny Holger's truisms. "I became very interested in these single-line aphorisms," Bono states. "So I got this character who could say them all, from 'A liar won't believe anybody else' to 'A friend is somebody who lets you down'. And that's where 'The Fly' was coming from." Flood contributed the distortion in the voice, creating the distance that Bono needed to get fully into the part. Daniel Lanois helped with the lyric.

"I thought it was a fascinating character," Bono recalls. "Because

Playful persona: On the Zoo TV tour, Bono parodied his old, sanctimonious image with a fun new personality.

there had been rumours of megalomania circulating and I thought – well, let's give them a megalomaniac! The faces of the people when that character walked on stage, was a sight to be seen. I couldn't see it as clearly as everyone else because I had the goggles and the boil-in-the-bag Elvis suit on. But it was a sense of 'Oh no, it's true'. And that was a great feeling."

Undercurrents had come together. 'The Fly' was about subversion. With its hip-hop beats, distorted vocals and industrial edge, Bono called it the sound of four men chopping down *The Joshua Tree*. It is packed with little explosions of truth, some of them universal, others personal. "It's no secret ambition bites the nail of success," 'The Fly' announces, and it's a powerful image that's rooted in Bono's own gnawed fingernails.

With the Gulf War erupting in the middle of recording, there was a sense in which 'The Fly' represented everyman on the run from the sheer craziness of the world around him. And then there was Bono playing the Fat Lady, crooning in a gospel falsetto: *"Love we shine like a burning star/We're falling from the sky."* We should have known it was all over when she began to sing.

The Fly Written: U2 • Duration: 4' 29" • UK singles chart position: 1 • US singles chart position: 61

Mysterious Ways

There is a feeling throughout *Achtung Baby* that man is but an awe-struck observer at the banquet of love. That woman is the superior being. That all she has to do is click her fingers – or crack her whip – and he will obey.

Images of submission abound. They're there in 'Zoo Station', 'One', 'Who's Gonna Ride Your Wild Horses?', 'So Cruel' and 'The Fly', with the narrator abasing himself in front of the woman, crawling around on his hands and knees. 'Mysterious Ways' continues in the same vein, with the celebrated couplet *"If you want to kiss the sky/better learn how to kneel... (on your knees boy!)"*.

"It's a song about a man living on little or no romance," Bono says. "It's a song about women – or about woman – but it's addressed to him." 'Mysterious Ways' is not about a particular woman. It is about women in general, and the way they entrance men. "Ali often says, 'For God's sake will you let me down off this pedestal?'" Bono laughs. "At times I do tend to idealise women. It's easy to fall into the trap of separating them into angels and devils for the sake of the drama."

'Mysterious Ways' is one of the album's most upful, optimistic tracks. It had begun with a bass riff, Adam kick-starting the musical framework and Larry laying down a suitably funky dance, rhythm groove. Then they hit a wall. "A load of different ideas were tried," says Flood. They accidentally side-tracked into 'One', and then came back to 'Mysterious Ways'. Daniel Lanois went into the studio in Berlin early one morning to try out a few ideas before the band got in. He didn't like what he was hearing. Then when Bono came in and started to sing, he seemed to be pushing the song in the opposite direction entirely. In a dark, tense period for the band, this was the nadir. Lanois and Bono argued solidly for over two hours – a bitter, intense argument during which no holds were barred.

"That's why I love Danny so much," Bono says. "He cares about the record he's making as much and more than any band or artist he's working with." But it wasn't funny at the time. Joe O'Herlihy remembers it as a brutal and bruising showdown.

"I really thought they were going to have a fight," Flood adds. "But I think it was just a product of the fact that this was such a hard record to make. Going into it everyone knew what we didn't want. It was like, you know what you want to throw out – but you're not quite sure of the place you want to go. It takes a series of mistakes, errors, learning, two steps forward, three steps sideways to actually get there."

Mysterious Ways Written: U2 • Duration: 4' 04" • UK singles chart position: 13 • US singles chart position: 9

Who's Gonna Ride Your Wild Horses

'Who's Gonna Ride Your Wild Horses?' had so many different incarnations. It was mixed a dozen different ways, and the pros and cons of each of them were debated in detail. Should Larry lighten up on the drums? Should he push them harder? What about that first rhythm track that The Edge put down? Where has the acoustic gone? The discussions went round in circles. And then it was time to be decisive.

Daniel Lanois was producing *Achtung Baby* but at times he seemed uncomfortable with what was going down. Eno was afforded the

Making *Achtung Baby* is the reason why we're still here now." Bono

luxury of being a dilettante. Flood was there all the way through, at the desk, keeping track of everything. And when things were getting really hairy, there was always the option of calling in Steve Lillywhite as a fresh pair of ears. And when it came to the crunch, when decisions had to be made about 'Who's Gonna Ride Your Wild Horses?', they brought him in again.

"Steve mixed it and he went for the sonic blast of it," Bono says. "It started out as one of those Scott Walker things but we felt it was too rich. Daniel probably felt that the way we went in the end was too FM." It had been more of a love song. Now it was about sexual jealousy. The lyrics may have been hurried but it has its share of telling psychological insights into the battlefield of love, all the same. "*Well, you lied to me/'cos I asked you to,*" Bono sings, and you don't need to be told what the context is. And it comes back, in the final chorus, to oral sex: "*Who's gonna taste your salt water kisses?/Who's gonna take the place of me?*" "It's been said to me, alright", Bono concedes, "that there's a lot of references to oral sex on the record. It's a very equal position. But I hadn't thought about the cumulative effect. I guess there's something for everybody. Don't try this at home! [laughs]."

Who's Gonna Ride Your Wild Horses? Written: U2 • Duration: 5' 16" • UK singles chart position: 14 • US singles chart position: 35

Trying To Throw Your Arms Around The World

Sometimes it could get too intense in Dublin. Everyone watching your every move. The stupidest things being reported on, often inaccurately. That was one of the reasons for deciding to stay in Los Angeles through the winter of '86. There was a sense of freedom there that Dublin didn't allow. When they began searching for a place to stay, the estate agents showed them a dozen fancy pads. "You don't want to see this place," they told The Edge. "It's more like a military compound. There's no air conditioning. No carpets. No en-suite toilets." The Edge said they'd take it. It was a massive place. They could do anything they wanted to it, because it was up for demolition in the not-too-distant future. So they put down roots and went through the full LA experience. "We started to live at night a lot more," Bono says.

Downtown LA is an extraordinary scene: people stepping over bodies on the way into banks in the morning. Bobby Fischer was rumoured to be living downtown in a box. At night the place was full of illegal drinking joints and other nefarious clubs. There was a small community of lost souls inhabiting this twilight zone, and U2 embraced it.

"It was really important for me," Bono says. "Things that other people were going through at 18 or 19, I was going through then. You know, getting loaded and being a bit of a tinker. Not caring where you woke up. Ali was really good about it. She was coming over, but she recognized that this was a stage I might need to go through.

On the lyrics sheet of *Achtung Baby*, 'Trying to Throw Your Arms Around the World' is followed by a thanks to The Flaming Colossus, the infamous Hollywood celebrity late-nite bar. It revives 'The Fly', presenting him this time from a somewhat more sympathetic guy who goes on the town and finds himself staggering home in the early hours like a lost soul.

"That's a song about drunk ambition," Bono says. "As in 'I'll be home soon'. There's just warmth in that image." And great insight. "*Nothing much to say I guess/Just the same as all the rest/Been tryin' to throw your arms around the world.*" Bono knew the character he was writing about very well.

Trying To Throw Your Arms Around The World Written: U2 • Duration: 3' 53"

Ultra Violet (Light My Way)

On most occasions it would pass unremarked. A bit of a chuckle, back to the top of the take and away we go again.

It was about half-way through when Larry dropped one of his drumsticks. You could hear it on the track, as clear as daylight. Everyone carried on. Larry got going again and they finished the take. Then someone threw a curve-ball. Maybe we should leave it in. That bit where Larry dropped the drumstick. He wasn't being funny.

"Given the choice," Eno would ask later, "how much do you allow a record to exhibit warts-and-all spontaneity and how much do you repair?" Put like that, it sounds like a reasonable question. But when you're the drummer and it was you who dropped the stick – at first, you think maybe they're winding you up. Then you realize they aren't, that they're for real about leaving this stupid little cock-up on the record. What are they trying to do? Make a record that, finally, ruins the band? That insults its fans? That exposes us all as incompetent? The debate lasts for three hours. At times it feels like people are trying to sabotage the record with dissent. When Bono first produces the chorus, it inspires a degree of mirth. "Baby, baby, baby," he sings, "light my way." What's so funny?

People hadn't heard Bono use the word "baby" like that before. He'd often scat things one way and then change them later, but it became obvious that this was the lyric of the song. It didn't feel right. And besides something was niggling about the smartness of it: was it not condescending to use the term for a woman anyway? "There was a lot of debate, and a good deal of laughter, about Bono actually coming out and going 'Baby'," Flood recalls. "It was less to do with the political correctness of it than whether he could actually get away with singing "Baby, baby, baby/Baby, baby, baby" and so on. That was very funny for a long time. But he got away with it alright."

Ultraviolet (Light My Way) Written: U2 • Duration: 5' 31"

Acrobat

During the run up to *Achtung Baby*, U2 had been listening to KMFDM, Sonic Youth, Young Gods, My Bloody Valentine. As far as rock 'n' roll was concerned, the emphasis was on a hard-edged industrial kind of sound. The Edge was particularly into some of the speedy metal stuff that was in vogue. At the time, they'd also developed an interest in Roy Orbison, Scott Walker, Jacques Brel – in torch songs.

In terms of lyrics, that was the way The Edge wanted to go, towards a more personal kind of writing. The challenge that U2 had set themselves for the album was to do justice to both impulses.

Everything was in flux. *Rattle and Hum* had been so successful it was embarrassing. It had also been savaged by the press. Having started out as a band in the slipstream of punk, U2 remembered what they had felt about the supergroups of the late '70s. Were they now about to become what they had despised?

Their strategy had been radical. Take everything you know and throw it out. Work with the music you don't know, in a place you don't know, in a way you haven't worked before. Disorientate yourself.

Well, they succeeded in that – but they succeeded in disorientating Daniel Lanois even further. 'Acrobat' was a case in point. "Daniel had such a hard time on that," Bono says. "He did so well, but he was trying to get us to play to our strengths and I didn't want to. I wanted to play to our weaknesses. I wanted to experiment. With hindsight, some of the experiments didn't come off so well, to be honest."

The Edge cranks up the guitar and does a part that's half 'Where the Streets Have No Name', half 'Bullet the Blue Sky'. Larry's drumming adds to the sense of urgency, whipped along by Adam's driving bass.

But it is the lyrics that make 'Acrobat'. Not for the first time on the record, Bono acknowledges his own weakness and inadequacy. He is more conscious now than ever before of the contradictions in his own position. *"And I must be an acrobat/to talk like this/and act like that,"* he sings. It was as far from the righteousness that U2 had so often been accused of as you could get. Or was it? "I think he was taking a swipe back at the press with that line 'Don't let the bastards grind you down'," suggests Gavin Friday.

Acrobat Written: U2 • Duration: 4' 30"

Love is Blindness

It was Gavin Friday who interested Bono in Jacques Brel. Gavin had run the Blue Jaysus club in Dublin's Waterfront cafe and for a few glorious months, it became one of the city's most celebrated nights-out with Agnes Bernelle, Maria McKee and Bono, among many musicians and comedians, likely to show up with something new to perform, in the spirit of the cabaret.

Despite its distinctly European flavour, 'Love Is Blindness' had been written during the *Rattle and Hum* period. It was Blue Jaysus material, a song that could have been performed with the accompaniment of a lone piano. In Bono's head, it might have been sung by Nina Simone, one of his all-time favourite singers.

It takes us back – again – to the shadowy world of deceit, infidelity and betrayal. It depicts love at the end, the very end, of its tether. It is as bleak and as despairing a view of the world as you're likely to get, reflecting the emotional climate in which the entire album had been made. "All one's relationships, with your family, with your friends, with the members of the band – everything started to disintegrate with that record," Adam Clayton told John Waters. In terms of its mood, 'Love is Blindness' had the dark, sensual and decadent feel of pre-war Berlin. But its sentiments made it the perfect conclusion to *Achtung Baby*. *"Love is blindness/I don't want to see,"* Bono sang – a desolate acknowledgement of the terrible reality that it is sometimes better not to know. The Edge plays a mournful guitar solo, stabbing out thick emotional blues notes that linger and then fall away like tears. "A more eloquent prayer than anything I could say," Bono reflects.

Love is Blindness Written: U2 • Duration: 4' 23"

U2 in America

Number one singles, multi-million album sales, two Grammy Awards and a global stadium tour. *Time* magazine put them on the cover, calling the band "Rock's Hottest Ticket". U2 had become the biggest rock band in the world.

Stars and stripes: U2 in America, 1986.
The Claw: The 360° tour at Giants Stadium, New Jersey in 2009. The tour is the most successful in history.

Record shops in the UK and Ireland opened at midnight on 9 March 1987 in order to cope with the demand for *The Joshua Tree*. Whereas U2 had threatened the top of the charts with previous albums, this time they delivered. The album went to Number 1 in the US for nine weeks and became what was then the fastest-selling album in British chart history. As some indication of how strong the eleven-track album was, five singles were released off it.

The much-respected music critic Robert Hilburn, of the *Los Angeles Times*, wrote that "U2 is what the Rolling Stones ceased being years ago – the greatest rock and roll band in the world." No one had expected quite this level of sales and critical acclaim.

The band had little time to savour their success as *The Joshua Tree* tour began in April and carried on until the end of the year. The band were now playing stadia and suddenly had to deal with logistical, financial and psychological pressures that were never there before. The band scrambled to beef up the U2 organization (touring personnel, press officers, etc.) and were finding out that "celebrity" in the music world was a double-edged sword.

On 27 April, the band became only the fourth-ever rock band (after the Beatles, the Band and the Who) to be featured on the cover of *Time* magazine. It was a massive endorsement of their relatively quick ascent to superstar status.

The Joshua Tree was notable for being released on vinyl, cassette and CD formats. The album was many people's first introduction to the new CD format and if ever an album was recorded to sound good on the new format, this was it.

The year-long Joshua Tree tour played to over three million people. Eight of the eleven album songs featured regularly and the bigger the audience, the bigger the message Bono had. Frequently raising social and political concerns from his "pulpit" on the stage, this was Bono becoming the activist – whether talking about the evils of apartheid or the moral bankruptcy of the Reagan administration in the US.

Continuing their fascination with learning about the roots of American music and broadening their own education, the band visited Elvis's Graceland as an act of pilgrimage and Sun Studios in Memphis to record new material. Almost everything on *The Joshua Tree* tour was filmed because the band already had ideas of a cinema film based on their American adventure. Such was the speed with which new material was arriving, a prompt follow-up album was also being confidently discussed.

U2's most wildly successful year ever was topped off by winning two Grammy Awards – one for Best Album and another for Best Rock Performance.

But just as the band had previously snatched victory from defeat, now at the very peak of their career old doubts were re-emerging. For the band the live show was always the priority. They always fretted that the bigger their audiences were becoming, how important it was for every single person to make that vital connection with the music. The band had broken through on word of mouth from their lives shows – and they intended to keep their standards just as high, no matter how many people were in the audience.

Larry Mullen summed up the band's doubts succinctly: "We were the biggest, but we weren't the best." It also had been only a few years since three of the band (Bono, The Edge and Larry) had almost walked away from rock 'n' roll because of the conflict it presented with their Christian lifestyle. That had all been resolved – with rock 'n' roll winning out – before the *War* album, but the band were beginning to allude to the fact that the stresses of an enormous stadium tour and their new-found status as rock's hottest ticket led them to embrace the rock musician's lifestyle.

Their lives were now being planned out for them, and they found themselves making commitments to projects they hadn't the time to really think through. The record label was ecstatic with the sales of the album, the fans loved the big, new stadium shows, but the band themselves were wondering just how this New Wave band from Dublin who were all about punk energy and self-expression had strayed from their core principles. They were just about to find out.

ADAM CLAYTON

BY BRIAN BOYD

Adam Clayton was always the bold boy of U2. Expelled from school as a teenager, he talked his way into the band and revelled the most in their success. But now he's the elder statesman of the group.

Born on 13 March 1960, Adam Charles Clayton spent his first five years in Oxfordshire before his family moved to Dublin. By a strange coincidence one of Adam's first friends as a child in Dublin was The Edge (both sets of parents were friends because both had relocated to Dublin from England).

It was always clear that the young Adam was somewhat of a misfit. Aged eight, he was packed off to boarding school, which he disliked intensely because he wasn't the slightest bit interested in sports and the students were not allowed to listen to music on school grounds. After he moved school but was then asked to leave because of his lack of interest, his parents decided to send him to the more liberal, arts-friendly Mount Temple School where Bono, The Edge and Larry were already students.

Cool Clayton: Adam during the Joshua Tree tour; his English accent won him the nickname "The Posh One".
Blonde ambition: Adam in Dublin, in the days of New Wave.

> “I do realize how unusual it is to be able to play large, sold-out shows 30-plus years into a rock ’n’ roll career. I don’t take it for granted.” Adam Clayton

Just before joining the new school his parents had bought him a bass guitar; Adam didn't know how to play it but liked it because it had a big, fat sound – and it looked cool. At Mount Temple he stood out – he wasn't the best academically and instead would swan around in a big Afghan coat, wearing sunglasses even in the Irish winter, as if he were the rock star he would later become.

He had briefly been in a band before reading Larry Mullen's notice in Mount Temple looking for musicians to form a band. He made a big impression at the audition in Larry's kitchen – he talked about "chords" and "frets" and about "amplifiers" and "feedback". He was immediately in the band for the simple reason that the others thought he knew what he was talking about.

Adam appointed himself manager of the new band. He was impressive – writing to DJs and music journalists and always quick to ask advice from anyone he came across who was even remotely connected with the music industry. When the band began to get serious, though, he ceded this role to Paul McGuinness.

It was difficult for Adam in the early days of U2. He retained a posh, English accent from his time in Oxfordshire and some people took him for being pretentious. Within the band, Bono, The Edge and Larry would frequently hold prayer meetings while on tour – Adam, though, never displayed any interest in the Christian grouping in which they were involved.

His bass playing improved dramatically over the first few years. From '11 o'Clock Tick Tock' to 'New Year's Day', he was developing a melodic style that would go on to underpin the band's later work. He gelled instantly with Larry Mullen as the rhythm section and if his bass playing sometimes goes unheralded it's mainly because it's difficult to be in a band with a virtuoso such as The Edge.

The early U2 were notoriously clean-living, but Adam always did his bit for the rock 'n' roll cause. Quite the party animal, he was arrested in 1989 for possession of marijuana. He avoided conviction by making a sizeable donation to charity.

But his drinking was beginning to get out of hand, particularly on the Zoo TV tour. He was so drastically hungover in Sydney in 1993 that he was unable to play that night's show. And it was an important show: the next night the band were filming their Zoo TV live DVD. This was the first time any member of U2 had missed a show and such was the shock and disappointment felt by Clayton that he immediately sought treatment for his alcohol problem. He has been sober ever since.

Known for his gentlemanly ways and his polite, good manners, he's had his fair share of blows. In 2012 his long-time housekeeper was sentenced to seven years' imprisonment after it was reported she had misappropriated 2.8 million euros of Clayton's money.

He has had a series of relationships over the years – including an engagement to the model Naomi Campbell. He has a child from a relationship that is now over and in 2013 he married the Brazilian model Mariana Teixeira de Carvalho.

Somewhat of the wise old man of U2 these days, Adam Clayton has travelled the furthest of all the members of the band. Now quietened down considerably since his rock 'n' roll excess days, he has found perspective and wisdom and has become an even more valued member of the band than he was previously.

Manager player: An early shot of Adam, when he was also the band's manager.
Bass break: Relaxing during rehearsals for the Joshua Tree tour.
Surround sound: Adam in Toronto, for the 360° tour.

ZOOROPA

Achtung Baby had a message. You thought you had us pigeon-holed: now try sticking all this in that little box. You want to see the real U2? Well, here we are. Even better than the real thing!

Zoo TV developed out of the same impulse. It began with the proposition "Everything you know is wrong". It concerned media distortion. The truth behind the lies – and the difficulty in ever being able to dig deep enough to find it. The Fly and MacPhisto came alive during the Zoo TV tour. It was U2 in disguise. But it was also U2.

Bono was enjoying himself. He discovered that he likes putting on masks. It was fun being MacPhisto, arriving in St Peter's Square to get the Pope's blessing, pushing children out of the way. Method acting!

The whole band were enjoying themselves in this crazy hall of distorting mirrors. The energy being generated was phenomenal.A break in the tour was coming up. They didn't want to come down. Better to turn this energy into noise. Better to make a record. *Zooropa* here we come!

Zooropa

One of the most important things is to find a location. Then you get a sense of who's actually singing the songs. What they're really about. The emotional as well as the physical terrain. The Edge and Bono had been reading William Gibson's cyberpunk futuristic novels. "He has this location," Bono explains, "the sprawl, he calls it, the city in the future where a lot of stuff is set." Bono wanted to paint a similar kind of picture with noise.

During the Zoo TV tour, the band had been working with Roger Trilling, and part of the deal was to create the sense of a future that would be attractive, as opposed to the typical sci-fi scenario where what's in store is a wasteland. But other undercurrents were at work too. With the collapse of communism and the expansion of the European Union, borders were coming down all over Europe. Not always to the good. Civil war was breaking out in the former Yugoslavia and the horrors that would befall Bosnia were beginning to take nightmarish shape. Nazism was on the rise in the newly re-unified Germany. "Looking at all that," Bono says "*Zooropa* seemed like a great image of a European location that was surreal."

During the Zoo TV tour, The Fly had taken on a life of his own. He had insisted on having his own dressing room. He began to crowd Bono's space, successfully replacing the singer as the band's frontman for a significant part of the set. He brought his friend MacPhisto on board. And between them they got to the designers who were putting the show together. They filled the gigantic screens with every conceivable kind of bizarre imagery. Some atrocity from the Gulf War? No problem. Bang it on. A clip from a blue movie? Go ahead, sweethearts. Do your stuff.

More of those mad aphorisms that had been premiered on 'The Fly'. TV ads. Copylines. Scenes from a Nazi movie. Members of the audience enjoying their 15 seconds of fame in the Zoo TV video confessional. Hey, this is the information age. We're on the brink of a tele-visual revolution. Let's put it all up there.

It was frightening. Fascinating. So much potential. So much potential for disaster. Not a time to lie down and leave it to the buccaneers and the pirates. Time to engage. Time to help to make the future according to your own vision.

"We were opening this kind of *Blade Runner*-type world," Bono says. "It starts with this neon winking and blinking and these two characters come out of it. There's this image of the 'overground'. It was a time when everyone was all indie and grey and dull – the 'underground'. The overground was like coming out into the bright light of the modern city. It's an amazing place to be, walking around these modern cities like Houston or Tokyo. And the idea was coming out into that, embracing it."

But first there was the small matter of re-appropriating the language on which *Zooropa* was being founded. Steve Turner, who wrote the book accompanying the *Rattle and Hum* album and film, had begun sending Bono a digest of articles from all around the world. "I kind of stopped reading books and novels so much, and I started reading more magazines," Bono recalls. "I wanted to get away from the weight of where I was going. I wanted to fly. There was enough melancholy around."

'Zooropa' begins with the Audi slogan "Vorsprung durch Technik", and in the first three verses there are references to advertising copylines from Daz, Fairy Liquid, Colgate and Zanussi, among others. "And I have no religion," the protagonist proclaims, "and I don't know what's what." But far from seeing that as a weakness, the thrust of 'Zooropa' was that uncertainty could be a positive point of departure.

There was certainly a touch of anarchy about how 'Zooropa' was put together. Joe O'Herlihy had captured a couple of good sound check jams at the beginning of the Zoo TV tour. The Edge took the best bits as the basis for a backing track, fed them into a digital editor and created a song structure. The band did a separate jam for the sombre,

Pure gold: The dollar bills on the floor around Bono's feet were thrown there each night during a barnstorming version of 'Bullet the Blue Sky'.

Release date: July 1993
Catalogue number: U29
Producer: Flood, Brian Eno & The Edge
Track listing: Zooropa/Babyface/Numb/Lemon/Stay (Faraway, So Close)/Daddy's Gonna Pay for Your Crashed Car/Some Days Are Better than Others/The First Time/Dirty Day/The Wanderer
Highest Chart position: No. 1 (UK and US)

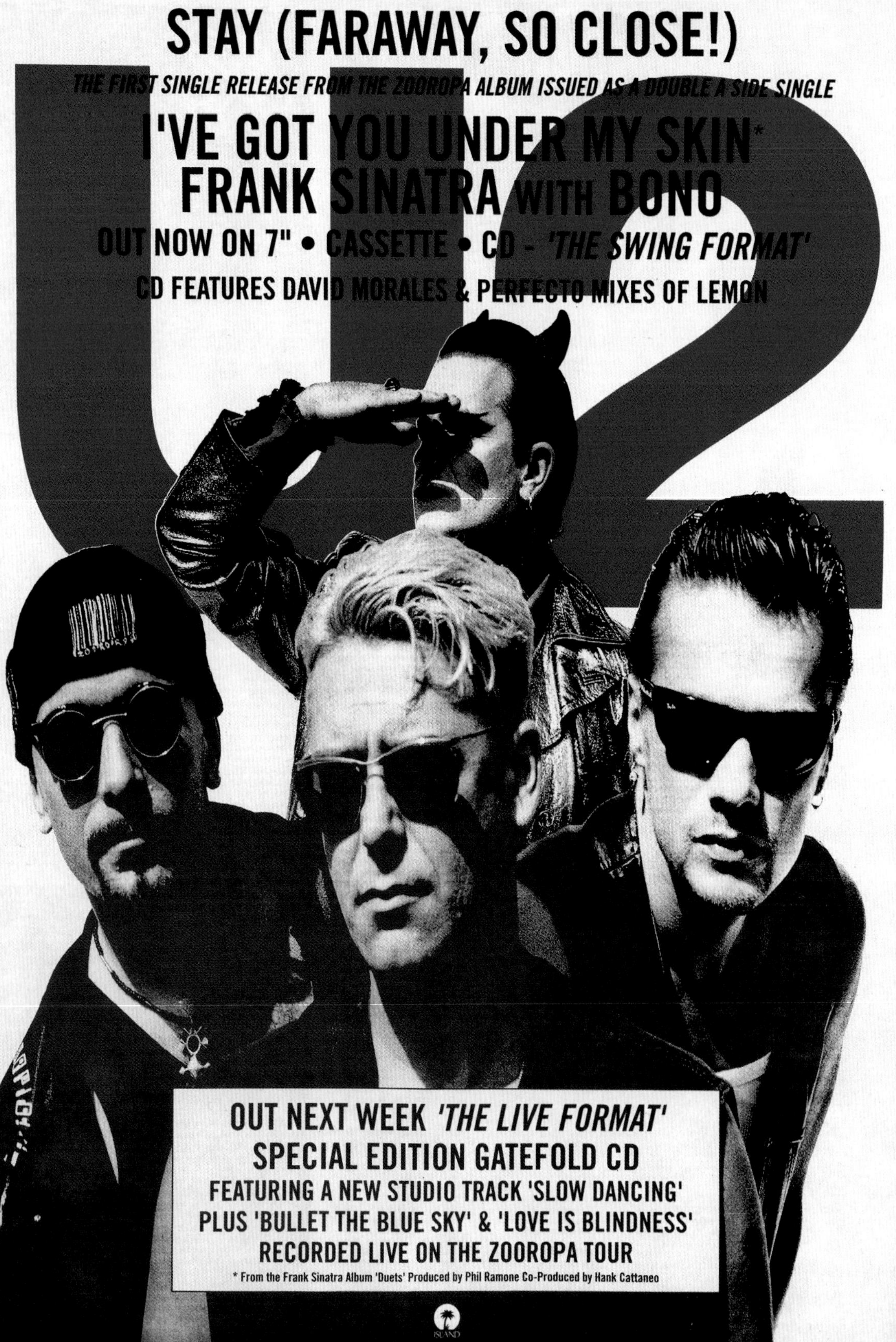

Staying power: Poster from 1993 advertising both the studio single release of 'Stay (Far Away)' and a special live edition.

ethereal opening. "I found sections of this jam," Flood recalls, "did a weird atmospheric mix of it and then when we were starting to piece the album together, I tried to cross-fade that into the beginning of 'Zooropa' as it stood then."

Everybody felt that Flood's intro worked. "The whole mad guitar stuff that happens on the second half was Eno treating a lot of guitars," Flood adds. That worked too. Then, at the last minute, everyone had misgivings about the original jam that formed the backing track for the first half. Now that there was a shape to the song, the band could play it through. Bono even tossed in an odd lyrical reference to 'Acrobat' as a coda. "In the end," Flood explains, "for the first half we just used what had been replayed and on the second half we used what was the jam, with some elements of the replay on it."

You can just imagine the producer at the console, as the band depart back into Europe for another date. "Don't worry, baby," he says. "It's gonna be alright."

Zooropa Written: U2 • Duration: 6' 30"

Babyface

During the Zoo TV tour, U2 had entered another kind of celebrity zone. *Achtung Baby* had been their hippest album to date, claiming a place for them at (what was perceived to be) the contemporary cutting edge of rock. The successful Paul Oakenfold remixes of 'Even Better Than the Real Thing' and 'Mysterious Ways' had won U2 a new cult respectability in clubs. They'd begun to understand the appeal of glamour, of fantasy. Glamour had begun to understand the appeal of U2 too. Adam had hooked up with Naomi Campbell. Kate Moss and Christy Turlington had become friends of the band, visiting Dublin frequently. Bono was on the cover of Vogue in his Fly gear in the company of Christy Turlington.

In some ways it was a natural drift. When you're operating at high altitude, you tend to make friends with other people who are operating in the same rarified sphere. But, on Bono's part at least, it was also a conscious decision. You can embrace this stuff or be ashamed of it. What was there to be ashamed of? Why not live the contradiction and report back on it? 'Babyface' – "cover girl with natural grace" – could have been written with any of the band's new model friends in mind, The Edge explains. But it was done with a twist. Bono had always been intrigued by the way in which the media turn consumers into voyeurs. It had been highlighted by the CNN coverage of the Gulf War, which had reduced human catastrophe to a video game.

By comparison, pornography – beamed into your home by satellite television – could seem like a benign calling. In the narrative of *Zooropa*, the camera moves up away from the couple in the opening song and goes in through a window in one of the high-rise buildings in the imaginary city of the future. There's a guy inside, watching a television. He has a remote control and he's slowing down the images. He's turning up the contrast and playing with it. "It's a song about watching and not being in the picture," Bono says. "About how people play with images, believing you know somebody through an image – and thinking that by manipulating a machine that in fact controls you, you can have some kind of power. It's about the illusion of being in control."

The irony is that 'Babyface' is delivered with all the tenderness of a love song. And, in its own way, maybe that's what it is.

Babyface Written: U2 • Duration: 4' 00"

Numb

The band took a mid-tour break at the beginning of 1993. Yet The Edge needed to keep going. His marriage had split up. It drove him back into the studio, where he began to demo new material. He came across a song called 'Down All the Days' that had been intended for *Achtung Baby*, but didn't make the cut. He liked the backing track, with its loop taken from the passage in Leni Riefenstahl's Nazi propaganda film, *Triumph of the Will*, where an 11-year-old boy is shown playing the drum at the 1936 Olympic Games. There was a hard, dirty, industrial feel to the instrumentation, making it a prime candidate for some kind of rap. They had considered the possibility of Bono reading 'In Cold Blood', his poem on the dehumanising effect of media coverage of violence and war, over it. But when that didn't work out, The Edge took over.

He had become more involved in the lyric-writing, acting at times as Bono's editor, suggesting cuts and bouncing couplets off him. 'Numb', however, was entirely his own, and the chorus probably reflected his emotional frailty at the time, with Bono adopting his fat lady voice to testify "I feel numb" in a soulful falsetto that contrasted oddly with The Edge's flat delivery of the main vocal. Yet it also suggested that he was on the road to recovery because 'Numb' was an exercise in surreal humour, capturing the jaded rock star frozen into physical and emotional immobility by the self-imposed strictures of his position.

"It's arcade music," Bono said, "but at base it's a kind of dark energy that we're tapping into. It's us trying to get inside somebody's head. So you hear a football crowd, a line of don'ts, kitsch soul singing and Larry singing for the first time in that context. What we're trying to do is recreate that feeling of sensory overload."

The video for 'Numb', produced by Kevin Godley, was equally over-thetop, an absurd send-up of bondage games with The Edge being subjected to all kinds of arbitrary humiliations. But the song achieved its apotheosis when the band performed it in the Olympic Stadium in Berlin, where the Riefenstahl film loops had originally been recorded.

"That was a trip," Bono reflects. "There was uproar. There were people at the gig who could be – and probably were – the sons and daughters of the people in the film. But we wanted to point out, before anyone else did, the similarities between rock gigs and Nazi rallies."

Numb Written: U2 • Duration: 4' 18"

Lemon

You wouldn't have any inkling that 'Lemon' was about Bono's mother unless you were told. "Here's one for you," Gavin Friday had said conspiratorially. "The lyrical idea for that developed out of an old home movie that Bono saw."

It happened by chance. Someone had approached one of Bono's family at the airport and told him about the existence of this ancient footage in which Bob and Iris Hewson featured. Turned out it had been packaged by one of those companies that put kitsch music on top. It was eerie watching it. The image of his mother, on-screen, haunted Bono. "She was wearing lemon," Gavin recalled. "That's where the title came from."

From that starting point, the song became something else entirely: a meditation about film itself and the pleasure of looking. "The cinema is where we get to be nosy," Bono reflects. "Where we go to look into people's lives, without them minding. People like to stare at other people up close. But because of my position, I don't get to stare at people so much, so film is important for me, in that it allows me to do that."

'Lemon' is a complex song that flickers with different meanings depending on how you view it. But it is about seeing yourself more clearly through seeing someone else. "Through the light projected/He can see himself up close," Bono sings, and it doesn't involve a huge leap of the imagination to picture him seeing his own reflection in the poignant image of his mother in her youth.

He borrows a line from John Boorman about the film-making process when he talks about *"turning money into light/To look for her"*. And in that phrase, it becomes a song about imagination itself, about the muse, about the female spirit with which U2 have always associated creativity.

There are hints of voyeurism too. "It's about the experience of looking rather than touching," Bono says. "I think my favourite image is the image of glass, where he melts the sand so he can see the world outside." The end product may sound fluent but it came together in fits and starts. "It began as a crude form of thing," Flood recalls. "Eno decided that there was a bassline he didn't like, so he just took it out."

With the band flitting back and forth between various European cities in which they were gigging, and the studio, that was the way they had to work. They'd play for four or five hours in the middle of the night and Eno and Flood would divide up the end product between them. They'd work separately, pushing the songs forward, tinkering with stuff, adding whatever they saw fit and getting down rough mixes. The band would come back in, repeat the process and hope they were going somewhere.

The Edge added a piano part at the bridge. Then he and Eno

contributed the Talking Heads-style block vocals. They were getting down to some serious mixing when Bono finished the lyrics and did a vocal. Then, finally, Flood decided that they'd have to replace the drum machine with a real drum track and Larry obliged.

It was the last track to be finished. There was a deadline alright, but the days when they'd had to stick down '40' inside an hour were long gone. Sometimes they wondered if the greater latitude had actually made things harder for them.

"They were on tour and flying back after each gig," Flood recalls. "They'd come in to the studio about midnight. I'd have been mixing. They'd listen and make suggestions, maybe do some music. They'd go home to bed. I'd carry on till about 4 or 5 in the morning. Then they'd come in at midday, make some suggestions on the mixing or do some more music. There was a whole two-week period where it was like that, which was absolute lunacy.

"With 'Lemon', I was mixing all night and I knew, by 9.30, 10 in the morning, that all the madness had come to a point where this is it. This really worked. Then I left. They heard what I'd done and really liked it. That was my last day on the album because I had other commitments. After I was gone, they spent another three days trying to perfect the balance, but ended up going back to the one that I had.

"It was a very strange sensation because for me it had been the ultimate feeling of everything coming together. You're digging through the dirt. You have all the frustration, all the lunacy that was going on. And, finally you reach a moment where you know that that's it."

The Edge had doubts about it all along, the way it drew so many disparate elements together. When it was finished, however, he too knew it was a U2 song. Whatever that is.

Lemon Written: U2 • Duration: 6' 56"

Stay (Faraway So Close)

During the mid-'80s, Bono had read one of Wim Wenders' books, *Emotion Pictures*. Wenders wrote about the way in which the USA had colonised the unconscious of the rest of the world through popular culture.

Bono was also reading Sam Shepard's plays at the time. Shepard had worked on the screenplay of Paris, Texas with Wenders and when it came to making *The Joshua Tree*, U2 had in mind a landscape similar to that depicted in that extraordinary film. When Bono met Wenders, he mentioned this. A bizarre synchronicity was revealed. "He told me that when he was driving across America," Bono relates, "and preparing for Paris, Texas, he was listening to *Boy*. He had just one cassette in the car and that was it."

Wenders and Bono established a firm friendship, so it was no surprise when the director asked the band to do the title track for his *Stay (Faraway, So Close!)* movie.

The band watched the film and used it as a jumping off point for their own take on the theme. "The film was about angels who want to be human and who want to be on Earth," Bono explains. "But to do so they have to become mortal. That was a great image to play with – the impossibility of wanting something like this, and then the cost of having it."

In Bono's lyrics, it isn't clear where the lines can be drawn between fantasy and reality – if indeed they can be at all in the world of *Zooropa*. It isn't clear whether the girl who stumbles out of a nightclub – "Out of a hole in the ground" – into the grey morning is a stranger, a friend, a wife or a lover. Or if she's just another image on a screen, a chimera with whom the narrator presumes an intimacy that doesn't exist.

The action happens in a curious dreamscape in which nothing seems certain except uncertainty itself. And yet the performance is full of languorous beauty, a gentle understated kind of emotion that seems at odds with the disorientation in the lyrics.

It ends with a start, Larry Mullen emphasizing the downbeat on the cymbal as the dreamer suddenly sits up, staring into the black night, the image of a fallen angel burning in his imagination. And a curious bang and clatter ringing in his ears.

Stay (Faraway So Close) Written: U2 • Duration: 4' 58" • UK singles chart position: 4 • US singles chart position: 61

Daddy's Gonna Pay For Your Crashed Car

There's a suspicion that *Zooropa* is largely about nightlife, and the obscure and often empty liaisons that fertilise in that artificial universe. 'Daddy's Gonna Pay For Your Crashed Car' is about a woman who's protected from the consequences of her own actions by an indulgent sugar daddy.

Bono originally conceived it as a blues. "John Lee Hooker is the person I'd love to sing that," he says and launches into a slower, rootsier version of the song. "*You're out on your own/You know everyone in the world/But you feel alone/Daddy's gonna pay/for your crashed car/*

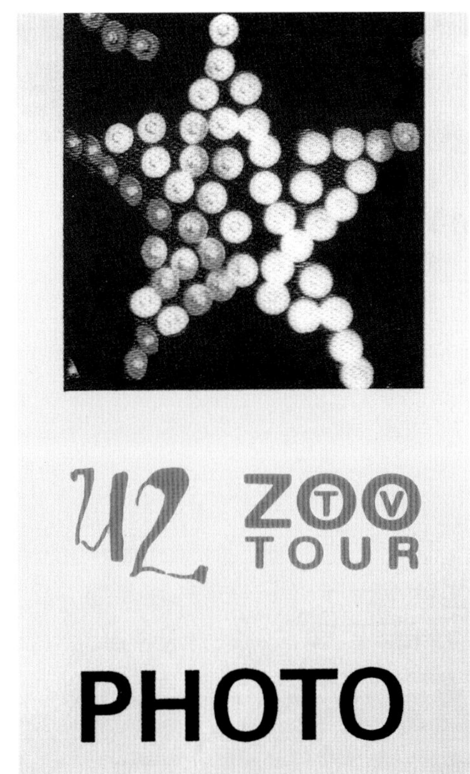

MacPhisto strikes again: Bono and Adam Clayton on the Zoo TV tour in Rotterdam, May 1993.
Access all areas: Backstage pass for the Zoo TV tour.

Daddy's gonna pay..." You can hear Hooker hollerin' it out alright.

"God is a sugar daddy, as well," Bono muses. "Is it God or is it the Devil? Who's gonna get you out of the mess? It's a song about being strung out. You can be strung out on a lot of things, not just smack. The thing you need is the thing you're a slave to. How much do you need this? How much do I need to be in a band? How much do you need anything?"

The fanfare which introduces the song is taken from the album Lenin's Favourite Songs, on what was formerly the state-owned Soviet label, Melodia. There's a sample in there too from the song 'The City Sleeps' by MC 900ft Jesus. But hey, why this sudden interested in crashed cars, Bono?

"They're Berlin images," he explains. "There's a piece of waste ground outside Hansa that's inhabited – or was inhabited – by a bunch of gypsies and crusties. They'd collected bits of F11s and tanks from Russia and wrecked cars. There's dogs and ducks flying around there. It was the Trafalgar Square of Berlin, and these travellers were living there almost in holes in the ground. Of course, now that Berlin has been reunited, they want to rebuild the centre but these gypsies had been given this place to live. That's where the crashed car imagery came from."

Daddy's Gonna Pay For Your Crashed Car Written: U2 • Duration: 5'19"

Some Days Are Better Than Others

Zooropa is probably U2's least emotional record. It's something that Bono observes unprompted about 'Babyface', about 'Daddy's Gonna Pay For Your Crashed Car', about 'Numb'. And 'Some Days Are Better Than Others'? "They sure are," he says mischievously. "I think that's just one of those songs. It's like a summer song. It's just fun."

In fact Bono sends himself up royally in a track that reflects some of the turmoil that surrounded the making of the album. "It was mad," Bono laughs. "You can't imagine what it was like. We would fly out to Rome, play to 60,000 people and I'd still be dressed as MacPhisto with the makeup running, and we'd get into the cars, out to the airport, onto Zoo Airlines and all that. We'd get back to Dublin at 4 o'clock in the morning, work till 8, sleep till noon and then go back on tour. So a few things suffered, but the record has a nice kinetic energy to it."

Between Bono, MacPhisto and The Fly, the main man was becoming an increasingly split personality. Bono felt that he needed some privacy, a way of keeping something for himself.

"Depending on the person I wake up as, one day I can be verbose, the next quite shy," he says. "But with this thing, it was great. Whether it was The Fly or MacPhisto, it was like put the batteries in and off he goes! I got through the whole tour like that. Also people thought we were just mocking rock 'n' roll stardom and all that, but I was actually owning up to it. It was owning up to the side of yourself that is an egomaniac.

"So then we put out a whole bunch of characters from the preachers in the travelling show, through MacPhisto to The Fly. Suddenly there was a lot of versions of the singer in the band. Now which one is for real? And of course they're all for real."

There's a bit of owning up on 'Some Songs Are Better Than Others' too. "Some days I feel like a bit of a baby," Bono confesses, and you can imagine Ali nodding in agreement. And then there's the line about bouncers that won't let you in. "I think The Kitchen might have to take credit for that,"he laughs. "But it's just throwaway." And I thought it was a profound statement about the human condition... "One of the things I have to deal with every day is the fact that I'm very moody, so I'm just having fun with that."

Some Days Are Better Than Others Written: U2 • Duration: 4' 15"

The First Time

This was one that Bono heard in his headfirst. He'd been listening to a lot of Al Green and it had influenced his singing: the Fat Lady was his version of Green's sweet high-pitched tone pushed a notch further.

Sometimes the inspiration sneaks up on you like that: you hear the chorus in someone else's voice. It can be easier to write if you come at a song in that way. The self-editing, the self-censorship that frequently comes into play when you imagine the words coming out of your own mouth, doesn't happen. You're free of baggage. People aren't going to be listening to Al Green and thinking that it's some kind of confession on your part, some kind of soul-baring.

It was intended to be an "up" song. Bono gives a demonstration of how the chorus might have sounded, and you can hear the soul backbeat and the swirl of imaginary strings.

It's hard to avoid the impression that the song was written in two separate bursts. It almost certainly began as a straightforward testifying song, but became something quite different in the third verse. Here, 'The First Time' abandons its symmetry and offers a new twist on an old parable.

"We decided to keep it for ourselves," Bono says. "Brian really loved it. But instead of doing an 'up' version, we just emptied it out, deconstructed the song and ended on this line about throwing away the key, and the prodigal son doesn't go back. He sees all this stuff there for him and he doesn't want it and he goes off again. That's a really interesting take on that story."

Cash machine: During the Zoo TV tour Bono's character, MacPhisto, threw Zooropa dollar bills into the crowd.
After show: A backstage pass for the Zoo TV tour.

"There are many rooms to see/But I left by the back door/And threw away the key." It's a line that captures Bono's own wanderlust, the urge that's always there to light out, leaving all the obligations and responsibilities of his role behind.

"It's about losing your faith," Bono adds. "I haven't lost my faith. I've a great deal of faith. But that song expresses that moment a lot of people feel."

The First Time Written: U2 • Duration: 3' 45"

Dirty Day

In some ways *Zooropa* was taking U2 right back. The imaginary city of the future had long been abandoned as a theme. Now, it was down to finishing an album that hadn't been planned, in the middle of the most demanding tour the band had ever undertaken.

'Dirty Day' was born out of a band improvisation. It was one of those murky numbers, with the band reflecting the tiredness they felt and the pressure they were under in a sulky, brooding performance. Bono felt a crushing sense of sadness in the music. Every time he went to improvise, an idea kept flashing up in front of him of a father giving surreal advice to his son.

On the mic, it was back to the influence of Iggy Pop and the way he'd make up songs in performance. He kept seeing Charles Bukowski in his head, and remembering the kind of advice he'd give, like "Always give a false name." He had the sense that there was some blackness at the heart of all this. Maybe the father had disappeared and left the son and the mother behind. That idea was preying on his mind. It was like a guilt thing about having been away from his own children so much when the band were on the road. It had become a bit of an obsession.

Things gel in funny ways. Sean Penn had come out to the house one night and they were talking bullshit about poetry and God knows what else until 6 in the morning. Bono told him he was a fan of Charles Bukowski and Penn said hang on a minute. Dialled Los Angeles on the spot and got the author on the line. Bukowski was in good form, laughing and joking. "I've got someone here wants to talk to you," he quipped. "It's my wife, Linda. And, by the way, she really wants to fuck you." It turned out she was a U2 fan who'd been to every concert the band had played in LA . She was also the backbone of this great writer.

The next time the band were in town, Bukowski came down to the gig. Larry got up to sing 'Dirty Old Town', which was dedicated to him. It meant a lot, even to a hard-ass like Charles Bukowski. Co-written by The Edge, 'Dirty Day' is also a song about passing the torch. About taking on responsibilities you don't know if you're cut out for. The days run away like horses over the hills, it ends, borrowing a phrase from Bukowski. Bono had a feeling it was out of control.

Dirty Day Written: U2 • Duration: 5' 24"

The Wanderer

Zooropa was a trip. It took you into this strange terrain where nothing seemed quite to add up. Perspectives were constantly changing. Voices kept shifting. Gradually you realized that there was nothing you could rely on. Nothing you could believe in. Not even fantasy itself.

U2 had plunged you into this moonscape. Now they had to get you out. Bono thought he'd found the way. He'd made Johnny Cash's acquaintance a few years previously. They'd been promising to write a song together and had worked on something tentatively entitled 'Ellis Island'. It would be familiar Cash country, when it happened. If it happened.

In the meantime, Bono had another scam in mind. At first Eno and Flood opposed the idea, but he pushed it through. In the middle of recording *Zooropa*, Bono spotted that Cash would be arriving in Dublin for a gig. This is how it would work with Willie Nelson later: hook up with him in the studio while he's in town. No harm in seeing if the Man in Black could spare a few hours.

"If you imagine the album being set in this place, *Zooropa*," Flood reflects, "just when you're expecting the norm, to finish the album you get somebody who's outside the whole thing, wandering through, discussing it. It's like the perfect full stop."

The working title was 'Johnny Cash on the Moon'. But Bono was thinking of The Book of Ecclesiastes, which translates as The Preacher. That was the first real title. The Edge suggested that it would connect better with the rest of the album to call it 'The Wanderer'. Bono had no problem with that. Wanderlust was still on his mind.

The band wanted to end the album on a musical joke. They took on the identity of the ultimate Holiday Inn band from hell and produced an anachronistic noise to match. The Edge had the musical ideas. Eno made a few suggestions along the way to help it flow. But the track is dominated by Adam's wonderfully absurd arcade-game bass that sounds like some mutant cordovox programme on a cheap Casio. It is diabolically effective.

It might sound potentially like a thin joke – until Johnny Cash opens his mouth, that is. The result is awesome and eerie at once,

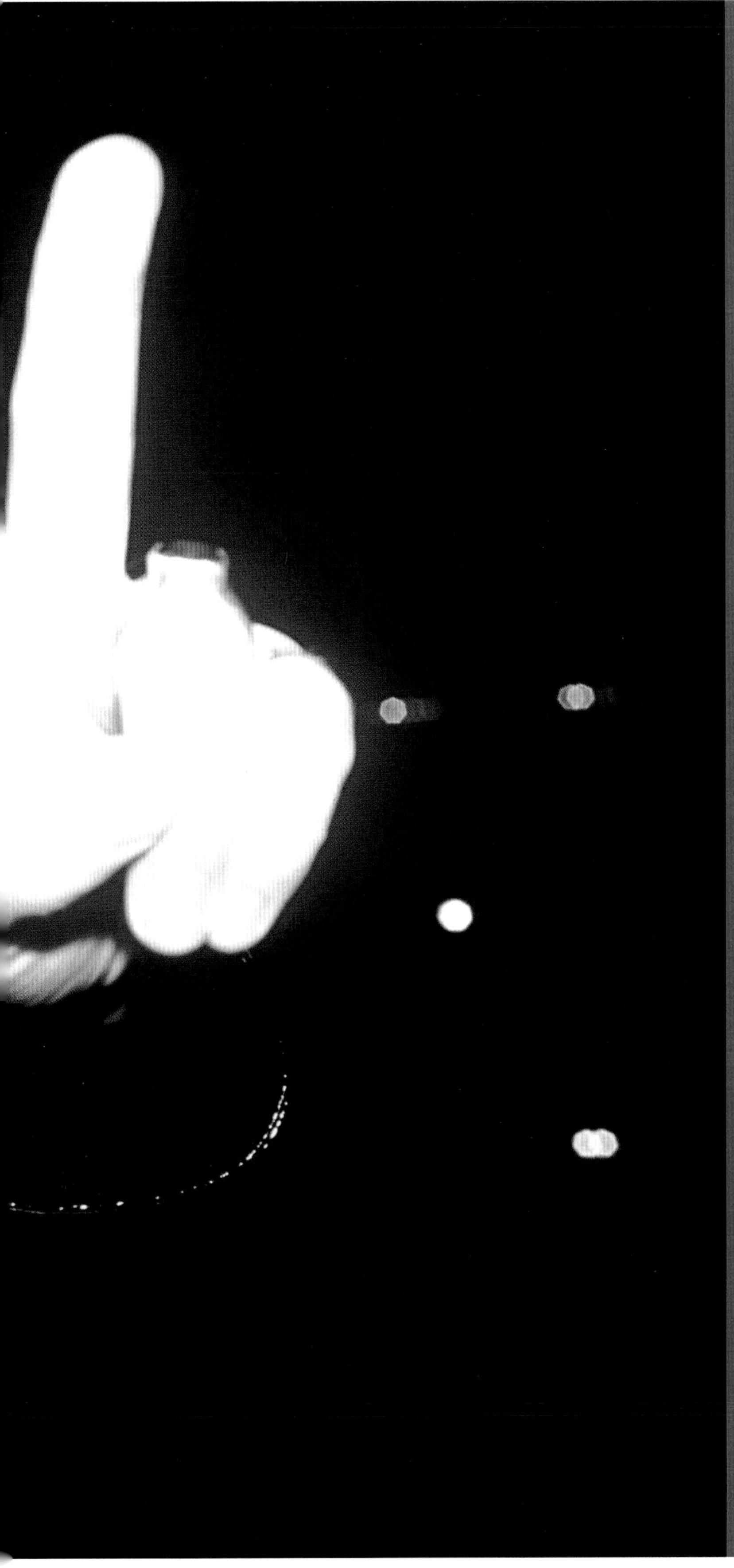

the contrast between the cheap throwaway backing and Cash's monumental delivery lending the whole a thoroughly skewed power that's entirely appropriate. It's the story of a preacher who embarks on an epic journey and experiments on himself at every level: knowledge, sex, gold, whatever's going, he's taking it. The setting is a kind of surreal, post-nuclear Paris, Texas world in which loyalty, faith and honour have become virtually extinct. Bono had Flannery O'Connor in mind – the way she writes about the strangest American characters and their do-it-yourself religion with humour, sympathy and love.

"I suppose, in our picture, I want to have that kind of crackpot in there," Bono told John Waters, "who's off to save the world and, at the same time, he's just up for the ride."

Bono knows when he says that kind of thing that he could be describing a song about himself. But Johnny Cash had reservations. He wouldn't have appreciated The Fly's phone-call on the run to his poor neglected partner at home on *Achtung Baby*. He wouldn't have been too keen either on the shyster falling off the sidewalk at 6 in the morning in 'Trying to Throw Your Arms Around the World'. Or the guy in 'Ultraviolet (Light My Way)' who sometimes feels like checking out, who wants to get it wrong – the bastard! Not at this stage of his life. And he never liked singing the line in 'The Wanderer', *"I went out for the papers/told her I'd be back by noon."* The jokey line: it was Bono through and through. The same old restlessness. The desire to cut and run. The need to be irresponsible.

"He used to leave that verse out because he liked it much heavier," Bono recounts. "I always liked that, you know, bottle of milk, newspapers and he's off. He's got God's work to do. He's looking for knowledge as well, and experience. He's on tour [laughs]."

There's a kind of freak energy that follows a band home after a spell on the road. It can take weeks to come down from it, months even. During the break in the Zoo TV expedition, U2 hadn't wanted to come down. "We have all this energy," they'd agreed. "Why not use it? Why not go into the studio and see what happens?" Now they knew.

The Wanderer Written: U2 • Duration: 4' 44"

Light up: These particular sunglasses were originally given to Bono in the studio while making *Achtung Baby*, to lighten the mood of sometimes fraught recording sessions.

U2 REINVENT TOURING

BY BRIAN BOYD

Lights, camera and sensory overload action. The Zoo TV tour rewrote the rulebook for the live music tour. ABBA, Trabant cars and an order for 10,000 pizzas were bonus features.

The Zoo TV tour ran for two years, 1992–1993, but such was its scale and scope that intense planning for it had begun months before *Achtung Baby* was released. For The Edge, it was a thrilling adventure for the band to "smash U2 up and start all over again". Everything was up for grabs; the only ideas that were ruled out were anything to do with U2 in the 1980s – Stetson hats, white flags and over earnestness.

The band wanted to reflect the "new Europe" in their stage set-up (with the Berlin Wall gone, Europe was busy reshaping itself) and also wanted an acknowledgement of how crucial their time in Berlin was to the *Achtung Baby* album. While in Berlin, they had been watching coverage of the First Gulf War on television and were struck by how images of death and destruction were interrupted by ad breaks – the agony of war side by side with the crassness of consumerism.

Technology was advancing rapidly in the early 1990s and the show would also nod to the emerging new media. Zoo TV would feature video banks and pre-recorded film material to add to the feeling of "sensory bombardment" and audio-visual excess.

While in Berlin the band had formed a bizarre attachment to the Trabant car – for many the symbol of East Germany and the wall coming down. The idea was to buy up as many old Trabants as they could, fit them out with lighting systems and hang them from the ceilings during shows. As the band went on a shopping spree for the Zoo TV stage, the costs mounted – but it was all or nothing for the band at this stage. Live television transmissions, Bono making live prank phone calls from the stage and a "confession box" for audience members were all added to the mix.

The first two legs of Zoo TV (in the US and Europe) were indoors and featured a "B" stage – a smaller platform off the main stage used by the band for more acoustic-style numbers. To adequately capture the new songs live, the band seriously considered bringing in other musicians, but ultimately they were reluctant to do away with the classic four-piece lineup, so some pre-recorded backing music was used instead.

The show was spectacular and despite some hardcore U2 fans being confused by this very different band doing a very different live show, the critics agreed that live rock music was being presented in an exciting and dynamic new way. Nearly all the tour shows opened with either six or eight *Achtung Baby* songs before the band even thought about using any back catalogue material.

Bono was in character throughout – either as "The Fly", "Mirror Ball Man" or "MacPhisto" – all of them grotesque but humorous rock star caricatures. "I became this identikit rock star, an assemble-ityourself rock star, it was incredibly freeing. The characters could say things I couldn't," he said of his nightly transformation. The preaching "Hello, is this Speedy Pizza? I'd like to order 10,000 pizzas for Detroit. Yes, I am serious. My name is Bono."

Bono orders pizza for everyone in the audience when Zoo TV played Detroit in 1992 (Speedy Pizza managed to make 100 pizzas and couriered them to the venue) and flag-waving of previous tours had been replaced by a multi-media circus in fancy dress and such was the visual assault of the show that demand for tickets was soon outstripping supply.

There was fun – members of ABBA joining the band in Stockholm for a version of 'Dancing Queen' – intermixed with serious matters – the band conducted live satellite link-ups with people in Sarajevo during the Bosnian war to hear about the trauma visited on the city.

As successful as Zoo TV was, it leaked money at every turn. U2 saw the huge costs of their travelling carnival as an investment – not a financial one but a musical one for their future wellbeing. But the margins were so slim that Bono was to later reveal: "When we built Zoo TV we were so close to bankruptcy that if five per cent fewer people went (to the shows), U2 was bankrupt. It was terrifying." Manager Paul McGuinness put it more bluntly: "We grossed $30 million in T-shirt sales. Without those we'd be fucked." The second two legs of Zoo TV went outdoors in the US and Europe. By the time the tour finished up with a final set of shows in Australia and Japan at the end of 1993, the tour had been seen by well over five million people. In between all the madness, there had been time for a new album.

Wall of sound: With its banks of video screens, Zoo TV was the precursor of the stadium rock show as we know it now.

Rock carnival: Lasting two years, the Zoo TV tour remains the band's crowning artistic achievement. And *Achtung Baby* remains the band's favourite album.

Devil in disguise: Bono in his treasured gold lamé suit from the tour – here in the guise of the shady underworld figure of "MacPhisto".

POP

Backstage at some celebrity charity bash, a plum-accented classical conductor is talking at Bono. "You're involved in a pop group," he says, one eyebrow arched like an accusation. It isn't what he says, it's the way that he says it. There's a pause and then it comes out like... pop group. His contempt for the very thought of it is palpable. A lower form: pop music. The encounter plays on Bono's mind. The condescension rankles. Who the fuck do these guys think they are? The implicit assumption seems to be that there's something unworthy in being in a rock 'n' roll band. Pop music. A term of abuse.

It crystallises something for the U2 singer. Pop. Your man thinks it's an insult. Well, fuck him. It's time to reclaim the word. Turn it into a badge of honour.

They had thought of calling the album Pop For Men or Pop Pour Hommes. In the end they simply called it *Pop*. You can interpret it as defiant or ironic – or simply as a statement of fact. But it's not a bad title for an album destined to chart at No.1 in 21 territories around the world in the week of its release. Not a bad title at all. *Pop*.

So let's talk about – pop music...

Discothèque

If Howie B had known how it would end, he might never have started it. 'Discothèque' originated in a jam between himself and Edge, 15 minutes of rhythmic surfing that would provide a launching-pad for the opening single from *Pop*; the first, cleverly-pitched trailer to what was to become U2's most widely acclaimed album ever.

With 'Discothèque', U2 took the art of disguise to a new level of sophistication. It's a conjuror's trick. If it is tactically desirable to use an idiom, use it. While you're using it, learn how to use it well. Use it well and you'll enjoy it. Enjoy it, but don't let it absorb you. Stamp your own authority on it. And, in case all else fails, make sure that your tongue is somewhere in the vicinity of your collective cheek. Now, have fun!

And so they did. Howie, who had worked on the Passengers record with them, had programmed up a selection of beats on his deck and at the end of a long evening he began to mess around with one of his favourites. Edge was hanging nearby and on impulse picked up the bass and began to riff along. Never one to be left out, Bono joined in on improvised vocals. "Virtually nothing remains from that original jam," producer Flood says, "but it was the inspiration."

To get the vibe right while they were recording, they dressed the studio up in mirror balls and disco lights – and gave it loads. Long before the final shape of the album had been decided, everyone knew 'Discothèque' was going to be the first single. That made it harder to finish. "It was going to be the first public statement, the first track that people were going to hear," Adam Clayton says, "so there was a lot of double-checking yourself to be certain that it was going to stand up as such."

'Discothèque' is an earnest little riddle about love, disguised as trash. "You know you're chewing bubblegum," Bono sings, "You know what that is but you still want some." Yes, there is an addictive quality about living for the moment. Yes, there is an undeniable pleasure in surrendering to the hedonistic buzz of the dancefloor. Yes, yes, yes!

Musically, the trick was to acknowledge those parts of your record collection you wouldn't normally own up to: "KC and the Sunshine Band, Boyz 2 Men, Donna Summer, Los Sex Pistoles," Bono lists them off. Village fucking People! The boys got to dress up like tarts for the video – and, mmm, they enjoyed that too. There's a soupçon of camp in all of us, girls. 'Discothèque' doesn't quite know what its chorus is. It mixes metal and dance in a cheesy hybrid. It is self-consciously kitsch. But it also undeniably rocks like a monster, particularly with the volume turned up to 11 on the Howie B or Steve Osborne mix, when a club is jumping at 2 or 3 o'clock in the morning. Boom Cha Boom CHA DISCOTHÈQUE. The implicit message to humourless U2 fans was "You didn't think you'd like this, now did ya?" Meantime, the style counsellors were goin' "Well, hello! U2 are far cuter than we thought. U2 are far fucking hipper than we thought." If it was going to be the first single, it had to be the first track on the album. The whole shebang in the bag, the entire entourage of band and producers set out for New York, further behind schedule than ever, to finally master the album. Even then, the job wasn't done. Even then, Bono couldn't let Howie be...

"It was outrageous," Howie says. "It had gotten to the stage where I couldn't speak, I was that ill. I was run down, my chest was caving

Pop star: Bono with his treasured red guitar when PopMart hit Rotterdam in 1997.

Release date: 3rd March 1997.
Catalogue number: CID U210/524334-2
Producer: Flood
Additional Production: Steve Osborne, Howie B
Track listing: Discothèque/Do You Feel Loved/Mofo/If God Will Send His Angels/Staring At The Sun/Last Night On Earth/Gone/Miami/The Playboy Mansion/If You Wear That Velvet Dress/Please/Wake Up Dead Man
Highest Chart position: No. 1 (UK and US)

in, everything was caving in. It was Saoirse's birthday and she was in New York as well and I had to meet her and then at about 10.30 Bono turns around and goes 'Listen, it'd be magic if you could get a new intro together for 'Discothèque'. And it was just like... (groans).

"I got into a cab, went up the road to the Hit Factory. I was kicking things like you wouldn't believe, going 'Fuck! Fuck!' Like, we were in the middle of mastering an album and they wanted to change the intro! It was like, 'any ideas?' And swirl was the idea. That was what they came up with, a 'swirl' sound. For fuck's sake!"

Howie had a bash, thought he'd cracked it, phoned Flood at Master Disc and played it down the phone to him. Flood said nothing and Howie got the message. Fuck! Fuck! He threw down the phone, turned up the speakers, pushed all the faders up – and BAM! Blew the fuck out of them: two £30,000 speakers gone for a burton.

"After I'd got all that aggression out of me, I got what is now the intro to 'Discothèque' about ten minutes later. So I phoned them up and I went 'Come on 'round, ye fuckers, I'm ready'. So they all trooped around and I couldn't play it to them properly 'cos I'd blown the fucking speakers! I'm still annoyed about that evening but I got a good piece of work out of it." There were rumours that 'Discothèque' was about drugs. Well, no one's going to deny that but actually it's about something much simpler, and much more complicated too. It's about the pleasures of the flesh. And it's about the heart's yearning. In a way you could say it's as earnest as you can get. "U2 are just better at disguising it now," Bono says. And he laughs.

Discothèque Written: U2 • Duration: 5' 19" • UK singles chart position: 1 • US singles chart position: 10

Do You Feel Loved

How does a monstrously successful rock band, around for the best part of 20 years, get to grips with a whole new area of musical expression? U2 were facing that dilemma so they did the smart thing, not just immersing themselves in the new music, but getting a couple of its most livelier exponents involved. In addition to Howie B, they brought Steve Osborne – who'd later be dubbed The Man With The Golden Ears – on board.

Part of his role was to act as a catalyst. He'd take records into the studio and play them for the band to see if they sparked any ideas. 'Do You Feel Loved' was a case in point, growing out of a Naked Funk track that Howie opened his set with one night in The Kitchen when the band were on the town. Everyone got off on 'Groove Sensation' because it was a blast, so they got Howie to do his DJ thang with the track in the studio and the band jammed along. Howie spent a lot of time working with Adam on getting an extraordinary bass sound that, in the jargon of the studio at the time, seemed to vibe everyone up.

It was one of the first cuts to get close to its final shape, but there was still work to be done. That's where Steve Osborne came in. He'd made his name producing Happy Mondays' Pills 'n' Thrills and Bellyaches

Stage show: PopMart's centrepiece was a Golden Arch 30 metres (100 feet) high.

Golden ticket: A ticket for the Wembley Stadium date of the PopMart tour on 22 August 1997.
Counter culture: The extravagant PopMart tour opened in Las Vegas in April 1997. Early reviews were mixed, some critics confused by the band's attempt to satirize consumerist culture.

album and had been involved with Paul Oakenfold in remixing a few U2 tracks. When he got his hands on 'Do You Feel Loved' he felt that it needed a new groove and Larry came in to get that down. "Then I got Edge over, and we worked on the guitar line that comes in over the chorus," Steve says. "The core of the tune was there but we added a fair bit."

Bono talks about the lyrics as if they're playful and in a way they may be. But to someone coming at it fresh, they sound remarkably confessional. 'Do You Feel Loved' is nothing more or less than a love song, that strays into the erotic boudoir first mentioned by Bono in 'Your Blue Room', with its references to conversations and prayers amid the tangle of the senses. 'Do You Feel Loved' may be a smart thing to say to a lover – but it's an even smarter one to put to 50,000 people in an open-air arena.

"It's quite a question," Bono says, "but there's no question mark on it. We took the question mark out because we thought it was a bit heavy with it." Clearly a case for the grammar police to get working on...

Do You Feel Loved Written: U2 • Duration: 5' 07"

Mofo

It began as a conversation with Simon Carmody. Bono picked Simon up on his use of "motherfucker" and a philosophical debate ensued about the origins of the word in black slang and the way it went from a term of abuse into one of praise. "It's such a dumb cliché, you wanna have a good reason to use it," Bono smiles. And so they set about finding one, settling on 'Mofo' as a likely title and building from there.

Edge and Bono were in Nice on a song-writing expedition. They got a structure down. It had a blues feel until they took it into the studio and Adam added a Motown-style bass part. It was shaping up but as the lyrical ideas began to crystallise, they felt that it needed to become tougher. "We spent months farting around with it," Adam confesses, "and then we said to Flood 'Let's hip-hop it, let's strip it back, let's get a beat together, let's see where it goes'. And it rose from those ashes."

It became the hardest cut on the record, a techno assault reminiscent of the Prodigy, powered by a towering double-tracked drum attack from Larry Mullen. It's the track Flood singles out as the one he had most influence on. Steve Osborne did his bit by throwing in a blaring Moog line. Meanwhile, with Howie B acting as critic and catalyst, Bono had gone for broke lyrically, throwing references to Salman Rushdie ("Lookin' for to fill that God-shaped hole") and William Butler Yeats ("Still lookin' for the face I had before the world was made") into a song that otherwise trades in rock jargon.

"I was reading in a book on Jack Kerouac," he says, "about him smoking a bag of grass and praying, literally, for a vision of a language, or a way of writing that would be both precious and trashy. That's what I'm aiming for," Bono reveals. "'Mofo' is one of my favourite tracks," says Gavin Friday. "To me it sounds like Led Zeppelin after taking an E (laughs). But it's got real heart to it. I just love Bono's plea to his mother in it."

It's a song of which Bono is proud, oscillating as it does between the throwaway and the profound with consummate craft, and amounting, in the end, to his best shot yet at capturing the demon spirit that drives him.

"In the middle of it, when you go into that conversation piece, it's like WHAT?," he says. "It was as if my whole life was in that song. I think it was the first thing mixed on the album and when we were finished, we couldn't get over ourselves. I had a deck in the car and we were playing it, going on a kind of club-crawl – but we wouldn't go into the club because we just had to hear it one more time."

Mofo Written: U2 • Duration: 5' 49"

If God Will Send His Angels

'If God Will Send His Angels' had existed as a title at the time of the making of *Zooropa*. 'Stay (Faraway So Close)', on that album, had been inspired by a Wim Wenders film, which was about angels who wanted to be human and to live on Earth. The seed of an idea had been sown, and it lurked until the songwriting sessions for *Pop* began in earnest.

It was one that was written on an acoustic guitar, with Bono and Edge strumming away like latter-day Simon and Garfunkels. The tune reminded Bono of Fugees, or even Boyzone, and he became fiercely excited about its potential. "I thought – this is like pure pop. Now drop acid onto that."

What emerged is a classic U2 ballad, a song with a very subtle emotional tug that's brilliantly highlighted by the superb arrangement. Rhythmically, Adam Clayton and Larry Mullen supplied a light, lazy skank groove and then Howie B got to work. "He came on board about halfway through," Flood recalls, "and I think it's one of the tracks that's closest to his heart."

Howie B's imprint is there throughout but there is one sublime and quintessentially Howie moment. Having taken a sample of Larry's hi-hat, and lowered it a couple of octaves, he unleashed the resulting whoosh to magnificent dramatic effect.

Most U2 albums had been conceived with an imaginative location in mind. *Pop* was different. "The record doesn't seem to have any physical place that it's centred in," Bono explains. "Instead, to me the

songs feel like conversations. Overheard conversations. It's like a movie that opens in the middle of a scene. You're brought immediately into the action and there's lot of little arguments going on."

That's certainly the scene in 'If God Will Send His Angels', but there's an essential bleakness in the pictures being painted: loosely about a guy beating up his girlfriend. Bono describes it as being a sour song, "But you can still hear her somewhere in there, through the music," he adds. "You can feel there's light there."

Asked what the themes of the album are, Edge says: "Love, desire and the crisis of faith. The usual stuff." On 'If God Will Send His Angels', the crisis reaches epidemic proportions. In a world where love has taken a train heading south, the blind are leading the blond and God has got his phone off the hook, there isn't much left to hang on to. "So where is the hope and the faith and the love?" Bono asks. The eternal questions.

If God Will Send His Angels Written: U2 • Duration: 5' 22" • UK singles chart position: 12

Staring At The Sun

The band were working on another song entirely but they got stuck in an unproductive groove. A couple of bizarre loops were introduced, Larry got a really sweet pattern going against them and Edge made a significant call, out of the blue. It was familiar territory for U2: "Oh, I know another song that will work over this." It was a completely different speed and a completely different feel but the potential was immediately apparent.

"I had a great time with Edge on 'Staring At The Sun'. I got a mad wee sound out of his guitar," Howie recalls. "After we broke our first deadline, Edge and I spent a week playing around with the tune. We put his guitar through a Leslie and it was a nice little thing. What you think is an organ on 'Staring At The Sun' is actually Edge playing the guitar."

There's a Zen-like aspect to the lyrics, a sense of being immersed in the moment that's perfectly articulated through the euphoric music. Even after Howie was finished, however, there was work to do. Steve Osborne and Mark Grant got involved in the mixing and they did a lot of searching through tapes looking for different guitar parts. When Edge gets going he produces a lot of ideas and they found some discarded stuff that worked, enhancing the arrangement considerably.

The Something Happens album Stuck Together With God's Glue had been left lying around – it went into the song. Howie B had an abscess in his ear – it went into the song. The television was running in the background, newspaper headlines had been pinned on the walls, the marching season was in full swing – it all went into the song. The British presence in Northern Ireland is alluded to, as is the European Cup. And there's a modicum of self-mockery, too, in the line "Those who can't do often have to preach."

"If you're going to have a dig at someone, it might as well be yourself," Bono laughs. "But there are other things in there too. All

New look: Adam Clayton with mouth guard and industrial wear at a PopMart show in Oakland, California in June 1997.

Back stage: A guest pass for the PopMart tour, 1997.
Pop shop: Special editions of *Pop* were packaged in a 12" cube, containing the album and a brandad notepad and pen.

these references are quite personal but they wouldn't be there if they were just personal."

Ali Hewson had a tremendous influence on the lyrics of *Pop*, and not just because of the fact that she's the focus for Bono's ongoing affair of the heart. She is also a woman of great courage, who has been placed directly at risk, through her involvement in the Children Of Chernobyl charity. There is a sense in which 'Staring At The Sun' may be a reference to Ali's experiences. An attempt to reassure in the face of all the odds, it's a blast of defiant optimism, underscored inevitably by a sense of creeping paranoia. But what a blast!

Staring At The Sun Written: U2 • Duration: 4' 36" • UK singles chart position: 3 • US singles chart position: 26

Last Night On Earth

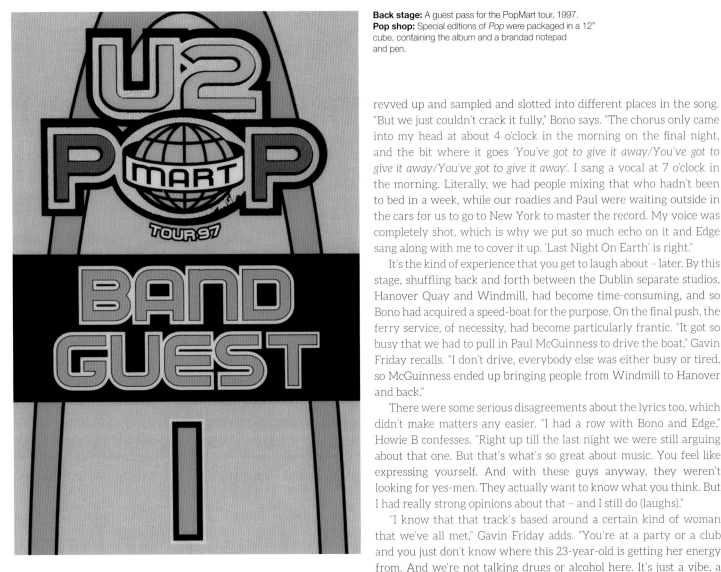

The song had been in gestation since early on in the recording of *Pop*. The backing tracks done, the search was on for riffs and moods and Howie slid in a couple of Don Cherry pieces. The guitar parts were revved up and sampled and slotted into different places in the song. "But we just couldn't crack it fully," Bono says. "The chorus only came into my head at about 4 o'clock in the morning on the final night, and the bit where it goes *'You've got to give it away/You've got to give it away/You've got to give it away'*. I sang a vocal at 7 o'clock in the morning. Literally, we had people mixing that who hadn't been to bed in a week, while our roadies and Paul were waiting outside in the cars for us to go to New York to master the record. My voice was completely shot, which is why we put so much echo on it and Edge sang along with me to cover it up. 'Last Night On Earth' is right."

It's the kind of experience that you get to laugh about – later. By this stage, shuffling back and forth between the Dublin separate studios, Hanover Quay and Windmill, had become time-consuming, and so Bono had acquired a speed-boat for the purpose. On the final push, the ferry service, of necessity, had become particularly frantic. "It got so busy that we had to pull in Paul McGuinness to drive the boat," Gavin Friday recalls. "I don't drive, everybody else was either busy or tired, so McGuinness ended up bringing people from Windmill to Hanover and back."

There were some serious disagreements about the lyrics too, which didn't make matters any easier. "I had a row with Bono and Edge," Howie B confesses. "Right up till the last night we were still arguing about that one. But that's what's so great about music. You feel like expressing yourself. And with these guys anyway, they weren't looking for yes-men. They actually want to know what you think. But I had really strong opinions about that – and I still do (laughs)."

"I know that that track's based around a certain kind of woman that we've all met," Gavin Friday adds. "You're at a party or a club and you just don't know where this 23-year-old is getting her energy from. And we're not talking drugs or alcohol here. It's just a vibe, a wild woman who gives you a charge of energy."

Maybe Howie felt so strongly about it because he saw a reflection of someone close to him in the lyrics. Someone for whom freedom is not just a by-word but a name, perhaps?

Last Night On Earth Written: U2 • Duration: 4' 45" • UK singles chart position: 10 • US singles chart position: 57

Gone

It's one of the things that makes Bono most visibly angry. The basic premise seems to be that once you're successful, you've sold out. Automatically.

"Right through the '80s this is what we had to put up with," he remarked, early on in the recording of *Pop*, "the idea that there was something morally superior in being an indie band. I've written a song now that's like a two-finger salute to the people who tried to foist a sense of guilt on us because we were successful. The thing is, we always wanted to be one of the biggest bands in the world."

'Gone' was one of the first tracks that the crew knew would make it to the album, but it went through many personalities before it finally made the cut. "At one stage," Gavin Friday says, "it was a hard rock thing, then a punk thing, then a hard rock thing again." But they still couldn't seem to get to the core of it.

The indecision may have had something to do with the death of Bill Graham, the Hot Press writer who'd been a friend and inspiration to the band from their earliest days. It was towards the end of May and they'd just been working on the song in Miami, where they'd gone to do a photo shoot or two and to record, when they heard the news of his death. The connection sounded an eerie resonance that fed back into the sinews of the song. Rather than being the fuck-you to the begrudgers whom it had originally been intended for, it became instead a meditation on the superficiality and transience of success itself, over which the spectre of death hangs like a stark premonition. "*Closer to you every day*," Bono sings, "*I didn't want it that much anyway*" – and the echo is unmistakably of the hymn 'Nearer My God To Thee'.

"The background is so atmospheric and disturbing," Gavin Friday reflects. "It's weird. The track conjures up all the things that make U2 what they are. You can't properly put your finger on it. A vocal line here, a riff there, a lyric – it just gets you."

Bono puts it in context. "The bridge, which was put in to make it more of a pop song for me – and for Edge too – ended up having this incredible emotional weight," he says. "It's almost like Gavin's 'The Last Song I'll Ever Sing'. That's what it felt like to me. It felt like the last song I'd ever sing."

Gone Written: U2 • Duration: 4' 26"

Miami

Recording for *Pop* had started in November 1996. The Christmas break was followed by a period of down-time as Larry Mullen struggled with a bad back. Howie B took up some of the rhythm duties and by March they were on full alert again. But they still lacked any real sense of what was going to give the record the sense of continuity they'd always striven for in the past. It needed a location – or so they thought.

For a while they toyed with the idea of heading for Cuba and inviting the spirit of Havana to infiltrate the grooves, but the cynicism they'd almost certainly have been confronted with as a result dissuaded them. As April turned into May, they upped camp and split for Miami instead.

There were a dozen reasons why it might have made a good location for the record. It's a crossroads between North and South. It has a glamorous side, a humorous side, a dark side – and the strangest underbelly. But in the end, the idea was more enthralling than the experience. Instead of leading them to the heart of the record, their sojourn there produced a small movie of a song that Edge wryly describes as a kind of "creative tourism".

It's an experience that no-one regrets. "We'd been in the studio, slugging it out with the direction of the record," Adam explains. "It's a nice place to be for six months or so, but I think we all needed a bit of fresh air. So we went to Miami and we had a very good time! We met a lot of very serious people and some very superficial people and enjoyed both. We were introduced to the art of smoking cigars. We went to this kind of Mafia late-night place – none of your old spit 'n'

sawdust here, this was shag-pile carpet all the way. We came, we saw, we conquered – it's in the lyric. It was all there and our eyes were wide open. Some of the time (laughs)."

Lyrically, 'Miami' exhibits a kind of holiday snap-book gaudiness, coming on like a handy-cam diary that slips into the themes of consumerism and violence with remarkable ease. Bono's sense of humour comes across on the oedipal pun of the chorus: "Miami! My mammy!" But the whole thing hangs together because it was a labour of love for Howie B. "That was very much Howie's bag," Flood explains. "After it had been recorded, he locked himself into a room for three days and he arranged everything."

Miami Written: U2 • Duration: 4' 52"

The Playboy Mansion

Roy Orbison was a master of form. He never felt constrained by conventional song structures, instead producing mini-symphonies in two or three movements. Having befriended him before his death, and written 'She's A Mystery To Me' for his 1989 album *Mystery Girl*, Bono and Edge had learned something from the master. "He was always way ahead of the pack," Bono reflects, acknowledging the musical lineage into which 'The Playboy Mansion' taps.

It started life as 'Hymn to Mr Universe', beginning with a jam, back in the early stages of making the record. It popped out and everyone felt confident about it – so much so that it was one of the last tracks completed. Over a looped trip-hop backdrop Bono was back on familiar turf, playing with clichés, truisms and advertising slogans. Having been alluded to in 'Miami', plastic surgery gets another mention here; Michael Jackson is also on the guest-list in an opening verse that recalls 'Even Better Than the Real Thing' before moving on: "*If coke is a mystery/And Michael Jackson... history/If beauty is truth/And surgery the fountain of youth/What am I do to/Have I got the gifts to get me through/The gates of that mansion*."

"I think surgery with Michael Jackson might have something to do with editing," Bono muses. "If you're in the studio and you're in control of what you hear – you can up the bass, down the snare – I think Michael Jackson started to do that to himself in some way. It's the critical eye that makes him such a genius being turned on himself – the knife turned around."

Its wry humour notwithstanding, 'The Playboy Mansion' is not intended to be smart. For all the warped values in evidence, the song is infused with a real sense of spiritual yearning, as if at some deep level the covetous protagonist knows that it's all fake, that far from being even better than the real thing, his desires are but a pale shadow of the heart's need for a more fulfilling kind of truth.

"People in America say 'if you don't have cash it's hard to believe in yourself'," Bono explains. "It's almost like prosperity as a religion." That's the territory we're in here. 'The Playboy Mansion' is a gospel song for American white trash but it ends in a sublime slice of gospel-verité, a la Al Green, which enables us to see the grace that is to be found in even the more mundane things – if you look hard enough.

The Playboy Mansion Written: U2 • Duration: 4' 40"

If You Wear That Velvet Dress

When the news first emerged that U2 were in the studio, the word was that they were making a trip-hop album. The assumption was based not just on the soundings they'd taken about Howie B's availability. After all, the first producer on board was Nellie Hooper, one of the lynchpins of the thriving Bristol scene and a man with a proven feel for a good groove.

They got together with him in London and stuck a number of backing tracks down. Among them was 'If You Wear That Velvet Dress', a song that comes from the same place as 'Your Blue Room', but which also dips into territory mapped out by Massive Attack and Tricky.

If there was any disagreement between U2 and Hooper, it doesn't show now. Though he isn't listed in the credits on the album, his involvement is openly discussed. "He started things off on 'Velvet Dress' but because of time constraints he couldn't stick with it," Flood says.

"Actually what happened," Hooper adds, "is that I sat down for a day and did my usual sort of fascist number: 'I don't like this, this or this. Now, how about trying this? And then Howie came in and did the same kind of thing, and the track began to take its final shape."

Bono reflects ruefully on the need for such strong-arm tactics. "We gave Flood a spiky helmet at one stage," he laughs, "because he had to become quite the gaffer. Flood was amazing at pushing things through. I don't know how anyone can be so anarchistic and yet so organised. Howie on the other hand is like music itself. There's no difference between him and the music he makes."

Which may explain what he brought to the song. "For me my main input was sexual," he says. "There was a lot of sex put into that one. Again, it was like a little bit of a throwdown from the band to me. 'OK , Howie, we want this to be on the album. Make this be on the album'. So I put a lot of jazz into it. Jazz and sex." A familiar combination.

"It's great to be able to get away with it," Bono says. "We can write sexy songs and spiritual songs – and songs that are both. This is the place we've made for ourselves after 15 years of making albums." And Adam always thought the song was addressed to him!

If You Wear That Velvet Dress Written: U2 • Duration: 5' 15"

Please

Anyone who thought that *Pop* was going to be a dance album was entirely wrong. "I'm sceptical about these reference points," Larry Mullen states. "I just like the idea of taking what's out there and fucking with it."

And so that's what U2 did, using techno, trip-hop and hip-hop as jumping off points for the different tracks. Ultimately they had to pass the Mullen test: if what the band produced was unmistakably a U2 song it could go on the record. Larry had been concerned about elements of *Zooropa*, which had been rushed. And he had been downright disgusted with what he saw as the self-indulgence of parts of the *Passengers* album. 'Please' was an example of how the synergy could work.

Howie B had been playing stuff to the band. Over one shimmering rhythm, Bono came up with an idea for a melody and everything flowed from there. "Once Bono got it – boom!" Howie reflects. "Once the band got it – boom! The actual backing track is the first take."

On the face of it, 'Please' sounds like a bitter song of personal disillusionment, set against an unsettling wider backdrop, where things are falling apart and the centre cannot hold. Bono acknowledges that it is hard, almost spiteful. It was written with someone specific in mind but there was much more at stake than the satisfaction of a well-crafted put-down.

It is a song about victimhood, self-indulgence and hypocrisy. Written against a backdrop of the collapse of the ceasefire in Northern Ireland and the summer of conflict that ensued, with the siege of Drumcree as its tribal nadir, it could be addressed, in different verses, to people on either side of the sectarian divide. "It's a mad prayer of a tune," Bono attests.

The lyric device that gives the song its form – a series of lines beginning 'You never' – was Edge's, linking back to the 'Numb' lyric and its use of lists. And the guitarist must also take considerable credit for the song's astonishing arrangement which builds from a relatively contained opening into one of U2's most molten – and moving – statements ever. 'Please' may be steeped in ambiguity but the finished painting is magnificent.

Please Written: U2 • Duration: 5' 02" • UK singles chart position: 7

Wake Up Dead Man

Pop begins on a high. 'Discotheque' is bright, contemporary and in your face. At least on the surface, it is a hedonistic celebration of the ephemeral. But from that acknowledgement of worldly addictions on, the record journeys down – from dance to despair.

As a lyricist, Bono emerges as a kind of Everyman desperately searching for something to hang onto amid the escalating din we're surrounded with: a hellish combination of political mayhem, consumerism gone crazy and the culture of the soundbite.

"*Jesus, Jesus help me*," the final song on *Pop* begins, "*I'm alone in this world and a fucked-up world it is too*." Bono has never sounded quite so hopeless. If *Pop* begins with dance, it ends with a slow danse macabre. The song was started during the *Zooropa* sessions under the title 'The Dead Man'. It had been a big rock song with distinct gothic leanings, but no one was too enthusiastic about that anymore. They did some work on it with Nellie Hooper in London and came up with what you might call a trip-hop version – but it still wasn't right.

It took shape during a jam, with Howie on the decks. "I think that was the first time I saw the band go 'Wait a minute, something interesting can happen here with these decks!'," Howie laughs. " 'How come he's playing a record on top of our record and it sounds OK? Not only does it sound alright, it sounds ho-ho!' So that was an interesting adventure for them."

It came together quickly. In the end it was unanimous. It made sense to tie the album up with an end of the millennium psychosis blues-song. Neither Protestant nor Catholic, neither working-class nor middle-class, U2 had started out as a band who would have to forge an identity without much of the familiar ballast of Irish cultural life. As a result, they could wrap rock'n'roll and religion up together in a way very few other bands would even have contemplated. It was inconceivable that an album as ambitious and searching as *Pop* would go out on any other note.

'Wake Up Dead Man' comes on like a call to arms, a plea for Jesus or God to reveal himself. But the strength of Bono's faith notwithstanding, there is something eerie and forlorn about the call, even amid the epic beauty of the music.

"People want to believe but they're angry," Bono says. "If God is not dead, there's some questions we want to ask him." 'Wake Up Dead Man' doesn't attempt to offer any answers.

Wake Up Dead Man Written: U2 • Duration: 4' 52"

Urban cowboy: The Edge bought a new look with him on the PopMart tour, along with his trusty old Rickenbacker. Pictured here in Rotterdam.

ALL THAT YOU CAN'T LEAVE BEHIND

After *Rattle and Hum*, U2 started playing their own kind of mind games. Dressing up. Wearing masks. Wrapping their songs up in hip threads. Throwing shapes. From *Achtung Baby* through to *Pop*, subversion was the order of the day.

You could say that this strategy worked too well: they succeeded in confounding legions of their own fans too, while failing to pick up enough hip young gunslingers to compensate. U2 were still huge. But ticket sales for their live shows were disappointing. Album sales were down.

You could take the pessimistic view and conclude that U2 was a brand – and a band – in decline, and that it would be better to bow out gracefully. Or you could go for the big one again.

U2 decided to go for it. On *All That You Can't Leave Behind*, they ditched the dance gurus and went back to their roots. The trip-hop techniques of *Pop* were abandoned. Instead, they called in Eno and Daniel Lanois, with whom they'd made their biggest-selling record, *The Joshua Tree*. This was a time for big hearts. This was a time for soul.

According to Lanois, it was a hell of a record to make – almost as black as *Achtung Baby* at times. With Bono's voice badly frayed around the edges, the approach had to be different: the conductor could no longer afford to bawl his heart out in the studio. Lacking this, the collective were plunged into uncharted territory and the strain was palpable. Making *The Million Dollar Hotel* exacerbated it. And, noble as it may have been, Jubilee 2000 turned the screw even further.

But U2 are made of stern stuff. It was fraught – and, hey, when has it not been? But they battled through and made it to the finishing line. And released a wonderful, exhilarating, triumphant and, above all, accessible record. Like as if it couldn't have happened any other way.

Beautiful Day

When Jimmy Iovine landed in Dublin, he was given a preview of what was going down in the studio. It wasn't finished but he was still overwhelmed by the power of 'Beautiful Day' in its formative stages. This was where U2 had come in all those years ago, on a silvery glistening guitar ride that spoke of exhilaration and of rapture. "It's a beautiful day a-a-a-a-a-a"! There wasn't an iota of doubt in Iovine's mind. "You've landed a big bass," he told them. Now all they had to do was to reel it in.

Brian Eno had come up with the beat. Edge found a guitar sequence that went with it. And in a moment of spontaneous invention, Bono yelled out the declaration that would take the song into another dimension. "It's a beautiful dayeeeeeee", he ejaculated, because the feeling was good. Daniel Lanois also had that feeling. "The track at

Beautiful night: Bono pictured at one of U2's smallest-ever shows – when they played to 2,000 people at London's Astoria Theatre in February 2001 ahead of their Elevation tour.

Release date: October 2000
Catalogue number: U212
Producers: Daniel Lanois and Brian Eno
Additional production: Steve Lillywhite, Mike Hedges, Richard Stannard and Julian Gallagher
Track listing: Beautiful Day/Stuck in a Moment You Can't Get Out Of/ Elevation/Walk On/Kite/In a Little While/Wild Honey/Peace on Earth/When I Look at the World/ New York/Grace/The Ground Beneath Her Feet
Highest Chart Position: No.1 (UK), 3 (US)

LANE
FIRE

The track at that point was really pumping," he remembers, "and the mix that we did had the power of shattered metal." Daniel Lanois, on 'Beautiful Day'

that point was really pumping," he remembers, "and the mix that we did had the power of shattered metal. And I had this image of Bono, singing about beauty in the midst of flying pieces of metal and mayhem." Lanois pushed Bono to consider what had been a throwaway interjection as the chorus and constructed the melody line. Edge came up with a harmony line and when they put them together and processed it they sounded almost like angels.

The Jubilee 2000 campaign that Bono got involved in was a distraction from making *All That You Can't Leave Behind*. This typical Bono crusade followed the indulgence of making *The Million Dollar Hotel* movie. Yet he experienced a surge of optimism. He'd sat down with arch-conservative Congressman Jesse Helmes in Washington and hit some kind of emotional nerve. Now the US had come on board, to the extent of $435m in cancelled debts. Maybe the world wasn't such a bad place after all. There was hope. It's a beautiful day! Edge reached for the Explorer – the Gibson guitar he'd used during U2's formative years – and the sound was complete.

When Steve Lillywhite arrived in at the death and polished it up even more with a sparkling final mix, they had the opening track, the lead single – and a monumental U2 anthem that would run and run, delivering them back to the top spot in singles charts all over the world. It would eventually be awarded a Grammy for Single of the Year.

There it was. A shimmering triumph.

Beautiful Day Written: U2 • Duration: 4' 08" • UK singles chart position: 1 • US singles chart position: 21

Stuck In A Moment You Can't Get Out Of

Bono first bumped into Paula Yates when she was just 17. She was an extravagant doll at the time, hanging out with Bob Geldof during the prime of the Boomtown Rats and making like a particularly chintzy rock moll. Bono was chalk to her cheese. "I ducked her for years," he says, "'cos I just thought 'Whoa, where's she coming from?' And then years later, I really discovered this thing that people who've had a lot of pain in their lives are not in pubs talking about it."

Magic carpet ride: To promote *All That You Can't Leave Behind*, released in 2000, the band played an impromptu show in Times Square, New York.

Smart and feisty, Yates spent her whole life trying to come across as a dizzy blonde. But there was substance there, and as Paula's life moved on through her own brand of celebrity, her path crossed Bono's with increasing frequency. Both the breakdown of her marriage to Bob Geldof and the ensuing battle for custody of their children were played out in the full glare of the tabloid spotlight. So was her romance with Michael Hutchence, the glamorous and flawed INXS frontman.

Excess was the defining quality in their lives. Drink and drugs were about the place and they indulged. Yet it still came as a shock, even to those closest to him, when Hutchence was found dead in his bedroom in the Ritz Carlton Hotel in Double Bay, Sydney, in his home country of Australia. Paula clung desperately to the belief that he had died accidentally in the course of an auto-erotic experience of some kind.

Bono read it differently. He had spoken to Hutchence along the way about suicide, and they had agreed how pathetic it was. Now Bono felt angry at the probability that Hutchence had chosen an easy way out. In the heat of his anger, not long after he heard the news, he wrote the guts of 'Stuck In a Moment You Can't Get Out Of', a song he describes as being a row between mates. "The greatest respect I could pay him," Bono reflects, "was not to write some stupid, sentimental, soppy fucking song."

And so he wrote instead what he describes as a nasty, little number which, in Bono's account, slaps his old, lost friend around the head. "It's like somebody's in a stupor and you're trying to wake them up," he says, "cause the cops are coming, they're sitting at the wheel and you're trying to get them out of the car 'cause they're gonna crash it."

But the song doesn't quite bear out that explanation all the way, sounding at times more like a plea written from the vantage point of Paula Yates, as she attempts to wrestle with the loss of her lover.

Stuck In A Moment You Can't Get Out Of Written: U2 • Duration: 4' 32" • UK singles chart position: 2 • US singles chart position: 52

Elevation

Bob Dylan once said that he never heard a good song that had a middle eight. Which just goes to show that even Bob Dylan can be wrong. It was also where Eno and Lanois parted company with 'Elevation'. The song had started out with a sound from Edge, fashioned on an effects pedal that Lanois describes as his secret weapon. "It's like a distortion pedal that has a warp, or a tone control, built on," he explains. "As you push the pedal down, you get the high frequency. It's a great little pedal. It has a lovely, specific personality to it."

Eno conjured up an electronic beat as an undertow and Adam and Larry played on top of it. Edge came through with a riff and they were halfway there. But the song still needed a bit of contrast to open it up – or so the band thought. When Eno and Lanois were slow to play ball, reinforcements were called in. The masters were taken across the river from U2's Hanover St. HQ to Windmill Lane studios. There the boys joined forces with ace pop producer Richard 'Biff' Stannard and his cohort Julian Gallagher to conjure up a kind of science-fiction middle-eight that provides a tender interlude, amid the onslaught of 'Elevation'.

A distant cousin of Sly and the Family Stone's 'Higher and Higher' and the Pixies' 'Levitate Me', 'Elevation' is scarcely the album's most original moment. The mole livin' in a hole diggin' up his soul in the fourth verse is reminiscent of the central character in 'The Fly' from *Achtung Baby* and there's a hint of the climax to 'Mysterious Ways' in here too. But from Adam Clayton's engorged opening bass figure onwards, the song captures well the murky terrain inhabited by a writer struggling with the attempt to make art of his or her experience. "Adam really came into his own on 'Elevation'," Edge reflects. "He's the hip hop man in the band, and there's a hip hop attitude in the rhythm section on that one."

'Elevation' achieves a quality that's reminiscent of the Rolling Stones, and their capacity to create epic muck. But there is an exhilaration to it that is uniquely U2 – a combination of primordial lasciviousness, ecstatic spirituality and soulful need – that renders analysis virtually redundant.

Elevation Written: U2 • Duration: 3' 47" • UK singles chart position: 3

Walk On

In March 2000, U2 were given the freedom of Dublin Among the previous recipients to be thus honoured by City Hall, in their home town, was Nelson Mandela. And there was another recipient of this somewhat arcane honour, on the same day that the achievements of Bono, Adam, Larry, Edge and Paul McGuinness were being acknowledged and celebrated in a civic ceremony in Smithfield Square, just north of the River Liffey that runs through the heart of the capital. In all probability, her name meant little to the vast majority of the 5,000 citizens who gathered in the square that day, but Bono had taken the trouble to find out as much as he could about her and knew that, like the black South African leader, she was a hero.

A Burmese academic based at Oxford University, Aung San Suu Kyi took her courage in her hands and returned to Burma. She knew that she was going back to a country controlled by a brutal and oppressive regime and that inevitably her life and her freedom would be under threat. But inspired by the belief that only by fighting – and defeating – fear can you be truly free, she became leader of the National League for Democracy and spearheaded the campaign against the corrupt controlling military junta.

"It was just one of the great acts of courage of the twentieth century," Bono reflects, "and it continues into the twenty-first."

Aung San Suu Kyi was placed under house arrest in 1989. She was unable to receive visitors or communicate freely. But neither her spirit nor her convictions could be broken and she has struggled on, and in the process has become a powerful and enduring symbol of the fight for democratic rights in the face of totalitarianism. Following international pressure, democratic elections were held in Burma in 1990, and over 80% of those eligible voted for the National League for Democracy. In the wake of that rebuke, the military tightened their grip, imprisoning newly-elected MPs and forcing others into exile. Awarded the Nobel Peace Prize in 1991, Aung San Suu Kyi remained under house arrest until 1995, and her movements have subsequently been severely restricted.

Pride of Ireland: The Freedom of Dublin was bestowed upon Bono and the rest of the band in 2000. To celebrate this honour, Bono brought sheep into pasture on St Stephen's Green, an area within the city's borders, an ancient privilege for holders of the award.

It was the human dimension of the story that captured Bono's imagination. As someone who has demonstrated his own sense of outrage at inequality and injustice, and taken some flak for it along the way, the empathy that he felt was in part at least political. But Aung San Suu Kyi's experience had a particular poignancy, leaving as she did not just the comfort and security of academic life in Oxford but also her husband, her son and the home they had built together to go back to the place that she grew up in, the place she truly thought of as home.

At first Bono tried to write the song from the point of view of the husband and son left behind – dreaming of what might have been and living through the pain of not knowing how Aung San Suu Kyi was, or even if she was still alive. But it seemed presumptuous. "So I kept it a little abstract," he explains, "and just let it be a love song about somebody having to leave a relationship for all the right reasons."

But of course it becomes much more than that, as Bono explores some of his own obsessions on what is clearly perceived by the band as one of the major songs on the record, giving *All That You Can't Leave Behind* its title and inspiring the sleeve artwork of a band in transit, apparently travelling light through an otherwise sparsely populated Charles de Gaulle Airport in Paris. You can sense a touch of envy on Bono's part in the shifting refrain, especially the second time around. "*Walk on, walk on,*" he proclaims, "*What you've got they can't deny it/ Walk on, walk on/ Can't sell it, can't buy it*" – and you know that he knows that the same can never quite be said of his own contribution to making the world a better place, heartfelt and immense as it might be.

And Aung San Suu Kyi's journey becomes a point of departure in itself, a springboard towards the realisation that in the end we're all going to have to leave the baggage that we create or accumulate behind, as we undertake the final journey to whatever home awaits us in the beyond.

The obsession with the meaning of the word home, and the way it impacts on our lives, is a familiar one for U2. It's also understandable in a man who has spent a substantial part of the last 25 years living in hotels. But Bono finds a new twist here with a freshly-minted aphorism of the kind that has been engaging him since *Achtung Baby*. "*Home*," he sings, "*Hard to know if you've never had one/ Home... I can't say where it is but I know I'm going home/That's where the hurt is.*"

That's what they say, isn't it – that home is where the hurt is?

Walk On Written: U2 • Duration: 4' 56" • UK singles chart position: 5

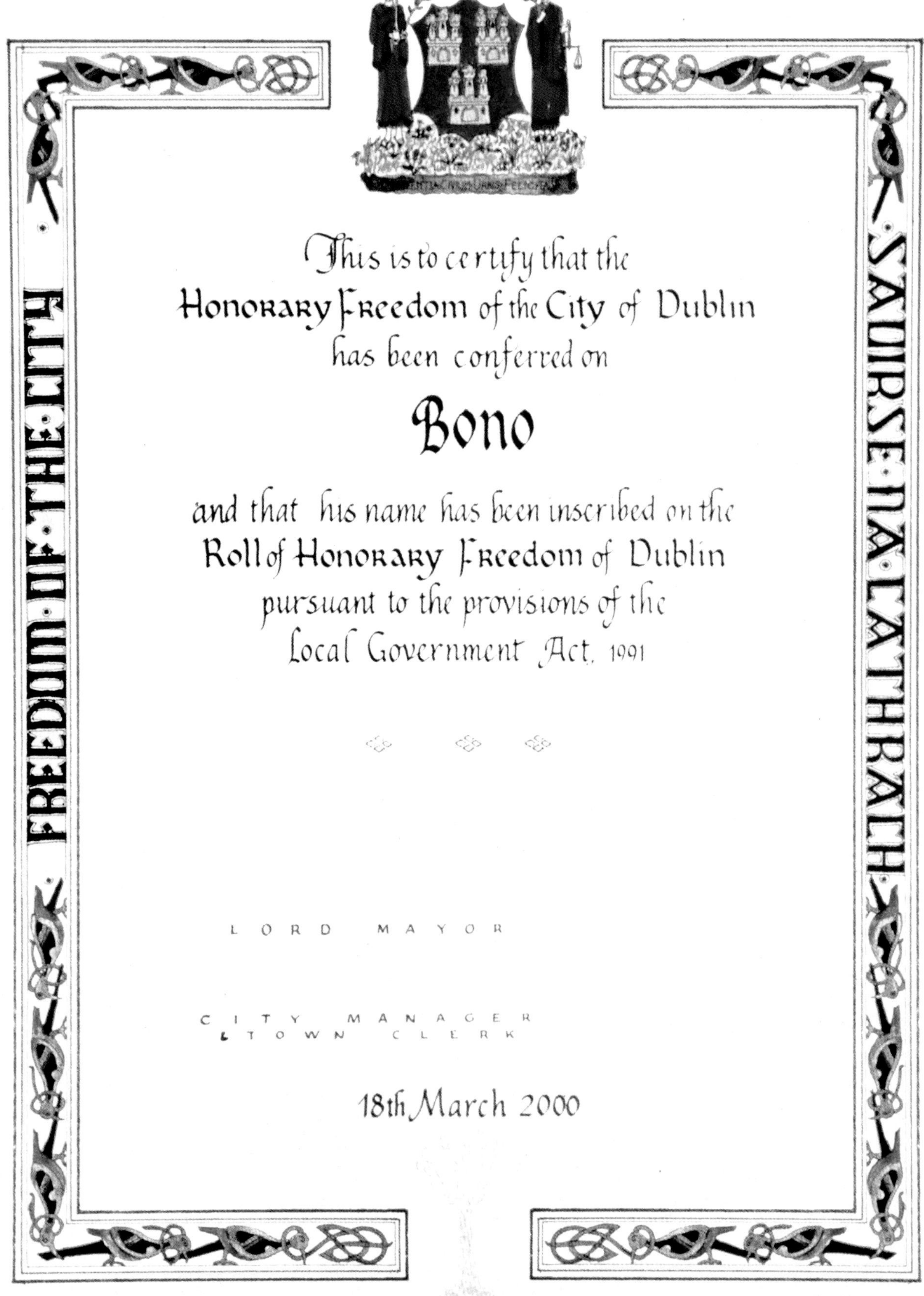

FREEDOM OF THE CITY
SAOIRSE NA CATHRACH
This is to certify that the
Honorary Freedom of the City of Dublin
has been conferred on
Bono
and that his name has been inscribed on the
Roll of Honorary Freedom of Dublin
pursuant to the provisions of the
Local Government Act, 1991
LORD MAYOR
CITY MANAGER
& TOWN CLERK
18th March 2000

Kite

It happens to most of us at some stage in our lives. The cards fall in a certain order, and suddenly people around us seem to be dropping like flies. And others are threatening to. That's the way it was during the recording of *All That You Can't Leave Behind*.

Death was in the air and Bono was confronted afresh with a visceral sense of his own mortality. Death had shaped him since his teens, when his mother was lost in tragic circumstances. Now, having himself passed the big four-oh, he saw his father in serious decline for the first time. Tributes to his mother litter U2's repertoire. Bono's relationship with his father is more sparingly evoked but now that there was cause for serious concern, it was a subject that could no longer be circumvented. It gnawed away at him, demanding that a song be written. But it needed something to give it lift-off, to get it airborne. It needed a metaphor to make it fly.

The rock star's life is a dislocated, disorientated one. Locked in the studio for months on end, and then – gone. For Bono's children – now he's here, now he disappears. And the minstrel feels guilty, he wants to do all the daddy-like things that he remembers from when he was a kid. And so he troops down to the beach at Killiney with Jordan and Eve to fly a kite. The expedition could hardly have been deemed a successful one. The kite went up, and it came down with a phhht, embedding itself in the strand. "Daddy, can we go home and play with the Playstation?" one of the kids asked. But when the kite hit the sand, a seed was sown.

'Kite' begins with a portent of doom. "*Something is about to give*," Bono ruminates. "*I can feel it coming... I'm not afraid to die*."He's seeing the world through the eyes of his father, and imagining how he himself will assess his own life, his own contribution, from the edge of the abyss. He's looking at his children and thinking about his father – who could be spirited away at any time. The voice could be his or his dad's: "*In summer I can taste the salt in the sea/ There's a kite blowing out of control on a breeze/ I wonder what's gonna happen to you/ You wonder what has happened to me.*"

It's a big subject: writing about it didn't come easy. Bono struggled with the verses. Edge got stuck in and gave him a hand, pushing the vehicle across the finishing line. "It seemed I knew what he was writing about and he didn't," Edge laughs. "It was one of those weird scenes. I was throwing in lines and he didn't like them at the time, but we went through this circular process where he was thinking, 'Oh yeah, that was a good line,' and so they went back in."

Kite Written: U2 • Duration: 4' 26"

In A Little While

'In a Little While' was an Eno line, one that he'd been playing with for some time. It's the measure of a hook with potential – it nags at you, and refuses to go away, till you just know that you have to do something with it.

It's part of the pattern when U2 record; the Thursday night drink. Bono may insist he's abstaining for Lent, but come St Patrick's Day, or someone's birthday or even any old Thursday night, he'll be slamming 'em down till 5 in the morning, better than the best.

It was one of those Thursday nights and the age-old ritual was being enacted. The gang were there, but Bono bumped into someone he hadn't seen in 15 years, maybe even 20. The conversation was an awakening, ricocheting into the morning. It was a long night, and the next day Bono arrived in the studio and blurted out most of the lyrics of 'In a Little While' – a spiritual song that draws on the legacy of Al Green, mating it with a high, lonesome keening figure that gives the track its special haunting power.

In fact, a few things came together in the song. Around the turn of the year, Bono had been thinking Millennium thoughts, watching old clips of the Apollo moon landing on TV and experiencing again the sense of awe that he'd felt when he saw those pictures for the first time as a kid, the ecstatic realisation of how tiny and insignificant we are as individuals. It was a mood that fed into 'Beautiful Day' with its vision of Bedouin fires, the Great Wall of China, the Grand Canyon and other earthly phenomena, as seen from above. It slipped in here too, in a metaphor for the restless spirit that's so often denied but that nestles dangerously even in the warmest embrace of the most committed relationships. "A man dreams one day to fly," Bono sings and you can tell that it's the Wanderer in him talking.

'In A Little While' drew a great vocal performance from Bono, aching, tender and full of longing and guilt. "*In a little while/I won't be blown by every breeze*," he promises. And he's got so much soul, you almost believe him.

In A Little While Written: U2 • Duration: 3' 39"

Wild Honey

There's a sub-text to any album – the story of what might have been. There were two or three big rock songs that everyone was committed to getting onto the album. A lot of work went in. But there's something in the dynamic of making a U2 record that defies logic. You're operating on instinct. "We reckoned people aren't buying rock records any more," Bono explains, "because of this progressive rock lurgy, where the single has been forgotten. In our heads we've written eleven singles for this record."

At the same time, there was another key complementary impulse: a desire to take a step sideways from the kind of dance-stances that U2 had experimented with on *Pop*. So they asked themselves the question that they have tried, consistently, to ask themselves each time it comes to making a new U2 record: what is it that you want to hear? And if you can get four people to answer that question in the same way, you're onto something.

The din of dance and the indulgence of progressive rock were to be avoided. And there was another foil that they identified, in the music that has dominated charts the world over these past five years and more. Pop! It's one of the oddest moments on the record, the neat little acoustic guitar intro to 'Wild Honey'. The technology is so sophisticated now that the temptation is there to use it all the time. 'Wild Honey' was captured in its raw state. "It was never monkeyed with," Lanois says. "That's why it sounds like that."

There's so much melancholy elsewhere on the album that it's a vital tangent, slipped in at the last minute to enable people to lift their heads up from the sheer weight of the surrounding sonic and lyrical material. It isn't just the rudimentary sound that makes you think of the '60s: there's a Beatle-ish flavour to the melody and the harmony lines. And it's impossible not to hear Van Morrison, not just in Bono's voice but also in the pantheistic flavour of the sentiments. "Well, Van sings in major keys a lot," Daniel Lanois speculates. And Bono sounds like Van now and again. They grew up in the same backyard, so he has a licence!"

"We thought it would be fun to include it," Lanois adds, "a nice, simple, clear song with a lovely sentiment. It does have a lightness to it but it's a song of appreciation. I think it's like taking time out to say a little prayer. That's what it is." A song of praise, indeed.

Wild Honey Written: U2 • Duration: 3' 46"

Peace On Earth

It was hardly a surprise that U2 responded positively to the call they received on the run-in to the referendum on the Good Friday Agreement – a historic document which set out a way forward for Northern Ireland which held the promise that paramilitary guns might, in the nuanced language of this most intricate of political processes, be placed permanently beyond use. As polling day approached, the referendum seemed to be in trouble: would they lend their support to the campaign for a 'yes' vote? And so U2 from Dublin travelled North, to join forces with Ash from Downpatrick in Northern Ireland, playing together at a historic rally in Belfast. The 'yes' campaign prevailed. Peace, for so long an impossible dream in Northern Ireland, seemed finally to have a context in which it might flourish.

That illusion was shattered in the most appalling, heart-breaking and gruesome way when a bomb went off at 2.30 in the afternoon, on 15 August 1998, in the town of Omagh in County Tyrone. The resulting carnage was the worst in the bloody history of the Northern troubles with 29 killed and dozens more scarred, maimed and wounded. The bomb had been planted by a new paramilitary grouping styling itself the Real IRA.

'Peace On Earth', an angry and bitter response, was written in the shuddering aftermath of the mass murder of innocent citizens. "It was written literally on the day the Omagh bomb went off," Bono recounts. "Nobody could actually believe it. In Ireland, when they read out the names of all the people who died on the six o'clock news, the city just came to a complete standstill.... People were just weeping – in cars, on O'Connell Street, all over the place. It was really a trauma for most people – because not only was it the destruction of lives, it was the destruction of the peace process, which had been put together with sticky tape and glue and tacks and a lot of faith. I couldn't believe that people could do that."

'Peace On Earth' is Bono's most agnostic song – "*Jesus, can you spare the time/ To throw a drowning man a line?*" he asks, knowing that the answer must be no. In 'Wake Up Dead Man' he had paraphrased Seamus Heaney, beseeching Jesus to listen as hope and peace try to rhyme. He returns to the same theme: "*Jesus, this song you wrote/ The words are sticking in my throat/ Peace on earth/ Hear it every Christmas time/But hope and history won't rhyme/ So what's it worth/This peace on earth.*"

"That Christmas, the whole 'peace on earth, goodwill to all men' struck a sour note," Bono observes. "It was very hard to be a believer that Christmas."

Peace On Earth Written: U2 • Duration: 4' 48"

When I Look At The World

At the start of the '90s, U2 had decided that in order to reach people and touch people during a new decade, they had to come in a different guise.It was time to don some mad glad rags and to top it off with a pair of shades. Or three. "We played it cool for about ten years," Bono reflects. "And we got quite good at it. I was surprised! Yet we always saw it for what it was. We always knew it was a bit silly."

Now, at the turn of the millennium, a new strategy was called for. They wanted an album of big songs that would be strong enough lyrically and subtle enough melodically to reach into millions of hearts. "We're going up against 'Bridge Over Troubled Water'," Bono jokes, "and we have our work cut out." This was a time for empathy, for tenderness – for love. It was a time for homage to the muse. It was a time for humility.

Bono's partner Ali has done extraordinary work on the Children from Chernobyl project that assists the children of a region that will remain infamous as the location of the worst ever peacetime nuclear catastrophe. At great risk to her own health, Ali and her co-workers have gone to Chernobyl and Belarus and spent time there working with people who are still being affected by disaster, and with their children, in an attempt to alleviate the suffering, isolation and neglect.

Written by Bono and Edge, 'When I Look at the World' acknowledges the special qualities that this kind of commitment takes. It isn't just the capacity that Bono's muse has to light up any room that she enters – it's the empathy of which she's capable, the composure that she shows, and the example that she gives to someone who by comparison feels flawed and impatient.

When I Look At The World Written: U2 • Duration: 4' 17"

New York

Friday is meeting day. The boys in the band sit down and wait for the bad news. We've been asked to do this. Yes. We've been asked to do that. No. We've got to find a way around this. Oh! It was a phenomenon throughout the making of *All That You Can't Leave Behind* that became a right royal pain in the ass for anyone outside the most inner of inner circles. It wasn't just Fridays anymore, it was every second fucking day.

Passionately as they might have felt like railing against it, Eno and Lanois had to live with it. The Friday meeting is on? Fine, we'll work away. Can we dig up that Larry rhythm thing? We might get something out of that. Frequently, Eno does his best work when he gets the hell out of the studio. "We're always glad when he goes away," Larry smiles, "because we know that when he comes back, he'll be back with some more goodies! Danny just stays in there and brings a different touch to it. So we're pushing one way, they're pushing others – and the results are always interesting."

On other occasions, it happens in the room, where the smell of

NME
CARLING
awards

the conflict and the frustration is fresh in everyone's nostrils. "Brian brings a very different thing to U2," Larry adds. "He gets onto those keyboards and he just takes songs in directions you wouldn't expect."

The meeting was a long one, but in the meantime Brian was in inspired form. He got a kind of a foghorn sound going over Larry's drumbeat. He conjured another chordal thing out of his bag of tricks and Lanois snuck in on guitar and they had a groove happening. The band came down from the meeting feeling itchy and scratchy. They grabbed their instruments and whaled into it. The chemistry worked. Eureka! "It all happened very, very quickly," Lanois remembers. "Bono thought 'This is going to be the home for my New York idea'!" A song was born.

Hearing it, it's impossible not to think of Lou Reed, of Frank Sinatra, of Ian Curtis and of P.J. Harvey, whose *Stories from the City, Stories from the Sea* is in part at least a paean to the city that never sleeps. Originally the song ended with a free-form conversation about Frank Sinatra, with whom Bono had the privilege of sharing a duet on 'I've Got You Under My Skin' before he died. Old Blue Eyes! Bono says: "I was at dinner once with Frank and he took a blue paper napkin from the table and he was just staring at it and he said, to no-one in particular, 'I remember when my eyes were this blue'. He put it, and kept it, in an inside pocket. It was very cool."

For the most part 'New York' is just that, the cool pulsing groove acting as a backdrop as the narrator confesses quietly to the terms of the mid-life crisis afflicting him, while all around nine million other, fascinating stories are being written. New York! New York! But halfway through it explodes in a grungy mess that's impressively appropriate to the theme of the song. That sonic thunderstorm was there in the track's infant state but Edge got to work on it and bent it into a different shape. "That's an overdub. It's very effective," Lanois comments. "He was right."

But was Bono? There's a line in it that's sounds almost boastful: "I just got a place in New York," Bono declares. "I was gonna change the line to something less consumerist," he admits, "but... I had just got a place in New York! And it made me smile. Even though the song is not autobiographical. Now you're thinking 'the bastard's got a nice place on Central Park' – but for the character in the song it could be a shoebox."

Obviously there are a bits of Bono in there. But only bits, he insists. No mid-life crisis here. "If anything I'm at the other end of that," he says. "I'm trying to calm down. I had a mid-life crisis much earlier, about age 27, for all the classic reasons. I just went downtown in Los Angeles, drank a lot of whiskey and made up for all the years pushing a rock up a hill. Or a rock band up the hill! I got quite good at being silly and that, in a way, prepared us for the silliness of the '90s – which I've thoroughly enjoyed."

Oddly, it ends on a glancing reference to 'The Stolen Child', a poem by William Butler Yeats. "*In the stillness of the evening/ When the sun has had its day/ I heard your voice a-whispering/ Come away child/ New York, New York.*" Unconscious? Maybe.

New York Written: U2 • Duration: 5' 30"

Grace

The mood starting out had been relaxed and positive. They went into the studio without a fixed agenda. The plan was to jam, to see what would come out of it without the pressure of actually making an album. It had worked well for U2, and for Eno and Lanois as their producers, in particular with *The Joshua Tree*. So they tried it again. It was kind of a fun time, but a fruitful one.

'Grace' was minted in that first loose flush of creativity. It was put on the shelf in embryonic form: one to come back to later. They did about mid-way through, but nothing gave. Bono hadn't linked it with any lyrical cue yet, and they had a frustrating time trying to move it along. It went into cold storage.

On one of his retreats to London, Eno took it with him. He was looking for a melody to open it out and help it take flight. Nothing. It went into storage for a third time. They were on the final countdown, with paranoia playing havoc all around, when the lightbulb went on. "Pretty much at the end of the record," Lanois recalls, "we pulled it out and Bono wrote something very beautiful for it. I came up with the guitar part and that sparked another keyboard part from Brian and Larry put some drums on it – it was kind of layered. And Bono just had this idea that we should approach the subject matter of 'grace'. It was lovely."

It's a tribute to womankind. You can sense the spirit of Ali informing it, but 'Grace' is not just about an individual, or about women – it's about a way of dealing with the world that offers intimations of a better place. An album that exploded into life on a wave of barely-founded optimism – the sky is falling but hey, it's a beautiful day! – ends on a deeper note. 'Grace' finds beauty in everything. It's a state we can aspire to. Not easily attained when you're trying to finish a U2 album, and the world is collapsing all around you. But worth chasing nonetheless.

Grace Written: U2 • Duration: 5' 30"

Best in show: The band on their way into the NME Carling Awards, in London 2002, to receive the award for Best Live Act.

LARRY MULLEN JR

BY BRIAN BOYD

Larry Mullen is the quiet one in U2. Not a fan of the celebrity lifestyle, he is the anchor of the band and an outstanding drummer in his own right.

Laurence Joseph Mullen was born on 31 October 1961. Long since known as Larry, he added the "Jr" to his name only when U2 started making money and his father (who has the same name) started getting his tax bills.

Originally a piano student, he was on his way out of a lesson in a Dublin music school when he heard someone clattering the drums in another room. Persuading his parents to allow him to switch classes, he soon discovered a natural gift for percussion. Continually practising by himself at home bored him, so his father advised him to put up a note at school looking for other musicians to play with.

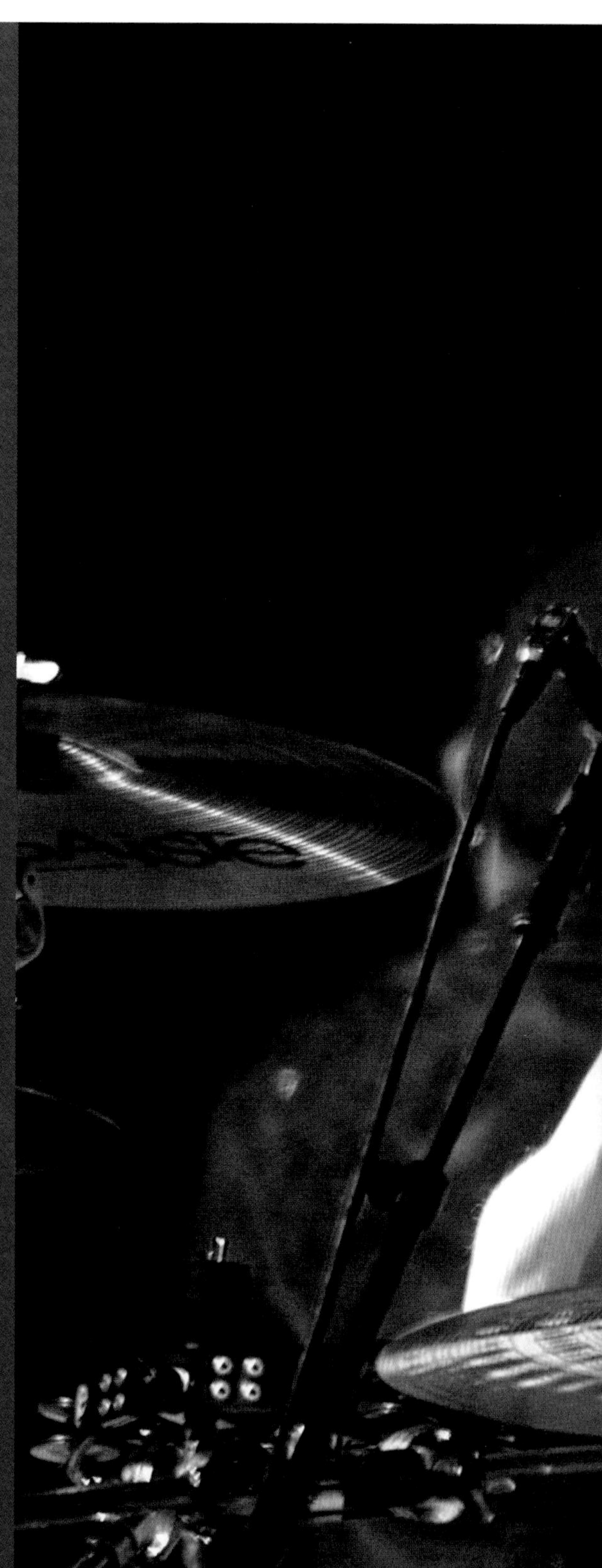

Left: The most down-to-earth member of the band, Larry, has, as Bono puts it, "saved us from ourselves, many a time". **Right:** Long-time U2 producer, Brian Eno, refers to Mullen as "a drumming genius"

> “[Larry] felt that the click track was out of time. Eno assured him it wasn’t, but Larry kept arguing it was. It was only later that Eno realized that the click track was two milliseconds out of time. Eno believes Larry’s drumming and precise sense of timing is “staggering”.

At the time of the first U2 audition in Larry's kitchen he was just 14, but he was the only trained musician in the band. It was also supposed to be the Larry Mullen Band since it was his idea and, unlike the others, he could actually play. However, within ten minutes of Bono arriving, the dynamic changed.

In the early days of U2, Larry and Bono were very close – they were the only two Irish-born members of U2 and came from similar working family backgrounds. They both endured the trauma of losing their mothers when they were teenagers. Larry, as with Bono, believes it was the grief of his mother's early death which led him to form a rock band. Larry's father was never entirely happy about his young son throwing in his lot with a rock band which didn't exactly display any promise in the early days. So the drummer was the only U2 member to have a day job, and Larry actually missed a lot of the early U2 photo shoots and gigs because of his work (his place was always taken by a stand-in).

With Bono and The Edge, Larry joined the Shalom Christian group while still at school. Just like the others, however, he left when a choice had to be made between his faith and his commitment to a touring rock band.

He is a very underestimated drummer: long-time U2 producer Brian Eno tells a story about how when recording the *All You Can't Leave Behind* album, the drummer felt that the click track (a computer-generated beat) was out of time. Eno assured him it wasn't but Larry kept arguing it was. It was only later that Eno realized that the click track was two milliseconds out of time. Eno believes Larry's drumming and precise sense of timing is "staggering".

Combining a number of styles – from his militaristic-style drumming on the *War* album to the more electronic syncopated approach on the *Pop* album – his drum loops have been the basis of many a U2 song.

Rhythm section: The engine room of U2 – Larry Mullen Jr at work on the Joshua Tree tour.

Junior drummer: A very youthful Larry in Dublin in 1977.

HOW TO DISMANTLE AN ATOMIC BOMB

The band came off the Elevation tour on a high. They were back at the top of their game, with over ten million sales of *All That You Can't Leave Behind* racked up, and the coveted title of Biggest Rock Band in the World successfully defended against all-comers. And they had a whole batch of new songs brewing, or at least that was the way it felt. Bring 'em on!

They began a new phase of recording in the South of France and got enough stuff down to feel that they were on the way. Then it was into the longer haul. With a ballsy rock'n'roll record in mind, they picked Chris Thomas to produce the album and the band ensconced themselves in their Dublin HQ to get the job finished. Well, started...

The best U2 record ever was on the way, we were told. It was a return to the band's rock'n'roll roots that would blow everyone away – a guitar album, with Edge leading the way. But those in the know sensed that all was not right down in Hanover Quay. The record – as yet untitled – had been scheduled to hit the racks in time for the Christmas rush, 2003, but the deadline for the delivery of the finished masters came... and went. The band decamped to the South of France again, and there was the by now almost de rigeur security scare when a CD of rough mixes was lost or stolen. Chris Thomas departed in ambiguous circumstances, the band later acknowledging that they had probably driven him mad. Steve Lillywhite was drafted in, and was still there as the finishing tape came into view, but by the time the album was fully done and dusted, no less than eight producers in all had been involved.

Sometimes it's necessary to do things the hard way. Over 25 years on, no one knows this better than U2. After a colossal and at times painful two years in the studios, the record was finished and put to bed. Someone joked that next time maybe someone should put a bomb under them.

Vertigo

It began with a riff, concocted at Edge's house in Malibu. He played it to Bono – Da da da da da da da dahn – and it registered. When you get a good one, it plays itself back to you when you're least expecting it, slipping in and out of your consciousness, until it claims its place in a song. Da da da da da da da dahn. This felt like a classic, one that might have been purloined from the Stones, the Pistols or even Led Zeppelin, but it was where Edge was leaning in the early stages of making what was to become *How To Dismantle An Atomic Bomb*.

It's only rock'n'roll but I like it. The Vines, the Hives, the Strokes and outfits like Black Rebel Motorcycle Club had thrust the guitar back to the centre of things. U2, ever aware of the zeitgeist, wanted to see any new pretenders off by coming up with an even bigger riff, a

Preparing to ascend: Rehearsing for the Elevation tour in Dublin in 2004.

Release date: November 2004
Catalogue number: CIDU214
Producer: Steve Lillywhite
Track listing: Vertigo/Miracle Drug/Sometimes You Can't Make It On Your Own/Love And Peace Or Else/City Of Blinding Lights/All Because Of You/A Man And A Woman/Crumbs From Your Table/One Step Closer/Original Of The Species/Yahweh/Fast Cars
Highest Chart Position: No.1 (UK and US)

Bono needs you: Poster for the Moscow date of the 360° tour. The band played at the Luzhniki Stadium, 25 August 2010.

I'd like to think this is a real classic U2 album and that there is this spine to it. I have a feeling that looking back on this album in a few years' time it will have a very strong identity from beginning to end and ultimately that's what an album is about." The Edge

harder one – something that would blast out of the radio like a calling card. Edge thought of the working title 'Full Metal Jacket' and that was how it started to take shape. There'd be blood on this track alright. Blood and guts.

Bono got enthused, thinking MC5 and the Stooges and deciding that the riff alone, and the rock'n'roll energy that blazed through it, was reason enough to make a new album before Larry and Adam had even heard it. He came up with an agit-prop set of lyrics about the plight of the native American Leonard Peltier, wrongly jailed for aiding and abetting in the killing of two FBI agents. He called it 'Native Son' and the song took shape in that guise.

Thinking that a blazing punky record was on the cards, they'd hired Chris Thomas to produce. Not only had Thomas worked with Roxy Music – an unacknowledged influence on U2 throughout their career – but he was the man at the control desk for the recording of the Sex Pistols' landmark album *Never Mind the Bollocks*, a record notable for its snarling guitars.

With Thomas in the production seat, they recorded 'Native Son', and the band loved it so much they sent it to their American label Interscope to get them equally fired up. It worked and everyone was buzzing about it, thinking they had a winner on their hands.

It was a fling that was destined to come to an end. The recording went into a slump and the band decided to bring in Steve Lillywhite to act as, in footballing parlance, the fresh pair of legs that was needed to get them through the second half. He immediately decided to change things around, to set the band a different kind of challenge. To take them out of the comfort zone, he turned the studio inside out, pushing them into the bigger of the Hanover Quay rooms to play. He found a more ambient room for Larry, to get closer to the early U2 sound and in the process to bring something fresh to the rhythm department. The track was still called 'Native Son' when they whacked down some great new parts in the re-organised set-up. Lillywhite asked Bono for a guide vocal and the frontman started to sing it – and something odd happened. "After 30 seconds he stopped," Steve Lillywhite recalls. "All of a sudden I realised 'he's imagining this as a stage and he's up there in front of 20,000 people singing this – and he doesn't want to'."

It's an ever-present consideration now for U2, and for Bono in particular. He writes a U2 song, especially one with a big stonking riff that's potentially an album opener and the first single, knowing that he's going to have to go out and play it live. 'Native Son', he had just figured out, wasn't one that he would feel comfortable doing that with.

Going back to the drawing board was hard. Larry talks about the fact that the song had to be deconstructed and put together again – and that's what they did. They changed the chords around, tried a variety of different lyrics and titles. It became 'Shark Soup' and then 'Viva La Ramone', a tribute to the great Joey Ramone. There was even a Spanish version that gave the track the mathematically challenged intro – "Unos, dos, tres, catorces" (One, two three, fourteen!) – bellowed by Bono at the start of the record. Eventually it transmuted into 'Vertigo', and even then they struggled to choose between a number of different potential choruses. They weren't sure which was the one, until a few outsiders had heard it and support for the "Hello, hello..." variation gathered momentum. "It's a club and you're supposed to be having the time of your life," Bono said in an interview on the U2achtung.com website, "but you want to kill yourself. Vertigo is a dizzy feeling, when you get to the top of something and there's only one way to go."

"In my head I created a club called Vertigo with all these people in it," he added (though there's a Club Vertigo in Boston and rumours of a place in Germany called Vertigo too), "and the music is not the music you want to hear and the people are not the people you want to be with and then you see somebody and she's got a cross around her neck, and you focus on it. Because you can't focus on anything else. You find a tiny little fragment of salvation there."

Whatever the origin of the imaginary club, they had found the fragment of salvation necessary to realize the full potential of the track. Steve Lillywhite took the unusual initiative of double-tracking Bono's voice on the chorus, which gave it added impact. Finally, after more heartache, indecision and grief than Edge could possibly have imagined when he came up with that first killer riff, they knew that this was the one. And the riff had survived. Da da da da da da da dahn.

"'Vertigo' refers back to their past," according to Neil McCormick, who conducted interviews for the album's accompanying DVD. "Bono sings at one point, '*Hello, hello*' and I said, 'You've used that line before' and he said, 'Have I? Where?' and I said, 'Well you used to use it all the time, basically when you ran out of words! And it's on 'Stories For Boys'. And that's on their first single, on U23.

"So 'Vertigo', the first single off the new album refers back to their first. It's like the early U2 pumped up in the 21st century, a really exciting record. It actually includes my name in it, so I definitely voted for that as the first single! At the end, Bono's singing '*Your love is teaching me how to kneel*'. And then he goes: '*Kneee-heel!*' He and Edge were playing this in the studio and at that exact moment they both looked up and saw me standing there and Bono went, 'Hey Neil!'"

But the break in the song also directly references the guitar part in 'I Will Follow'. Thus 'Vertigo' takes them back and forward at the same time, reclaiming their heritage and putting it in a modern rock context. According to producer Trevor Horn, the first overdub on the record doesn't appear until over two minutes into the song, making it essentially a live recording by the band – an incredible thought given that they were a full two years in the studio making *How To Dismantle An Atomic Bomb*.

"Adam is fantastic on that song," Steve Lillywhite says, "because on the verse there's nothing but bass and drums and vocals. Edge just does a couple of clicks, so Adam and Larry have to carry it. It's a really big song, as big as any of their songs actually." The ideal electric shock treatment, you might say, with which to open the record.

Vertigo Written: U2 • Duration: 3' 14" • UK singles chart position: 1 • US singles chart position: 31

Miracle Drug

When the first glow of the pounding rock'n'roll of the Chris Thomas sessions had dimmed and the hard labour they'd put in subsequently had worn thin, there was a feeling of uncertainty, bordering on depression, in the air.

There was a lot of stuff there, a lot of sweat in the tracks, but nothing was getting finished, no one was coming up trumps. Larry, who'd had his foot off the gas, listened to the material, and decided that what had been done didn't add up to the record he wanted to make. Exhaustion was beginning to take its toll, the band were feeling down, individually and collectively, and there was no guaranteeing that they'd get back up off the floor. There never is: the way U2 work, they're a catastrophe waiting to happen. The band had a creeping feeling now, that they might have been barking up the wrong tree all along. Originally scheduled to hit the shops late in 2003, the release of the record had to be put back. When Steve Lillywhite was drafted in, he had a good listen and tended to share the downbeat assessment: this gig wasn't going to be about mixing and fixing. A radical change of tack was needed.

Too often, what was there didn't have the spark; it was like, Lillywhite mused to himself, not-great versions of things U2 had done before. He girded his loins and said what nobody wanted to hear. "I think you need a few new songs," he announced, to the dismay of all concerned. But in a way it was liberating. Adam, for one, recognised that he was right. Having been so down, the only way was up. So they went away and wrote. 'Miracle Drug' was one of the first pieces under the new dispensation and it felt like another big song in the making.

The chord sequence was one Adam came up with, the band improvising their way to a song shape from there. Bono'd long had an idea in his head to write a song about Christopher Nolan, who went to Mount Temple, the school in north Dublin, at which the band originally formed. The working assumption had been that Christopher, in a wheelchair as a result of cerebral palsy, and unable to communicate, was just a spectator. But with the support of his mother, a woman of great dedication and love, and the help of a new drug – a miracle drug – he was able to move his head. At the age of 13 he began to write, using a unicorn on a band around his head to type. And when he did, hard as the tortuous process made it, the words began to flow. In 1981, his first book of poetry was published, and he called it *Damburst Of Dreams*, capturing with beautiful eloquence the sensation of finally being able to express the thoughts and feelings that had forever been racing through his mind. At 21, Nolan produced a powerful autobiographical novel, *Under The Eye Of The Clock*, that won the Whitbread Prize. Hard to believe! Such an unprecedented outpouring of intelligence and emotion from someone who hadn't been able to speak or walk or even move independently. Yes, there was a song in it, alright. "*I want to trip inside your head,*" Bono wrote, the image of Christopher Nolan in his mind's eye, "*Spend the day there/ To hear the things you haven't said/ And see what you might see...*"

Without the familiar presence of either Brian Eno or Daniel Lanois in the studio for any extended period, the band felt that they would benefit from having another musician involved in the production and brought in Garrett 'Jacknife' Lee to fill the role. A keyboard player, and a former member of Dublin bands Thee Amazing Colossal Men and Compulsion, as a producer Lee had hit paydirt with Snow Patrol's Final Straw, and the feeling was that he might now bring a bit of left-field sonic experimentation to the high table. He got involved, helping to push 'Miracle Drug' along. But, as it evolved, in Bono's mind it wasn't just going to be about Christopher Nolan. There was something else working its way through, something to do with AIDS and the drugs that have been developed to contain it.

There was a line he wanted to use, and it fitted. He'd had a conversation with Sean Lennon about Tibet, in which the younger Lennon asked him what freedom smelled like. "Like the top of a new-born baby's head," he'd said at the time. And he'd carried that around with him since. He'd tried it in a different context, but now, definitively, he'd found a home for it.

"*Freedom has a scent/ Like the top of a new born baby's head...*" he sang. And the melody and the mood took on an anthemic purpose, allowing the track to grow until it became a kind of prayer of hope about the miracles that can be wrought through science and medicine.

"Some people think it's a great lyric and some people think it's terrible," Steve Lillywhite reflects. "I think it's great. I think Bono does the things that make people question themselves and their responses. In a strange way, though, it works. It's a special song.

Miracle Drug Written: U2 • Duration: 3' 59"

Sometimes You Can't Make It On Your Own

Bono had known for a while that his father was dying of cancer. It was a tough time for him, the hardest since his mother had died. And so

he wrote a song for Bob, and called it 'Tough' because that was what his father had always seemed to him. "A tough old boot of a guy," in Bono's own words, "Irish, Dub, north side Dubliner, very cynical about the world and the people in it, but very charming and funny with it."

They worked on the song for *All That You Can't Leave Behind*, and it turned into 'Sometimes You Can't Make It On Your Own' during those sessions – but it wasn't ready. Bob died the week before the band's Slane Castle appearance. Bono sang the song at the funeral, a portrait of the artist as an old man – a working class guy who loved opera, and who had bequeathed something of his beautiful tenor voice to his son.

"He never talked about [our] the music," Bono said. "Oh, I do remember he liked the song 'The Unforgettable Fire'. He thought we were getting quite good around the time of *Rattle And Hum* but he didn't know where we were going in the '90s!"

They came back to the song for *How To Dismantle An Atomic Bomb* and it felt good. Everyone felt that they had it nailed. Except Steve Lillywhite. When he came in, he gave it a critical appraisal that was to prove, well, critical.

"My contribution to that song is that I was listening to it with Edge – and Bono was there as well – and I said 'Edge, this song doesn't have a chorus'. And they said 'What do you mean?' And I said, "Well, it just finishes the verse and then goes '*Sometimes you can't make it on your own*.'" And Bono immediately went 'Give me a guitar'. So he picked up a guitar and went '*And it's you when I look na na na na*' – he didn't have the lyrics yet – '*And it's you du du du du du du du/ Sometimes you can't make it on your own*'. And all of a sudden the song was finished. That song had been around for the best part of five years and no one had ever said to them that it didn't have a chorus."

Sometimes You Can't Make It On Your Own Written: U2 • Duration: 5' 08" • UK singles chart position: 1 • US singles chart position: 97

Looking down: Bono singing 'Vertigo' – the lead-off single from 2004's *How to Dismantle an Atomic Bomb*.

I told Thom Yorke two years ago, 'I know what the album's about and what it's going to be called, which is *How To Build An Atomic Bomb*'. That was the original title because the toothpaste was out of the tube." Bono

Love And Peace Or Else

How To Dismantle An Atomic Bomb was made against the backdrop of the invasion of Iraq. There was a song hanging over from *All That You Can't Leave Behind*. Now, every time they listened to the out-takes from those earlier sessions, it clamoured for attention.

Lyrically, inspired by Eno's end-of-the-world, subterranean guitar sound, Bono had in mind a preacher-type character, cracked but making sense. "It's like The Fly went to the seminary and became a priest," he revealed to u2achtung.com. Around the time of the album launch Bono enjoyed quoting couplets that he was especially pleased with to anyone who was writing about the record. In 'Love and Peace Or Else' it was this one; *"When you enter this life I pray you depart/ With a wrinkled face and a brand new heart."* Bono had set out to write a political record, in part at least with Iraq as a backdrop, but you can only write the songs that flow through you.

"I very much sat down to address it, hence the title of the album," Bono reflects. "It's worth reminding ourselves of those days after 9/11, and what they felt like. At no other point in history had there been a sense that people would commit that sort of mass murder as a terrorist act. That's no excuse for prosecuting a war in Iraq, but it puts it all into context. "I told Thom Yorke two years ago, 'I know what the album's about and what it's going to be called, which is How To Build An Atomic Bomb'. That was the original title because the toothpaste was out of the tube. There was an article in the *Guardian* newspaper with two college students discussing how easy it is to get your hands on this kind of weaponry.

"A private arms company in the US has developed this GPS-guided system made out of papier-mache and plastic, which for less than a $1m can fly 2,500 miles with anything you want attached to it. Somebody asked their CEO, 'Are you not worried about these getting into terrorist hands?' to which he replied, 'We've offered them to the Pentagon if they're prepared to buy in bulk, but the knowledge to make these things exists everywhere. We're just packaging it commercially'

"Someone who's paranoid, in my opinion, is a person in full possession of the facts," he says. "These are nervous times. After Bikini Atoll, after Mexico, after indeed Enola Gay was dropped in Japan, everything has changed – and the idea that the human race can destroy everything and remove all traces of itself is now in the air. What does it mean? Two things – you party hard, and you hold on to your loved ones a little tighter. I kind of enjoy forgetting I'm in a band."

Love And Peace Or Else Written: U2 • Duration: 4' 50"

City Of Blinding Lights

There are love affairs that never end. When U2 first went to the US, they were wide-eyed kids, open to what the world had to offer them. A lot of the other British and Irish bands of the time were deeply cynical and condescending about America. U2 crossed the Atlantic knowing that they had a lot to learn, conscious that they needed to establish a foundation there in order to further their ambition to become the biggest rock band in the world.

Their first trip to New York was a magical experience, and one they'd never forget. 'City Of Blinding Lights' is just the latest manifestation of an enduring crush. It's one of Steve Lillywhite's favourite tracks on the album. They came up with the idea as far back as the recording of *Pop*. The way they work is at once sprawling and instinctive. If something feels right for the time, it gets done. If it doesn't, it's filed away. The skeleton of 'City Of Blinding Lights' didn't have the necessary flesh put on it for *Pop* and it wasn't revived successfully for *All That You Can't Leave Behind* either. But it was one in reserve that they could turn to when the hits failed to do whatever they do to the fans. They plugged back into it for *How To Dismantle An Atomic Bomb*, and listening to it now, it's hard to believe that it could have waited so long to come good.

Talking about it, Bono name-checks Scott Walker but there's a hint of *Blue Nile* in here too, in the restrained visual evocation of the world, and the spirituality that's to be found in every sparkle of light. "You can hear that in our music," Bono attests, "that painterly side of the lyrics, that kind of melodrama." But it is an Ali song too, a love song to Bono's muse, that's shot through with a sense of the ravages of time.

"I've seen you walk unafraid," he sings, *"I've seen you in the clothes*

you've made/ Can you see the beauty inside of me?/ What happened to the beauty I had inside of me?"

"It's a New York song," Bono said. "About going there for the first time. We were the first band to play Madison Square Gardens after 9/11. During 'Where the Streets Have No Name', the house lights came up, and there were 20,000 people in tears. It was beautiful." 'City Of Blinding Lights' indeed.

City Of Burning Lights Written: U2 • Length: 5' 47"

All Because Of You

At times, it seems that momentum is the key. The Elevation tour was a triumph for U2, not least because in the dark days after 9/11 they decided to keep the show on the road. It would have been natural to retreat into their shells. Instead, U2 upped their collective game. What America, in particular, needed was a return to some semblance of normality.

The adrenalin from the tour was irresistible. They felt good about what they were doing, so good that they pressed ahead almost immediately into recording. They were on a high, and blasting into the sessions in the south of France they believed they were really onto something. They wrote 'Electrical Storm', a new track recorded for Best Of 1990-2000, and 'The Hands That Built America' for *Gangs of New York* there, and lashed some other stuff down too, full of punky energy, that gave them a lift at the time.

It seemed like maybe they were on their way to a new album already, but the initial buzz tailed off. In a way, in retrospect, that was inevitable. "That tour, playing indoors, doing the material from *All That You Can't Leave Behind*, we really seemed to connect with people'" Adam Clayton recalled. "But the one survivor from that session was 'All Because Of You'." It survived, but had to be revived. Steve Lillywhite took over the production. Jacknife Lee tossed in some keyboards. They changed the melody in the chorus, did some tinkering with the lyrics, changing a verse, and gave the lot to Flood to mix. They were in business.

One of the things that delayed the making of *How To Dismantle An Atomic Bomb* was Bono's involvement in issues relating to the Drop The Debt campaign and AIDS in Africa. In that milieu, the singer brings a sense of organisation and purpose to his work that is sometimes missing from his rock'n'roll adventures. "He is, as he says of himself in 'All Because Of You', an intellectual tortoise," Adam reflects. "He is a unique character. He is organised intellectually, but he wouldn't know where his car keys are. And to say he is disorganised is kind of derogatory. That stuff isn't important to him and it never was."

'All Because Of You' is another mother song, in a line from 'I Will Follow' and 'Tomorrow' through 'Mofo'. It could be addressed to his mother Iris, it could be to Ali, it could even be to God the Mother. But it is, without doubt, about the debt that man owes to woman, one that can never be dropped. *"I'm alive/ I'm being born / I just arrived/ I'm at the door/ Of the place I started from/ And I want back inside."*

Don't we all.

All Because Of You Written: U2 • Duration: 3' 39"

A Man And A Woman

It's a couple of weeks before the album is due to hit the shops and Bono is conducting another gathering of notables through *How To Dismantle An Atomic Bomb*. As the playback progresses, he's like a man possessed.

We're on 'A Man And A Woman' and he makes like a magician about to pull off his ultimate party piece, a conjuring trick to end all conjuring tricks. "Wait till you hear this," he yells again. "No one would know it, but I'm about to show you where this song came from – where it was stolen from. I'm going to sing it in a Phil Lynott voice and you'll get it. This is Thin Lizzy. Listen."

The languorous guitar strum and Latinised feel of 'A Man And A Woman' pour from the speakers, redolent of Burt Bacherach in its romantic pop-ishness. Bono starts singing. Through his nose, just a little bit, and in a Dublin accent. And you recognise the antecedents of the song, you see them perfectly. Caramba!

He goes back into character, in a way that is both funny and lovely and moving. The original Dublin rocker's presence fills the room. And a wonderfully beautiful song about "The mysterious distance between a man and a woman" – how come no one ever expressed that idea so perfectly before? – becomes even more mysterious and beautiful in the re-telling.

As far back as 2000, Bono was asked if he ever felt constricted in his writing and his interviews by the knowledge that Ali was going to be listening. "Ali doesn't read newspapers." Bono had answered with a laugh. "Or listen to the radio. (Laughs). There's a mysterious distance between us. And that's all I can say. I don't feel in any way constricted, though at times I have. Yeah.

I'm as honest as I can be in talking about songs but I'm really honest when I'm singing them. That's just the way it goes. It's a song for adults, for people who have been together for a long time and who are still together."

You know what he means when he sings: *"I could never take a chance/Of losing love to find romance/In the mysterious distance/ Between a man and a woman."*

A Man And A Woman • Written: U2 • Duration: 4' 30"

Crumbs From Your Table

Bono's initial intentions notwithstanding, *How To Dismantle An Atomic Bomb* isn't a political record. The more personal it got, the more often Bono would refer to it as 'How To Dismantle An Atomic Bob', the reference to his father reflecting the band's growing understanding that – more than anything else – it was a record about the ties that bind us to what we are.

But Bono's personal politics seep through it. There may be nothing on the record as virulently hostile to US hegemony as 'Bullet The Blue Sky'. But Bono insisted that this was not down to having to do business with George Bush and his aides in the cause of Drop The Debt.

"It's a real question and one that I can honestly answer with a 'No'," he said. "I don't really have much control over it – and if there are lyrics that offend some of the people I work with, so be it. 'Crumbs From Your Table' is one of the most vicious songs ever. It's full of

spleen about the church and its refusal to hear God's voice on the AIDS emergency."

He describes the recording, the band in full flow in the studio, when a call comes through from a friend. She's full of good humour and heart. Hard to believe that she's in a hospital in Africa, taking care of AIDS patients. It's Sister Annie, an Irish nun, and she's looking for a favour. "You're going into the song," he tells her. And so she does.

"I went to speak to Christian groups in America to convince them to give money to fight AIDS in Africa. It was like getting blood from a stone," he recalled. "I told them about a hospice in Uganda, where so many people were dying they had to sleep three to a bed."

The last thing U2 need is a return to the self-consciousness of the *Joshua Tree* era. But there are different ways to skin this particular cat.

Under the bridge: The band staged a free gig outdoors in New York City on 22 November 2004, to mark the release of *How to Dismantle an Atomic Bomb*.

"Whenever U2 gets specifically agitprop," Bono says, "the band here starts nodding off and Brian Eno or Daniel Lanois or Steve Lillywhite will start making people dance. 'Bullet The Blue Sky' is like U2 doing the Bad Seeds, it's biblical much more so than it's a polemic. We didn't make those kind of anti-personnel type songs to suddenly stop. There are moments when I keep my opinions out of the press – but not out of songs."

Crumbs From Your Table Written: U2 • Duration: 5' 03"

One Step Closer

Edge had been doing the prep work, burrowing away in the kitchen in Zen mode, coming up with some melodic structures, getting the possible recipe for a song down. There comes a time when you have to put it into the pan and see what the others think.

He produced the chord sequence with everyone in the studio and the band began to jam it. It's the most distinctive element in the creative process for U2, the stage where they all get to toss in different ingredients and see if they can come up with a signature dish. It's why the song credits run: "Music: U2". This one smelled good. Early on, it felt like a Velvet Underground song, with Bono delivering a melody that Edge loved, and the rest of the band responding in kind. Everyone knew that it had potential, but they still had to unlock it fully.

"The U2 working process is utterly unique to them and quite frustrating for everyone else," Steve Lillywhite observed. "It involves working tracks over and over and over again, dismissing every possible thing they don't like and ultimately ending up with the thing they like."

The theme was a big one. 'One Step Closer' ponders the meaning of death: shades of The Blue Nile in the picture of the tail lights glowing and the imminence of our inevitable demise captured in a plaintive question – 'Can you hear the drummer slowing?' – that sounds like it might have been tossed in first as a studio in-joke, but rises way above that.

They almost nailed this with Chris Thomas in the driving seat, aided first by Daniel Lanois, who put some extra guitars into the mix. Jacknife Lee added synthesizers, giving a stately backdrop to the throbbing heartbeat evoked by the band. But it is the beautiful simplicity of the idea around which the song is built that gives it its special resonance. Bono had been talking to Noel Gallagher of Oasis about the fact that his father, dying at the time, seemed to have lost his faith – that he no longer believed he knew where he was going in the after-life, if indeed there was one. "Well, he's one step closer to knowing," Gallagher had drawled.

"He's on a pint of Guinness and a packet of crisps for coming up with the title," Bono laughs.

One Step Closer Written: U2 • Duration: 3' 51"

Original Of The Species

Adam Clayton talks about the thematic threads that run through *How To Dismantle An Atomic Bomb*.

It deals with questions about how you fit into the world, about the power and strength of family relationships. Larry Mullen makes similar observations. That the world U2 are in now is one in which people recognize the value of family. That it's a dangerous world out there. That we are, to one degree or another, collectively living in a state of fear.

Sometimes what we have to fear most are the ghosts inside, the things that haunt us about who we are, about what we should do and be – and about how we fit into and around the images of ourselves that have been ingrained into us.

Bono was thinking about Edge's daughter Holly when 'Original Of The Species' took shape first, during the making of *All That You Can't Leave Behind*. Bono is her Godfather, and so he feels a special, different kind of closeness. Edge loved the lyrics when he heard them: it was a song that made him cry. "It started about Holly," he told Q magazine. "He's her Godfather. The lyric became more universal, about being young and full of doubt about yourself." Edge speculates that there is, in the song, an element of Bono looking back to when he was 20, and remembering his own insecurities: you have to have been there to know what it feels like, to identify with the confusion over self and worth.

Bono sees it as a melodic journey. There is something of Roy Orbison's mini-operas here, with Edge's piano adding to the orchestral flavour. "It's about seeing some people who are ashamed about their bodies," Bono explained, "in particular teenagers with eating disorders, not feeling comfortable with themselves and their sexuality. I'm just saying to them 'you are one of a kind, you're an original of the species'. So it's a 'Be who you are' song. I can't wait to play it live."

Original Of The Species Written: U2 • Duration: 4' 41"

Yahweh

"It just formed in my mouth, as a lot of U2 songs do," Bono explains. "There's the sound, and then trying to figure out what that sound is – and it was this word, 'Yahweh'." It's one of the biggest songs on *How To Dismantle An Atomic Bomb*. "I had this idea that no one can own Jerusalem," Bono said, "but everybody wants to put flags on it." "Yahweh is the name for the Most High," Edge elaborates, "which Jewish people do not utter. It is written, not spoken. It's a sacred name for God, and in this song it's a prayer."

"It's not meant to be spoken," Bono confirms, "but I got around it by singing it. I hope I don't offend anyone."

They recorded it with Chris Thomas, Daniel Lanois came in and added mandolin and they kicked it around with Steve Lillywhite – but eventually went back to the original.

"I played it to Jimmy Iovine of Interscope," Bono recalls, "who loved it up until the point where I told him it's the unspeakable word for God. And he said: 'Call it 'Mozza Balls'. Call it 'Ali'. Call it anything but that!'"

"It's the record company guy," Steve Lillywhite laughs. "It's like the guy who said 'Can you take the bloody out of 'Sunday Bloody Sunday', so that we can get it played on the radio?' That's a true story."

"A delegation came to see me from the Middle East to talk about the fact that there's no peace movement there," Bono reveals, "They asked would I give them a hand, and I said, 'Look, I'm at the point where the world will find it projectile vomit-inducing if I attach my name to another worthy cause.

"The only idea I had," he continues, "is a Festival Of Abraham, which will celebrate the three traditions that call Abraham their father. Out of that conversation there's another project – to build a sort of cathedral of understanding in Europe, called the Eye Of Abraham, where Jews, Muslims and Christians can watch each other worship. The two very inspirational people who are heading up the initiative were opposing negotiators during the Oslo Peace Accord, but are now friends."

It's an initiative for which the widescreen beauty of 'Yahweh' might yet make an appropriate anthem.

Yahweh Written: U2 • Duration: 4' 21"

Fast Cars

They needed an extra track in Japan. It's to do with release dates and the dangers of imported copies – and so it's a tradition with U2 to give their Japanese fans something extra as a kind of bonus for waiting.

So there we were on the last night, thinking, 'There, we've done it, we've got away with it, we've finished the album and there's no madness' and of course Bono walks in and goes let's re-record 'Xanax and Wine'." Steve Lillywhite

The UK and Ireland generally get the benefit – in this instance with the inclusion of 'Fast Cars' on the album release.

They had a track, 'Xanax and Wine', that everyone had agreed should be on the album. They spent weeks on it that turned into months. It gave them the title of the album. *"I'm going nowhere,"* the lyrics ran, *"Where I am it is a lot of fun/ They're in the desert to dismantle an atomic bomb."* That much established, there was a sense of 'fuck it, it has to make the cut' – so they spent some more time on it. And then a little bit more. They had taken it to a stage where it was ready for release – or not – but in the end the band came to the hard conclusion that, like the narrator of the song itself, it was going nowhere. Reluctantly, they decided to ditch it, though it would be used as part of the Apple iTunes Digital Box Set release of every U2 track.

"U2 albums at the end are always mad times," Steve Lillywhite says, "So there we were on the last night, thinking, 'There, we've done it, we've got away with it, we've finished the album and there's no madness' and of course Bono walks in and goes let's re-record 'Xanax and Wine'." Except now he had a new set of lyrics to work with. "Bono can sometimes use the same lines in different songs," Lillywhite adds. "Like, if it doesn't work in one, it might work in another. He likes the couplet, so he'll try to see how it fits into a few songs. So he had this line that had been the chorus of 'Vertigo' at one stage, when it had a different melody: 'I know these fast cars will do me no good'. So that came in handy. It was a bit weird calling a song 'Xanax and Wine' anyway, so we re-arranged it at midnight, that final night, as 'Fast Cars'."

The studio lay-out had been dismantled and so the band all set up around Lillywhite. They began recording at 2am and by 3.30am it was done. They came in the next day, did the vocals and mixed it – and ended up with one of the (extended) album's small gems.

"They're in the desert to dismantle an atomic bomb." Chunks were junked, including the Xanax and wine line, but the atomic reference stayed in. The album title rescued! A good job, well done. Thank you very much, ladies and gentlemen. Have a good night. Nobody even mentioned love.

Fast Cars Written: U2 • Duration: 3' 43"

Close to the edge: Bono and Edge harmonizing – their voices have blended better as the years have gone by.

NO LINE ON THE HORIZON

The original plan had been to work with Rick Rubin. The Edge went to LA and got stuck into some one-on-one sessions with the legendary producer. They picked up the thread with the rest of the band in Abbey Road Studios in London and made 'Window In The Skies', a new track to put on the U218 Singles album, which brilliantly crossed the Beatles, the Stones and David Bowie in a heady pop brew. They also worked up 'The Saints Are Coming', which was to become a collaboration with Green Day for a New Orleans charity, Music Rising. But they weren't sure if this was the direction they needed to take for the follow-up to *How To Dismantle An Atomic Bomb*.

Feel the noise: Although massive in scale, the 360° tour also allowed for acoustic, intimate interludes. Here the band perform 'Stuck in a Moment' in Rome 2010.

Somewhere in there, from all of the sessions, they had uncovered the bones of an otherworldly music that hinted at the Arabic. Bono had been invited for a few years running to the festival of sacred music in Fez, in Morocco. The thought occurred that he should go. Maybe, he said to Edge, they could all take a trip to get out of their comfort zone? "To our surprise, Adam and Larry showed huge enthusiasm for the idea," Edge recalls.

There was a feeling in the camp that this album needed to attempt something audacious, that they should write what Bono had taken to calling 'future hymns'. If there was a reference point it was *Achtung Baby*: masks and characters were back. They'd have to change the rules again, reinvent themselves, make a record that would chart new territory creatively, and sound like nothing they had ever done before. If Berlin had been the catalyst for what many people consider the band's greatest record, then perhaps Morocco could provide the magic spark for their next meisterwork.

They asked long-time producer collaborators Brian Eno and Daniel Lanois to join the expedition, only this time to sit in as part of the songwriting team. The group of six formed a circle in a riad right by the walls of the ancient city, the clear Moroccan skies overhead, and set to work, recording everything. Inspired by the setting, Brian Eno in particular came into his own. There was an atmosphere, an ambience, a spice to what they did that felt like the start of something special, if only they could bottle it! As ever, that would be the hard part...

No Line On The Horizon

It began with Larry. This time his drums served as the notice board, the rhythm he was toying with his statement of intent. It was a kind of Bo Diddley groove and he was nailing it down good. Eno, who was positioned in the station beside him in the studio, sampled it. Now they had a bedrock. The Edge began to improvise over that. It was

Release date: March 2009
Producer: Lanois/Eno
Track listing: No Line On The Horizon/Magnificent/Moment Of Surrender/Unknown Caller/I'll Go Crazy If I Don't Go Crazy Tonight/ Get On Your Boots/Stand Up Comedy/Fez – Being Born/White As Snow/Breathe/ Cedars Of Lebanon
Highest Chart Position: No.1 (UK and US)

coming together, but what did it sound like? Space age rock 'n' roll, Lanois said. Edge, who had become acquainted with Benjamin Curtis, ex- of Secret Machines and now with School of Seven Bells – the man who got him into Death By Audio's latest fuzz pedal – knew exactly what Danny meant and went for it. When he heard the track later, Curtis couldn't believe what the U2 guitarist had done with the pedal on 'No Line...' churning out a grinding rhythm guitar part that Edge himself conceptualised as 21st Century distortion. Eno, in his element, added Germanic Krautrock touches.

The vocal happened early: Bono had lyrics sketched out that seemed to suit. "In my head it happens over 24 hours," he told *Q* magazine. When he gets up at six in the morning to work in his Killiney home, Bono looks out the window across Dublin Bay, over the Irish sea. It's a privileged view and an inspiring one. At times the sea and the sky blend in an otherworldly way that seems to erase the horizon, leaving a vision of infinity, a sense of the immense possibilities of life. But its Zen like qualities notwithstanding, more than anything else 'No Line On The Horizon' is a love song to Ali, for whom the sea becomes a metaphor. *"One day she's still, the next she swells/ You can hear the universe in her sea shells."* Oh oh oh oh oh oh oh oh-o...

No Line On The Horizon • Written: U2/Eno/Lanois • Duration: 4' 12"

Magnificent

Listening to the playback, Bono is excited. The intro sounds like it could be a show-opener. Then the guitar sweeps you back to 1979 and the sound of the fledgling U2. The vocals, too. *"Ooooooh/Oooooh/Oooh"*: a return to *Boy*. Over the exhilarating clamour of Edge's repeat echo, arms pumping as he listens, the singer namechecks The Magnificat – a passage from the Gospel of Saint Luke that was put to music by Bach. "This is our take on that idea," he says, "It's devotional disco. This is a gospel song that transforms into the carnal, then into a song for family, for children."

But that wasn't how it started. Steve Lillywhite came to the album late. "There's a lot of Brian Eno on the album," Lillywhite told PBS radio in the US. "He's an incredible man. His job is to sort of destroy U2. He'll take one of their songs and go off and work on it and erase everything they've done. But then it'll be handed over to me. They bring me in towards the end. What's that baseball person? The closer. That's how they see me. It's like a relay race. I'll come in and add back in some things that were there before and try to make it into some sort of cohesive thing."

The track had originally been called 'French Disco'. It was slower. Not as visceral. Lillywhite encouraged them to work it up a bit. Adam Clayton conjured some Motown-inspired bass, Larry pitched in a sustained drum roll on the extended pause that becomes one of the song's most ingenious hooks, and Edge and Lanois evoked the spirit of Ennio Morricone with the reverb drenched guitars. Then Edge added a beautifully mellifluous slide solo. "It's new U2 because of the wonderful sounds on it," Lillywhite says. "But it also reminds you of old U2."

Magnificent Written: U2/Eno/Lanois • Duration: 5' 24" • US singles chart position: 79

Moment of Surrender

Bono began the album with two words in his head: reverie and revelry. 'Moment of Surrender' was connected to the first part of the equation. The title borrows a term from Alcoholics Anonymous for the moment an addict admits his or her helplessness. For inspiration, Bono could look at Adam, who has been over 10 years on the dry. But the U2 bassist is just one of the many who have had to deal with their demons the hard way. "I've been surrounded a lot in my personal life by addiction," Bono says. The song turns the idea into something broader, however, that simultaneously suggests love, sex, war and religion. It is at once unapologetically modern and dreamily mystical. Bono had played with the phrase "vision over visibility" before; now, he'd found a home for it in a song that is suffused in a kind of meditative, Sufi yearning for selflessness, subtly embroidered with Middle Eastern grace-notes in the melody. Healing music.

It started with a rolling hand-drum pattern courtesy of Eno and Larry Mullen. The song started to emerge in earnest as the final chord sequence, constructed by Eno with appropriate nudges from Edge, took shape. Adam snatched a leaf out of Grandmaster Flash's 'White Lines', before switching to a trancey bass part. In a moment of collective inspiration, the six-piece U2 improvised the entire structure of the song in real time, effectively a first-take backing track that stood proudly, unbelievably intact at the end of the session. "They're supposed to be spiritual," Eno told Rolling Stone about the recording of 'Moment of Surrender'. "They don't spot a miracle when it hits them in the face. Nothing like that ever happened to me in my whole life." It is Lanois' favourite track on the album. "The original sketch had me in charge of the chorus," he says. "Bono would point to me: 'OK, Lanois: you sing the chorus'. It's very much a Canadian sound there, a tribute to The Band." Even more so, it recalls another great Canadian, Neil Young, in the aching use of the major seventh in the final line of the chorus. And at the heart of it, there's a wonderful George Harrison-esque guitar solo, courtesy of Edge.

"Eno was obsessed with 'Moment of Surrender'," Gavin Friday observes. "He wanted it to be the first single." An edited version that dispensed with a verse was hammered into shape and Eno was outraged. He argued passionately for the complete seven minute epic to be included and in the end it was: a soulful masterpiece that Friday describes as "Al Green on Irish steroids, so guttural and so true." A modern rock classic, it will stand forever as one of U2's most inspirational creations.

Moment Of Surrender Written: U2/Eno/Lanois • Duration: 7' 24"

In demand: Adam Clayton pictured in New Jersey in 2009 on the 360° tour. Such was the request for tickets the first time around that the 360° tour had to go back to the US for a second leg two years later.

Unknown Caller

The band was working on 'Unknown Caller' when the birds of Fez shat on Larry Mullen's drums. "It was just one of those great moments," Larry says. "This idyllic place – everything is perfect or close to it. The roof is open. The sun is shining. And suddenly the birds are shitting on you! That suddenly brought us down to reality." It was a moment of surreal humour amid the serious business of making great art. It's an essential part of what U2 do. They find a groove, work a potential song into shape, hammer a few different ideas together, to see if – like the birds – it'll fly. Then they do it again only differently. There were two versions of 'With Or Without You' and the band stayed up in the studio till five in the morning on the final *Joshua Tree* session, trying to figure out which one to go with. They got it right – but what if they had chosen the other one? Sometimes they'll have as many as three or four versions simmering.

The initial surge of creativity on 'Unknown Caller' had been impressive. "It came together in about four hours," Edge says. "It was a live performance and once we had hit the arrangement, we only ever played it once." Towards the end of the recording, when the process of selection was getting intense, Lillywhite came in – a pair of fresh ears. Free of the preciousness of having been involved in the improvisational stage, he saw what needed to be done to make 'Unknown Caller' brilliant. "I thought the drumming needed changing, and so we did that," he says. "And we redid some of the bass as well. I could say 'this is the chorus, but we're not expressing the chorus in the way it should be'." Listening back to a track that unfolds like a piece of choreographed Moroccan soul, Bono hints at echoes of Joy Division. There are elements of Talking Heads too – that Eno had a hand in it is clear. The song's narrator has lost his bearings: "3:33," he recounts, "when the numbers fell off the clock face" – a reference to Jeremiah 33:3 ("Call unto me and I will answer thee and show thee great and mighty things, which thou knowest not"). The song is a conversation, with the protagonist's phone taking on the role of deity, as it offers him instructions on the chorus. The language is borrowed from the world of computers. It is a song about alienation and identity, shot through with grains of optimism. "*Shout for joy/ If you get the chance,*" Bono sings and the massed voices gather on the chorus, in a very male display of togetherness, Greek chorus style: "*Oh oh oh oh/ Oh oh oh oh oh oh oh...*"

The guitar solo delivers a heavy emotional payload. What Gavin Friday describes as "a new age 'Bad'" is, without doubt, another U2 classic.

Unknown Caller Written: U2/Eno/Lanois • Duration: 6' 02"

I'll Go Crazy If I Don't Go Crazy Tonight

The album had been leaning towards reverie. Everyone loved what had been done in Fez and beyond, but as the summer deadline approached it bacame clear that the album was missing something. Where was the revelry? "We needed patience," Edge says. "We went down a few blind alleys before we got songs like 'I'll Go Crazy'." The fifth track, it's the beginning of what Bono calls the *Rubber Soul* section of the record. The title had been just a line in a verse until Will.i.am of Black Eyed Peas got involved. "That line – that's a T-shirt," he told Bono. The singer thought about it. "OK, he said. "I'll make that the song!" He started to see it as this album's 'Beautiful Day' – one of the brighter, more upbeat, tracks that would make a good single (and accompanying T-shirt). The LA rapper helped with putting the original demo together, and was called in later to assist in putting the finishing touches to it, with Steve Lillywhite in charge of production. But ultimately, as the classic pop middle eight – "*Baby, baby, baby/I know I'm not alone*" – confirms, it is essentially a Bono and Ali love song boasting a title that makes you think: it's so right that it's hard to believe that no one ever wrote it before...

Let's go crazy!

I'll Go Crazy If I Don't Go Crazy Tonight Written: U2 • Duration: 4' 13"

Get On Your Boots

They'd gone so far out on the Sufi singing – the ecstatic music – that they had to rein it in. 'I'll Go Crazy' was one counterpoint. 'Get On Your Boots' was another, a shot of shamelessly hedonistic sexy, danceable, night-time electro rock, written by U2 sans Lanois and Eno. It began as a demo recorded on Garageband by Edge. "I put the original version together really fast, playing over a drum loop of Larry's, it sounded like punk Funkadelic," the guitarist says. "At first Brian and Danny hated it. The breakthrough in making it our own was finding the right guitar sound. The fun-fur synth treatment took us into new territory and the Eno hip hop loop gave it some hips."

For Bono there's a hint in there of the Damned, but you can hear the Rolling Stones, the Beatles, T.Rex and Primal Scream in the musical mix, too. It went through a phase with 'Four Letter Word' as the title, before metamorphosing into 'Sexy Boots'. In the end it became 'Get On Your Boots' – at 150bpm, the fastest U2 track ever.

The 'Let me in the sound' chant – delivered in a sort of Lee Dorsey 'Working In A Coalmine' rhythm (Gavin Friday describes it as Happy Mondays on acid) – came late in the process. "It was a chant we all loved," Lanois says and it makes a great additional hook. It's a moment of visceral, horny, carnival pop: yet strangely, according to Bono, it is another earnest love song in disguise, based on a family holiday in France at the start of the war in Iraq when, after a night at the fun fair, husband and wife were lying out under the stars worrying about the rumble of the air force high above them on the way to war. It was the first single release...

Get On Your Boots Written: U2 • Duration: 3' 25" • UK singles chart position: 12 • US singles chart position: 37

Guitar duel: Adam Clayton and The Edge perform in Gelsenkirchen, Germany in August 2009.

The problem was there was no pop song on *No Line on the Horizon.* People say 'Get On Your Boots' was the wrong single, but it's great live. We only figured out how to play it when we were on the road, and it became a much better song."

Bono

Stand Up Comedy

Some of the songs are in character. Not this one. It is Bono having a laugh at himself. "Stand up to rock stars," he sings. "*Napoleon is in high heels/Josephine be careful of small men with big ideas.*" It started as a very Moroccan-influenced rhythmic thing, but gradually took on a more rock 'n' roll character. Lanois remarks that it would be a great study in itself of the evolution of a U2 track – it was about six songs along the way. But it felt too crafted, and so they went in search of soul and found it in a groove where John Lennon meets Led Zeppelin meets David Bowie, with a touch of the Stone Roses thrown in. "What are you going to stand up for?" Bono asks. "What are you going to stand against? I love the idea of standing up to rock stars. Because they're a bunch of megalomaniacs." And what better weapon to use than a huge, barnstorming riff – probably the most powerful in U2's entire history – and, risking a double-entendre, the exhortation to "stand up for your love."

Stand Up Comedy Written: U2 • Duration: 3' 49"

Fez – Being Born

The start of the album's third movement, it's a miniature symphony, in three parts. 'Fez – Being Born' (original working title 'Tripoli') opens like morning, through an exploratory eastern-inflected, painterly sonic squiggle. Edge had a symphonic guitar moment that was 'free time'. Lanois put one of Eno's library of beats to it; now they had something to go on! There was separate high-speed piece they'd been calling 'Being Born': it became the main body of the song, an inspired reworking of an Edge composition that led the band into one of the most original moments on the album. Marrying the two, 'Fez – Being Born' was a feat of genius. "I always look for outstanding transitional moments like that," Lanois says. "They can't be taken for granted. They have to be thought of scientifically."

The lyrics tell the story, in impressionistic strokes, of a Moroccan-French cop who's going AWOL: the lost soul of 'Stay (Faraway, So Close!)' in another gender, time and space continuum. He drives through France and Spain, Bono explains, to Cadiz at the southern tip of Europe, from where you can see the fires of Africa burning. The track shifts a gear as the journey develops, Adam's bass hitting the high notes. With Eno providing Kraftwerkian keyboads, it resolves itself into a chanted unison vocal reminiscent of Talking Heads. As the lyrics recall the emergence of a child from the womb ("*A speeding head, a speeding heart/ I'm being born, a bleeding start/ The engines roar, blood curling wail/ Head first then foot/ Then heart sets sail*") musically it is quite staggeringly beautiful.

Fez – Being Born Written: U2/Eno/Lanois • Duration: 5' 16"

White As Snow

Daniel Lanois was working on a piece with the idea of 'future hymns' in mind. His friend Lori Anna Reid, a singer from Toronto, had begun digging up some spirituals for guidance. "One stood out to me," Lanois told The National Post, "It's an old church hymn called 'Oh Come, Oh Come, Emmanuel'." Dating from the 12th Century, and put to music in the 15th, coincidentally it was recorded by another Irish artist Enya on her *And Winter Came* album. Lanois put down a piano version and found a rhythm. It might have gone nowhere, but when Jim Sheridan asked for a song for his movie about the US war in Afghanistan, Brothers, Bono felt he had things to say on the theme. There was the war itself, the reality of invasion ("*The road refuses strangers/ The land the seeds we sow*") and the sense of desolation it provokes in those unlucky enough to find themselves in the frontline. But the movie is also about the theme of brotherhood. Bono looked at a rough cut and was inspired: with the minor key air Lanois had unearthed in mind, he constructed the story from the perspective of a soldier in Afghanistan, and delved into his own childhood memories of life alongside his elder brother Norman for the lyrics, retaining an optimistic Christian thread ("*Where might we find the lamb/As white as snow?*") in a desolate story.

Edge had been listening to Fleet Foxes, and their CSNY influences, with wonderful harmonies to the fore, crept into a song that harks back to the folk leanings of *Rattle and Hum*. Its inclusion meant that another ballad that Eno loved, entitled 'Winter' was left off: these are the trade-offs that are involved in shaping a U2 record.

White As Snow Written: Traditional/U2/Eno/Lanois • Duration: 4' 41"

Breathe

Musically, this was one that Edge cooked up. Based on the early demo, Eno proclaimed it one of his favourite U2 songs of all time. Chord-wise, it was effectively fully composed before being brought to the sessions. The waltz beat presented interesting problems, and after a few failed attempts at cutting the track, the final version was recorded without fanfare. Bono's scatter-gun vocal suggested a surreal stream-of-consciousness lyrical approach. Two completely different sets of lyrics were completed and Bono and Edge agonised over which to go with during the final recording sessions. One of the lyrics vying for inclusion was about Nelson Mandela.

And the other? Bono had been reading Cormac McCarthy and came up with an impressionistic word painting, rooted in paranoia, and based on the idea of a runic encounter with an enigmatic early morning caller. It was in the mould of Dylan's 'Subterranean Homesick Blues' and RE M's 'E-Bow The Letter', but the lineage goes even further back to the beat poets and Allan Ginsberg's seminal raps, the verses teeming forth in an urgent orgy of colour and detail, observing a world that's busy turning itself upside down.

The song takes place on Bloomsday, 16 June – the day on which James Joyce set his Dublin masterpiece Ulysses. But the character at the heart of it – a Bono alter-ego if ever there was one ("*Coming from a long line of travelling salespeople on my mother's side*") – ultimately finds redemption.

The band re-recorded it and Steve Lillywhite provided the finishing touches. "What have they done to the Fez version?" Eno asked. Turned it into a monster, that's what!

Breathe Written: U2/Eno/Lanois • Duration: 5' 00"

Cedars of Lebanon

Of all the characters on *No Line On The Horizon*, the journalistic narrator of 'Cedars of Lebanon' is the most clearly drawn. "I'd just kind of got worn out with my own biography," Bono says. "The last two albums were very personal. The irony, of course, as Oscar Wilde taught us, is that the mask reveals the man."

From Sarajevo to El Salvador to Addis Ababa, Bono has spent time with the men and women who deliver the news from the frontline, and so he feels an unusual empathy with them. Danny Lanois got the musical inspiration for the mood of the song from a piece he and Eno had done back in the 1980s with an artist by the name of Harold Budd. "It's really thick with ambience," he says. But the track fully kicked into life when Larry came in with a killer drum part. "I've a deep conviction that were I not doing what I'm doing now, I'd be doing what you are," Bono told Olaf Tyaransen of *Hot Press*. "I'd probably be writing about music and art and all my other interests, but I can imagine I'd also find myself in very unsafe places because that's my tendency."

It is a powerful song, rich in observation and detail that reminds us of what rock stars and war correspondents might have in common ("I'm here 'cos I don't want to go home.") There is a lot of Bono and U2 in the portrait of the journalist, not least – as Bono has acknowledged – in the closing verse: "*Choose your enemies carefully 'cos they will define you/ Make them interesting 'cos in some ways they will mind you/ They're not there in the beginning but when your story ends/ Gonna last longer with you than your friends.*"

But 'Cedars of Lebanon' is a less than veiled criticism too of the war in Iraq. "I think of all the energy that went into that," he told *Rolling Stone's* Brian Hiatt, "and the bravery of the men and women who served, and I think of what those resources could have achieved, if only the lives of the poorest of the poor were as valuable as the idea of bringing democracy to the desert." Amen to that.

Cedars Of Lebanon Written: U2/Eno/Lanois • Duration: 4' 16"

Weapon of choice: Bono uses the microphone to spread peace, love and unity.

SONGS OF INNOCENCE

Shaken by the response to *No Line on the Horizon*, the band took more than five years coming up with their new album. It was released quietly with just family, friends and 500 million people getting to hear it at the same time.

Songs of Ascent was Bono's idea. It had been imagined as a companion piece, and follow-up, to *No Line On The Horizon*. Gorillaz and Gnarls Barkley man Danger Mouse, aka Brian Burton, was drafted in as producer. They did some solid work on songs that had been left over from the earlier sessions, but gradually everyone felt it: they weren't getting lift-off.

There's a moment when you know something isn't working. The way U2 operate, you can always pick up the thread later. Time to move on, to pursue a different line of enquiry. Besides, there was another idea that was starting to feel more urgent. Bono had gotten seriously into William Blake as far back as 1987 when U2 were making *The Joshua Tree*. He'd first mooted *Songs of Innocence and Experience* as an idea in 1992. They wouldn't have been ready for it then. The thought had been simmering away though. Maybe they were now.

The notion of tunnelling back to the days before U2 sprang into life appealed to him. He'd been thinking about Dublin. Where they'd come from. What it had meant to him. How it had shaped the band. All they really couldn't leave behind. What they might learn about themselves now by exploring those early, uniquely tumultuous times and asking: what the fuck happened to you? "We have to have very good reasons to put out a new U2 album," he'd said. "There are 150 million of them out there. Why would anyone want another one?" In some ways, the response to *No Line on the Horizon* had felt like a slap on the cheek. If they were going to make another record, he wanted – they all wanted – to be sure that it'd be a great one. That it'd be airborne. That it'd fly, hopefully in more ways than one.

Conceptually, *Innocence and Experience* would work best as two albums. That way, U2 would get to mirror what Blake had done, issuing *Songs of Innocence* first, and then addressing similar themes with the benefit of hard-won wisdom – or not as the case might be – in *Songs of Experience*. In 2012, my partner-in-crime, Máirín Sheehy of *Hot Press* went to meet Bono. The magazine had a U2 book in mind. Bono saw the connection. He outlined his burgeoning plans for the album. Suggested we make the book about the early days. Do it as a U2.com special. Time it just ahead of the album release – it'd set the scene. We got stuck in and *U2: North Side Story* was the result. The album took a little bit longer, but that's how it goes.

Bono's affinity with William Blake was clear. Spirituality. A deep interest in the bible. Scepticism about organized religion. A passion for social justice. An abiding fascination with words and images. A love of nature. An awareness that we've got to free ourselves – of, among other things, the mind-forged manacles depicted in Blake's 'London' – in order to be ourselves. Danger Mouse, Declan Gaffney, Paul Epworth, Ryan Tedder and Flood all put their shoulder to the wheel. Edge, Adam and Larry were seriously revved up. Gradually the base metal of the idea was, like the copper in Blake's etchings, transformed into the imaginative currency of art, into the stardust of songs.

There was another question looming large. How best to embrace the digital revolution and the fact that, by late 2014, album sales were in terminal decline. It seemed like an inspired idea when someone suggested hooking up with Apple. It'd be the ultimate partnership deal. Apple would pay a sizeable chunk of change for the opportunity to make a present of a digital version of the new U2 album to everyone with an iTunes account. It would, as Apple CEO Tim Cook put it, be the biggest album launch in history.

It sparked huge controversy. A lot of people said no thanks. What had seemed like a win-win scenario instead became a major bone of contention, with U2 bashers spitting nails about corporate collusion. But when the band went out on the road for the iNNOCENCE + eXPERIENCE Tour, a huge number of people including lots of young ones who'd never seen U2 before, knew the songs inside out. Maybe it hadn't been such a bad idea after all...

The Miracle (of Joey Ramone)

The punk explosion erupted in 1976 in New York – and at the forefront of that musical revolution were The Ramones. Famously dumb by choice, the alleged brothers made a gleefully simplistic racket on songs, which – by law! – could never exceed two minutes and 35 seconds. All fourteen tracks on their eponymous debut totaled an exquisitely economical 29 minutes and four seconds.

In Dublin, the ground started to shift in earnest in 1977, when The Clash played Trinity College. But the ninth month of 1978 would come to be remembered as a seminal moment nonetheless. On September 9, the Stranglers played the Top Hat in Dun Laoghaire. The support act was a fledgling outfit from the north side of Dublin, who had begun to trade under the oddly hyphenated name U-2. Legend has it that, on

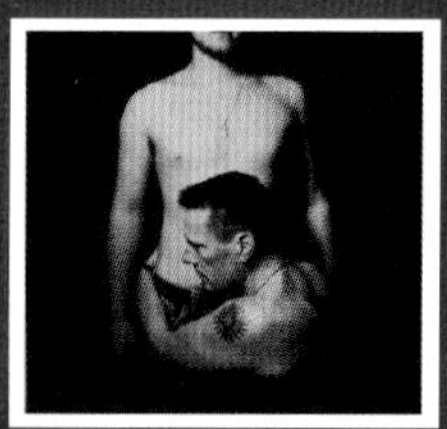

Release date: September 2014
Producer: Danger Mouse, Paul Epworth, Ryan Tedder, Declan Gaffney, Flood
Track listing: The Miracle (of Joey Ramone), Every Breaking Wave California (There is No End to Love), Song For Someone, Iris (Hold Me Close), Volcano, Raised by Wolves, Cedarwood Road, Sleep Like a Baby Tonight, This is Where You Can Reach Me Now, The Troubles, Lucifer's Hands (Deluxe edition), The Crystal Ballroom (Deluxe edition)
Highest Chart position: No. 6 (UK), 9 (US)

the night, certain members of U2 attempted to prevail on Jean Jacques Burnel of the Stranglers to wear a U-2 promotional button badge. Someone should have warned them that it was not the kind of thing the notoriously belligerent Burnel was likely to embrace. He refused point blank. In response, it has been passed down in local rock lore, Bono, Adam, The Edge and Larry decided to misappropriate the wine that was in the headliner's dressing room. At *Hot Press*, we always suspected that the real culprit was our man, Bill Graham, who was there with U2 on the night, and was rather fonder of a good red than anyone in the band. Either way, fisticuffs were threatened and the Irish fab four had to beat a hasty retreat, mildly disillusioned at least by the rebuff from these representatives of the swaggering UK punk rock hierarchy.

By 1978, most of us knew The Ramones schtick inside out and were well aware that it was far from swaggering these stick insects were reared. Thus, when their first-ever Irish gig was announced for 24 September, the imperative was obvious: you had to be there. Not every aspiring musician could afford a ticket, of course, but there were ways and means. "We had no tickets and no money," Bono recalls. "Guggi let us in through a side exit he prised open. Even though we only saw half the show, it became one of the great nights of our life."

Almost 40 years later, Bono remembers the gig as a revelation. There was the basis of a song in it. "I found my voice through Joey Ramone," he recalls. "I wasn't the obvious punk rock singer, or even rock singer. I sang like a girl – which I'm into now, but at 17 or 18, I wasn't so sure. But when I heard Joey Ramone, who sang like a girl, that was my way in."

Sky lines: U2 play their first new single in five years, 'Invisible', live on *The Tonight Show* in New York, February 2014.

Globe trotters: The band after receiving a Golden Globe award for their song 'Ordinary Love' in January 2014.

"I was young/not dumb," 'The Miracle of Joey Ramone' goes, *"just wishing to be blinded/By you, brand new/And we were pilgrims on the way."*

Pilgrims is a good word.

"When I was standing in the State Cinema," Bono riffs, "listening to Joey sing, and realizing that there was nothing else that mattered to him, pretty soon nothing else mattered to me. The Ramones were the best punk rock band ever, because they actually invented something."

For The Edge, in the process of looking back, acknowledging the band's influences was important. But *Songs of Innocence* was never going to descend into pastiche.

"We listened to the music of that time (again) really to remind ourselves of the milieu, and what was the soundtrack of that particular moment in our lives, both personally and as the band," Edge recalls. "We didn't set out to make an 'homage' album, by any means. What we kind of bumped into was the unbelievable life-force and vitality of that era of music. And, lo and behold, also some amazing songwriting – like The Buzzcocks. Fantastic melodies and really interesting work. The Ramones, also. So, that was inspiring. But *Songs of Innocence* is not in any way an attempt to recreate the sound of that time."

"The Ramones," Bono says, "were the beginning of something new. They stood for the idea of making your limitations work for you. This was a really important moment, because suddenly imagination was the only obstacle to overcome."

It was a stance that U2 – or rather U-2 – adopted with a reformer's zeal. Imagination was the only obstacle. It was a philosophy that would serve them very well indeed.

The Miracle (Of Joey Ramone) Written: U2 • Duration: 4' 16"

Every Breaking Wave

A figure dressed all in black walks along the beach in Killiney, on the eastern edge of a well-to-do enclave on the south coast of Dublin. He is wearing light shades to protect eyes that suffer from glaucoma. The wind is blowing hard to the extent that his eyes water. Beneath his feet, tellingly clad in pointy rock 'n' roll shoes, is the crunch of sea-shells breaking. There are moments when the water rushes in around his feet and he dances around the white foam and laughs. Doing his best to be normal, which of course in so many ways he is.

Even staring through the window of his house, which overlooks the beach from the hill above, Bono's eyes are drawn to the horizon. On a hazy day, that line retreats into obscurity. He often wishes that he could replicate that particular trick, but it isn't an option.

Still, when the mood takes him, and the coast is clear, the U2 singer slips down past the bottom of the garden. It is hard to resist the lure of the nearby sea, and the comforting sounds that roll on endlessly, through the day and night there, the plash and suck of water on sand and shingle. On a wilder day, watching the waves advance, crash and retreat, with a mineral fizz and gurgle, he is drawn inevitably back to childhood. We have all, or most of us anyway, danced along the shoreline as kids, and like the pull of the moon, the memory runs deep. There is a song playing in his head as he walks, which seems to fit the oceanic theme of album-in-the-making, *No Line On the Horizon*, but the shape and heft of it remain elusive.

It has ever been thus. U2 get an idea for a song. They kick it around, press it into service, get a narrative arc sorted, mould it a bit more, and figure they have it nailed – well, almost. There is inevitably more work to be done, and the problem is that no one knows precisely how much. 'Every Breaking Wave' was meant to land on *No Line On The Horizon* as the autumn of 2009 turned to winter. It was Jimmy Iovine's favourite track as the finishing touches were being put to that record, but Coldplay's Chris Martin heard it and insisted it wasn't finished. Better to keep it for later. The band agreed and it was shelved.

At the time, the intention was to follow through quickly with an album that had the working title *Songs of Ascent*. In the end, heaven could wait. Life got in the way. *No Line On the Horizon* may have been one of U2's least successful albums commercially, but the accompanying 360° Tour went on to become the most lucrative live show in the history of rock 'n' roll. U2 played a stripped-back version of 'Every Breaking Wave' during the tour, only to realise that a bit of extra polishing would be needed. When they kicked into working on *Songs of Innocence*, it was one of the sketches that appealed most to producer Ryan Tedder. But there was, he figured, something awry with the structure.

Tedder played around with it. There were lyrics that lacked flow. *"After every peak, the trough/ I can feel the energy drop/ Will we ever know when to stop/ With this chasing every breaking wave,"* Bono sang. This was hardly Bono, the lyricist, at his most eloquent. A different consideration was weighing on Bono's own mind: that the song shouldn't ring too finally of despair. And besides, those lines sounded rather ominously as if they were about U2's own ongoing dilemma: will we ever know when to stop? All Bono knew for sure was that this wasn't the moment for that.

What had been the chorus of the song was shifted to become the bridge. Ryan Tedder then got stuck into what was the crucial task: defining what the new chorus might sound like. The repetition of lines gave it an emotional weight: *"If you go/ If you go your way and I go mine/ Are we so/Are we so helpless against the tide..."*. With Tedder playing devil's advocate, The Edge and Bono created a new melody, and left the final line hanging, on what feels like a kind of suspended 4th, adding to the slightly uncanny, circular modus operandi of the track.

On the surface, it was a love song of sorts: Bono explained that it was about the difficulty of giving yourself completely to another person. The characters in the song are addicted to failure, prompting the question on which the entire edifice hangs: *"Are we ready to be swept off our feet/ and stop chasing/Every breaking wave?"* But these songs are seldom rigidly about one idea – and the more I listened to 'Every Breaking Wave', the more it reminded me of 'One'. Ostensibly a straightforward love song, I understood it also as being about relationships within U2, the chorus hinging on the kind of question that the members of a band that has been around for 40 years, more or less, inevitably ask of one another.

There is a tendency for groups, in their search for continuing relevance, to cast around for new influences that might help to immunise them against the threat of sounding dated. Having concluded that *No Line On the Horizon* had missed the mark by some distance, U2 were convinced that they needed fresh inspiration. The decision to work with a variety of producers was in part at least a product of that quest for new fire. Curiously, however, in the end, 'Every Breaking Wave' functions like an antidote to all of that. It is a classic U2 ballad, and the chorus reveals the insecurity that is often at the heart of great art. This, Bono genuinely believed as he crafted the lyrics, was the song, which might sweep U2 fans all over the world off their feet. But finding the essence of its potential would involve the band going back to more traditional values. The end result is a beautiful song, sung purely and without contrivance.

"I can't even begin to tell you what it's like to sing that song," Bono said at the time of the album release. "You have to steel yourself. A funny thing happened today, because we performed the song in the studio for whoever – and then had to do a few interviews, but the wounds are still open and so I got quite messy in the interview. There was a few black eyes, and I found myself quite raw and emotional on a few things – because that song had done that to me. So it's not something you can put on and off very easily. A lot of the songs on this album are like that..."

Maybe. But none are quite as rich and emotionally powerful as 'Every Breaking Wave'. It really is a U2 classic, the equal of anything the band had recorded since 1979.

Every Breaking Wave Written: U2 • Duration: 4' 12"

California (There Is No End To Love)

If anyone had suggested back in 1979, when *Hot Press* first put U2 on the cover, that the band would record a song that sounds like a tribute to the Beach Boys, there would have been no end to the laughter. Back in those determinedly obscurantist days, the very concept of musicianship was routinely sneered at. Was there a better musician on Planet Pop than Brian Wilson? It's doubtful. To their eternal credit, unlike so many of their post-punk contemporaries, U2 realised that, if they kept their eyes and their ears open, they were more likely to learn, and grow. Doubtless, on some sub-conscious level at least, Bono, Adam, Larry and The Edge were aware of the series of extraordinary records that the Beach Boys unleashed through the 1960s, almost as if by routine. The pinnacle was probably 'God Only Knows' or 'Good Vibrations' – but there was a sweet, masculine innocence about the surf-pop songs that were their early to mid-'60s stock-in-trade.

The opening line of 'California (There Is No End To Love)' reaches into that less recondite, formative terrain, evoking in particular the magnificent simplicities of 'Barbara Ann' – remarkably, the Beach Boys' fifth single of 1965. Further on, there is a reference to Zuma, which brings to mind both Neil Young, who was at the heart of the neo-hippy singer songwriter movement of the late '60s and early '70s – and whose *Zuma* album is regarded as one of his finest; and the Rolling Stones, who reference Zuma in their classic single 'Some Girls' (itself a nod to the Beach Boys 'California Girls', also from 1965).

Ostensibly, 'California (There Is No End To Love)' is about U2's first ever trip to the US, and the sheer exhilaration they felt when they finally hit the west coast. "I remember Edge, Adam, Larry and me getting off a plane in California and looking at each other like 'this is better than the movies' and that was just the airport," Bono said in the liner notes for *Songs of Innocence*. But, in a way, surely that was just a decoy. 'California' is really about the need that U2 felt to strike out beyond the limitations of being from Dublin. "*Everyone's a star in our town,*" Bono sings, not about Hollywood, but about his own place. "*It's just your light gets dimmer/If you have to stay/In your bedroom, in a mirror/Watching*

U2 LP: The surprise dramatic release of *Songs of Innocence* at an Apple event in Cupertino, California on 9 September 2014.

yourself cry like a baby." It is a line reminiscent of the Animals: we gotta get out of this place, if it's the last thing we ever do.

"It's like the sun itself," Bono says of the song. "The whole album is first journeys – first journeys geographically, spiritually, sexually. And that's hard. But we went there. It's about our first trip to Los Angeles." It feels joyous, in a summery, Beach Boys kinda way, but it has its moments of despair too. *"California, blood orange sunset brings you to your knees,"* Bono sings. *"I've seen for myself/There's no end to grief."* The 'I've seen for myself' is crucial. Bono is thinking about his mother, Iris, and the way in which her loss, and the grief that surrounded it, inspired him – not just to become an artist, but also to believe. In a song about California, you might conclude that the hippie spirit ultimately prevails. *"Whoa,"* Bono croons, *"Oh, all I know/All I need to know is/ There is no, yeah/ There is no end to love."* But really, 'California (There Is No End To Love)' is another U2 song about love as a higher law.

California (There Is No End To Love) Written: U2 • Duration: 4' 00"

Song For Someone

Ryan Tedder pushed Bono and The Edge to create a new melody for the chorus in 'Every Breaking Wave'. That was what the band wanted from the One Republic man. "The popsters are beating the others on melody," Bono told *Q* magazine. "They're writing better tunes. When Brian Burton (Danger Mouse) ran out of time to work with us, we got to work with Paul Epworth and Ryan Tedder. Their only interest is in melody that you haven't heard before, and the uniqueness of it. So that changed the game for us."

It isn't a bad starting point for a songwriter who wants to write a standard. 'Song For Someone' certainly sounds like Bono having a stab at that particular songwriting holy grail and Ryan Tedder made a good foil. It is the U2 singer's umpteenth song to his muse and the love of his life Ali – though in this instance he was going back to where it all started. "More first journeys," Bono scrawled in the liner notes, "...sex... note to songwriting self: when dealing with this subject – must. try. harder."

That is both right and wrong. There are aspects of the lyrics, which might have been finessed more effectively, for sure. But the chorus is a thing of real beauty that wants to be sung by a stadium-full of fans: in the context, it's no surprise that the song was performed every night, throughout the iNNOCENCE + eXPERIENCE Tour.

Bono recalls meeting Ali at the age of fourteen. "She agreed for me to take her out on a date in the same month I joined U2," he recalls. "The north coast of Dublin has dunes that are as unknowable as any great beauty, and is home to seaside towns that are even more beautiful in the winter... when a young man might bring his girl to (re)visit the scene of his summer crimes."

What happens on the occasion of the epoch-making 'first time' is never made entirely explicit in the song itself, but that it took a powerful hold is made abundantly clear. *"You let me in to a conversation,"* Bono sings to his young lover, *"A conversation only we could make/ You break and enter my imagination/ Whatever's in there it's yours to take."*

Of course, nothing is ever as simple as Bono tries to make it sound. The chorus isn't just thing of beauty; it's songwriting-smart too, in that it enables any woman to become its subject, making it the kind of song that could be hauled out on *American Idol* or covered 250 times by acts of any genre. Up to a point. That potential mass appeal is tested on the final verse, when – in that familiar U2 way – the line between sex and spirituality becomes blurred. *"And I'm a long way from your Hill of Calvary,"* he sings, *"And I'm a long way from where I was and where I need to be."*

The image of Jesus dying on the cross casts a long shadow, giving a different meaning to the exhortation: *"And there is a light/ don't let it go out."* No matter. In the long run, the pull of the secular was stronger here, in Bono's mind at least. To have found someone with whom he could share the highs and the lows through the kind of crazy life he has led, and Ali in her own way with him, is surely some fine kind of achievement.

"There've been times when it would have been sensible for either of us to go our own way," he reflects, "but we have not and we are not (sensible)... when it comes to song-writing, not sensible is almost as good as a broken heart and far more romantic than a full one."

'Song For Someone' bears rich testimony to that.

Song For Someone Written: U2 • Duration: 3' 43"

Iris (Hold Me Close)

Some themes, writers are drawn back to, like the proverbial fly to the light. They become a kind of obsession. And Bono knows it. "The mother is so, so important in rock music," he has said. "Show me a great singer and I'll show you someone who lost their mother early on. There's Paul McCartney. There's John Lennon. Look at Bob Geldof and what happened to his mother. In hip-hop, it's all about the father – being abandoned by the father and being brought up by a single mother. But for me, it's all about the mother."

We have been here before. The lyrics of 'I Will Follow', 'Another Day', 'Tomorrow', 'Lemon' and 'Mofo' were inspired, to one degree or another, by the loss of Bono's mother, Iris Hewson (nee Rankin), when the U2 singer was just 14 years of age. The circumstances must have deepened the psychic wounds: Iris collapsed at her own father's funeral, struck down by a cerebral aneurysm. She died two days later. That double loss is a cross that he has borne ever since. But even as his world was falling apart, something else began to come together.

"That was September 1974," Bono recalls. "And that's when I met my future wife, Ali. I didn't date her for a few years, but I saw her. And the song deals with some kind of transference of the female energy – because the way I would look at women, from that point on, was forever changed."

It was inevitable, in the construction of an album, like *Songs of Innocence*, which was designed to delve into the origin of the U2 species, that Bono would want – would need – to find a way of paying tribute to his mother. He had written 'Iris', but was riddled with doubt about whether it was good enough; and whether, in any event, it should even be allowed into the frame, to compete for a place. Then he read a letter written by James Foley, the American journalist who had been taken hostage in 2012 by ISIS and murdered two years later – beheaded in a grisly spectacle played out before the cameras for noxious propaganda effect. The journalist's heart-breaking missive was delivered, by another prisoner, to the family of James Foley. In it, James said the most poignant thing to his brother. "I remember," he wrote, "playing werewolf in the dark with you." It is a line that must have crushed his brother's heart. Gently. "I realised," Bono said later of the letter, "that we will be remembered by the least profound moments. The simplest moments."

'Iris' has been described as perhaps the most excruciatingly personal song in U2's history. That is to do it a huge disservice. In truth, it derives its unique power and beauty from the deeply personal backstory that drives it.

"I did think about whether it should be on the album or not," Bono confirms, "and three, four days after we finished the album, I thought it shouldn't. Even though the song is a beautiful tune, and everything, I just thought it was going a bit far and it's not very punk rock, singing about your mother."

Life was about to get even more complicated.

"Here's a wild thing," he confesses. "Two days before we were going to launch this album – and, indeed, this song – out there into the universe, I woke up feeling embarrassed about the song. And I thought: 'It's too late'. And I started to think back: how long was this ago? Why is this important? Oh god, this is 40 years ago. I really hadn't thought of that. I really hadn't. I was thinking: what date was it that it happened? I texted my brother. He didn't know! It's very Irish, in that we don't talk about things like that. We never talked about my mother, which is why I don't have many memories of her. So he didn't know either. I texted my uncle Jack – and he came back with, 'She collapsed at the grave of her father as he was being lowered into the ground on the 8th of September'. Which was the day I had texted my brother. Two days later, her spirit passed on. And on that day, we were putting this song out into the universe. I thought: that's amazing. What a blessing. I'm not superstitious, and the idea that my mother is looking at me, I just hope it's not true – because she would have seen some terrible stuff that I've been up to over the years! I'd be reeeeally embarrassed (laughs). But it was a beautiful cosmic rhyme."

What might have happened if Iris hadn't died? Could she have exerted a different kind of control that would have channeled Bono's creative energies down a more conventional route? We can never know, but there is a distinct sense that Bono feels he might never have become what he is, if his mother had lived; that he owes his success to her death.

"I sing this verse," he says, "which has the line: '*Iris standing in the hall, she tells me I can do it all*'. And then there's a typical mother's line, when she says to me: '*You'll be the death of me*'. It's a big moment, at puberty: you're just discovering girls, and this woman who brought you into the world leaves you, abandons you. And you think it's your fault, because that's something that kids do."

There is a sense in which he is trying to close the circle, to make sense of that contradiction.

"*A boy tries hard to be a man/ His mother takes him by the hand*," he sang in 'I Will Follow', on U2's first album *Boy*. Here that memory is sifted again, with different results. "*You took me by the hand*," he sings, "*I thought that I was leading you*."

The memories flood in.

"*Iris playing on the strand*," he lilts, bringing us back into close proximity with the waves chasing one another along the shore in 'Every Breaking Wave'. "*She buries the boy beneath the sand/ Iris says I'll be the death of her/ It was not me*."

It is a phrase he repeats, as if he needs to convince himself: "It was not me."

"I wasn't the death of her," he says now, and pauses, before repeating it (again). "I was not the death of her. I have very few memories of my mother, but all of them are in the song 'Iris'."

Live, on the iNNOCENCE + eXPERIENCE Tour, the yellow dress that inspired 'Lemon' was seen in the wonderful accompanying video imagery, Iris herself running around the garden in a fairground flourish. It was a stunning tour-de-force: an extraordinary rendition of one of the greatest songs ever in the U2 canon. Finally, Bono had truly hit the motherlode.

Iris (Hold Me Close) Written: U2 • Duration: 5' 20"

Volcano

Has there ever been a U2 album that wasn't stuck together in the end with God's glue – or even with a roll of gaffer tape or sticking plaster? Bono jokes that if The Edge were in charge they'd still be mixing *The Joshua Tree*. Larry doesn't really think that's funny. All the messing around in the studio can sometimes get on the drummer's nerves: Bono making lyrics up on the mic as the clock ticks down; three different producers doing remixes of tracks that, a few weeks ago, had definitely, definitely, definitely been finished; someone else adding keyboards to a different track, in a faraway studio, on a separate continent entirely. Always the same old shit. In another time, Adam might have got a bit angsty too, but now he puts his Zen hat on and shrugs. Life will take its course. What's the point in getting uptight?

Hallelujah! A finished version of *Songs of Innocence* was delivered a week before its official release date – which, of course, was scheduled for that moment of shock and awe, when Apple would make a gift of it to everyone who had an iPhone. "Then we ended up having a bit of a crisis. The 10-track record was sounding a little bit lopsided," The Edge says. He grimaces.

"And so we added 'Volcano' at the end. The reason why it wasn't in the shuffle originally was because the cut-off date arrived and it was like, 'Well, we can't have it on the album. It's not finished. It's not done." Larry was okay with that.

Not that piffling concerns like being finished on time had ever stopped U2 before. And they didn't this time either. "We managed to convince Apple to give us a few more days," The Edge adds, with the hint of a grin, "and in that couple of days, we finished 'Volcano' and it made the cut. It balanced the album out in a great way."

The opening line suggests that we might be about to be treated to a reprise of 'Out of Control'. "*The world is spinning fast tonight*," Bono sings, before getting down to brass tacks. "*You can hurt yourself tryin' to hold on/ To what you used to be*." And then the sucker punch: "*I'm so glad the past is all gone*."

A song with a single-word title in the tradition of 'Elevation' and 'Vertigo', and with similar priapic inclinations, it is about a different realm of vulnerability.

"*Volcano, you don't wanna, you don't wanna know*," the frontman shrieks, while The Edge scrawls his rock 'n' roll graffiti in the margins. "*Volcano/ Something in you wants to blow/ Volcano, you don't wanna, you don't wanna know/ You're a piece of ground above a volcano*." It isn't a question of if, but rather when, there'll be an explosion.

"When I ask Mullen," Bono told the *Guardian*, "if he remembers the teenage Bono as the cannonball of fury and grief portrayed in 'Volcano',

We went back to the very beginning to ask ourselves why did we form U2 in the first place and what [does] the band still mean to us today? We went home to Dublin for the answers." Bono

the drummer instantly replies: 'That's the guy I know now'." You can imagine Larry winking at the camera.

"I owe Iris," Bono says of his mother. "Her absence, I filled with music. After grief comes rage... the molten lava that turns to rock if it can. This kind of fire in the belly cannot sustain. If you're lucky, it burns out. Before it burns you out..." So far, he has gotten away with it. Just about.

Volcano Written: U2 • Duration: 3' 15"

Raised By Wolves

17.28. Parnell Street, Dublin. 17 May, 1974. A metallic green 1970 Hillman Avenger, hijacked in Belfast that morning, explodes. Had those responsible for manufacturing the car bomb chosen the vehicle for its name? A ball of flame scorches its way across the road. An Austin Mini is slung onto the path at right angles. Shattered glass is fired through the bruised air. Amid the hurtling cars, the falling debris and the apocalyptic flames, there is human debris too, bodies flung into the air, some of them their last breath gone. Ten people are dead, among them a veteran of World War I.

17.30. Talbot Street. Outside Guiney's venerable department store, a Ford Escort, registration number 1385 WZ, stolen that morning in the Docks area of Belfast, goes BOOM. The air is compressed furiously. A blast wave races through the evening light. Heat and fire erupt spontaneously. A head is sent flying, ripped from the neck that has supported it since birth. An arm lies on the street, covered in glass shards. Four bodies are strewn on the pavement outside Guiney's. A dozen people stone dead. Two more will drift away over the coming days. Unlucky 13 women gone.

17.32. South Leinster Street. Hijacked in Belfast earlier in the day, an Austin 1800, registration number HOI 2487 explodes. Just around the corner is Leinster House where the Irish parliament, Dáil Éireann, sits. Two women are blown to kingdom come. There are dozens injured.

18.58. Monaghan town, close to the border with Northern Ireland. A 1966 Hillman Minx, stolen in Portadown that day and parked outside Greacen's pub, explodes. Five people are killed on the spot. Two more die over the coming days. The bomb does its job, distracting security forces just when those responsible for the Dublin bombs were approaching the border on the road taking them back into Northern Ireland.

The working assumption was that these four co-ordinated explosions were carried out by Loyalist paramilitaries. But, we would later discover, the British Army were involved too, providing both the bombing expertise and the support mechanisms required to mount what was the greatest atrocity of the entire Long War in Ireland. The death count on 17 May 1974 was the highest ever, during the entire history of the Troubles.

"On any other Friday, at 5.30pm, in 1974, I would have been on Talbot Street in a record shop," Bono recalls. "On May 17th, I rode my bike to school – and dodged one of the bloodiest moments in a history that divided an island."

Many were not so fortunate. In addition to those who died – twenty-five in Dublin alone – there were dozens more scarred and maimed badly. With others, the wounds were less visible. Among these was Andy Rowen, brother of Bono's best friend Guggi. "Gus Pants Delaney, we used to call him," Bono remembers. "He was locked in his father's van as his father ran to help save the victims, scattered like refuse across the streets. The scene never left him. He turned to one of the world's great painkillers to deal with it. We wrote about him in our song 'Bad'." Now they were writing about him again. Which wasn't easy for a man of faith like Bono. *"Blood in the house/ Blood in the street,"* he sings, *"The worst things in the world/ are justified by belief/ I don't believe anymore."* This was much more than a political statement.

"'Raised By Wolves', like a lot of the songs on the album, is about personal experience," The Edge says. "It's about an event that we ourselves felt the impact of – acutely – at the time. Larry lost a neighbour in the bombing on Talbot Street. That street is where my bus stop was. We'd have been in town often, trying to get the bus home, and Bono just saying, you know, 'Literally, right there'. We really felt that... We're not drawing from it as simply reflecting a moment in history: it's part of our personal narrative."

In terms of the iNNOCENCE + eXPERIENCE show, it represented a challenge: could they, would they, play the song in Belfast?

"Bono and I wrote it together," The Edge told *Hot Press* at the time. "It's written from Andrew's perspective. We want to maintain the show and we don't want to start taking out key things. What we want to do, is to be sensitive. We always are. It's going to be very interesting, not only playing Belfast, but playing in Dublin because, of course, the album is very personal. It name-checks a lot of people and places in the city."

Bono had come to the conclusion that looking back – in anger or otherwise – was a grim and chastening experience.

"It was very disturbing," he confessed, "to realise that my teenage life was largely dominated by memories of violence and that my worldview was shaped by that. It might mean some sort of psychological flaw in me, but I feel most comfortable in the middle of the biggest, noisiest, most chaotic, howling argument."

Often, it has to be said, with himself.

Raised By Wolves Written: U2 • Duration: 4' 06"

Cedarwood Road

It started with a riff. The Edge at work on GarageBand, tinkering over a Larry drum loop. Threads woven into the beginning of a fabric. A demo of sorts. The process is a familiar one for the band. Characteristically, The Edge won't push the pattern too far. He wants to kick an idea into just the beginning of a shape. Create, maybe, a vital kind of energy. Establish momentum. The purpose, then, is to inspire the rest of the band. Collectively they'll do a better job than the guitarist on his own. Or that is the credo at least.

The intro came from the band working together. They hammered a chorus into shape. They recorded an early version of it, but the lyrics weren't what the album needed. Bono went back to the drawing board. From 'Sunny Googe Street' to 'Warwick Avenue', and dozens more, songs about streets have resonated through different rock 'n' roll eras: why couldn't U2 write one? Why shouldn't they? 'Cedarwood Road' might not seem like the most promisingly musical name, but it was an essential part of the story that *Songs of Innocence* set out to tell. Bono grew up there. So too did his best buddies Gavin Friday and Guggi. It was a relatively new suburb back then. The large families, which predominated in Ireland at the time, meant lots of teenagers coming to adulthood more or less simultaneously. The arrival of clans from the inner city, re-housed just up the road in the seven towers of the Ballymun flats added a harder edge to the local youthful truculence. If you were different at all, you became a target. The skinhead gangs of the mid-seventies enjoyed a rumble. Someone like Gavin Friday, flirting with teenage gender fluidity, or Guggi with his long hair and feminine physique, were obvious targets. There was a dog-eat-suburban-dog aspect to it all. Equally an outsider in his own stray way, Bono stood foursquare with his mates. All the while, behind the closed doors of pebble-dashed estates across Dublin, the grim realities of family life – as well as the joys – were hidden, but not unknown. It was a great place to grow up, and a terrible one.

"A lot of my early memories of teenage years were of violence," Bono told Hrishikesh Hirway, the musician and composer behind the *Song Exploder* podcast, "and the sheer fear of leaving the house, going to catch the bus." He also talked about the kind of violence experienced at home by Guggi – and the rest of the Rowan family – under the strict hand of their authoritarian, religious father.

"I grew up on Cedarwood Road," Bono said, in his liner notes for the album. "A nice street full of nice families. People who shaped my world-

Unplugged: The band performs 'Ordinary Love' at the Oscars in March 2014.

view. People I still admire and love. Like Gavin Friday, who lived up at the top of the road.

"But there was a lot of violence nearby in my teenage years," he adds. "Skinheads and boot-boys, blades and knuckledusters. Teenage parties where boys would turn up with hammers and saws." Same shit I'd had to deal with in Rathfarnham on the other side of the city a few years before. "I remember a lot of 'hidings' – I remember taking them and I remember giving them," Bono adds. Or as the song puts it: *"It was a war zone in my teens."* The truth at the heart of 'Cedarwood Road' is that those formative experiences are hard to shake off, no matter how hard you try: they are who you are. *"I'm still standing on that street/ Still need an enemy,"* Bono sings. *"The worst ones I can't see,"* he adds, in what sounds like an ominous reference to the inner demons that still haunt him.

Behind all of this lies the unspoken brute reality of the institutionalised violence, largely based on a traditional, patriarchal view of the world, that was widely accepted and festered like a tumour, perilously close to the heart of Irish society.

"None of that," Bono says of the street clashes, "compared to the violence behind front doors of a husband towards a wife, a brute father towards his children. Cedarwood Road had some dark and hidden sides like all places. Like all people."

In the end, it might have been called 'Song for Guggi'. *"I was looking for a soul that's real,"* Bono recalls, *"Then I ran into you."* Together, these young men retreated into art, the only way they might lift themselves beyond the stifling, oppressive realpolitick of Irish suburban life.

"I think that we were a group of artists in the middle of a jungle," Guggi observes, "who happened to be attracted to other people who weren't like everyone else. We thought we were a bunch of oddballs on the street, but in fact we were a group of artists."

"Symbols clashing, bibles smashing," the lyrics run, referring to Guggi's family after his father had converted to become a member of the Plymouth Brethren, *"Paint the world you need to see."*

As an artist, that is precisely what Guggi has done. It is what Gavin Friday has done as a musician and composer. And it is what Bono has done too, in his own unique way.

Cedarwood Road Written: U2 • Duration: 4' 26"

Sleep Like A Baby Tonight

Institutional violence. Adults must have known about it. Teenagers smelt it. Saw it some of the time too. Hardly knew what to say or do, because it was secretive. Hidden. Happening behind closed doors. In school. In the sacristy. At the sports ground. And children were the victims. How could they possibly know how to react when adults remained silent? All the more so when those who were doing it were figures of authority.

"I remembered the violence meted out to women by their husbands," Bono revealed. "The beatings children experienced from their fathers – and how priests were sexually abusing young children."

These were the sinister secrets that shaped Ireland in the 1960s and the 1970s. It ran like a poison through the bloodstream of the country that U2 grew up in, and that none of us has yet escaped completely. People bear the scars, some more than others. "Secrets can make you sick," Bono observes. And they did.

Bono doesn't usually do darkly satirical lyrics, but sometimes a different kind of language is needed to evoke the horror. He describes a bishop having breakfast and reading the paper. *"You dress in the colours of forgiveness,"* he sings, *"Your eyes as red as Christmas/ Purple robes are folded on the kitchen chair."*

There is an immense gulf between the burgeoning spirituality that flooded through Bono's teenage veins and the callousness of organised religion, with its instinct not for justice but for silencing those desperate for justice. "When the children of any church aren't served," he said of the song, "but are instead enslaved by an abuse of power, extraordinary acts of atonement are required to put things back together." Unfortunately, these have been far too slow in coming. The song has the flavour of a U2 lullaby, but in a way that feels ominous and creepy. Edge plays dirty low down guitar riffs. *"You're gonna sleep like a baby tonight,"* Bono accuses the shadowy religious figure, *"In your dreams everything is alright/ Tomorrow dawns like a suicide/ But you're gonna sleep like a baby tonight."* There is a nod here to Lou Reed's *Berlin*: towards the end, Bono does a strangulated version of the 'Lemon' falsetto and, to see the song out, Edge produces a bawling baby effect on guitar, reminiscent of that album's gut-wrenching 'The Kids'. It is one of the most deeply disconcerting tracks U2 have ever recorded, oozing an eerie atmosphere of claustrophobic menace. There was a lot of that in Ireland in the 1970s.

Sleep Like A Baby Tonight Written: U2 • Duration: 5' 02"

This Is Where You Can Reach Me Now

In the latter half of the 1970s, there was an understanding that joining a rock 'n' roll band was like enlisting, but in an alternative army that used guitars instead of guns. Part of the mission, volunteers figured, was to change the world. In exactly what way, or to which end, no one might have known for sure, but being against the existing machinery of state was good enough to get started.

Across the water, the Sex Pistols, with a first generation London-Irishman Johnny Lydon out front, sang *"God save the Queen/It's a fascist regime"* and did a tribal war dance to the clattering rhythms of 'Anarchy In The UK'. The Pistols didn't make it to Ireland in their early incarnation, but their closest London rivals, The Clash, did. They shaped up in the regulation spiky hair, leather jackets and torn jeans, and posed for photographs alongside military installations in Northern Ireland – and most fans thought that was pretty cool. Their Dublin debut was scheduled for 21 October 1977, in the hallowed confines of Trinity College, in the centre of the city. The band's planned gig in Queen's University, Belfast, the previous night had been cancelled at short notice, at the insistence of the college's insurance company, leading to a minor riot. Trinity College wanted to follow suit by banning the gig, but the Students Union – under Ian Wilson as President and Paul Tipping as Ents Officer – resisted fiercely. It lent the two shows, when they did go ahead that night, an even greater sense of 'us' against 'them'. Inside Trinity, with barricades freshly installed to keep the crowd under control, it looked like a war zone. For a bunch of Irish teenagers from Dublin's Northside, the occasion provided a glimpse into another, alien but utterly magnetic, world. Imagine what it'd be like to get up in front of a crowd like that – and make the kind of racket that'd have them throwing themselves around the hall, jumping, dancing, scrapping and pogoing like lunatics! A fuse had been lit. "We knew we were sleeping in the wrong beds," Bono says. "After we had seen The Clash, it was a sort of a blueprint for U2." In a sense this is when the band's campaign for world domination really started. *"Soldier, soldier,"* the song goes, *"We signed our lives away."* And later in the same verse: *"We knew the world would never be the same."*

Parents didn't like punk rock. It was loud, raw, aggressive, dirty and frequently obscene. In general, they wanted their kids to sign up to something far more conventional. Bono felt this more than most. *"Old man knows that I never listen,"* the youthful character given a voice in 'This Is Where You Can Reach Me Now' complains bitterly. *"So how could I have something to say?/ Old man knows how to cheat ambition/ You don't lose if you don't play."* It was a mantra sung in thousands of houses all over Dublin – all over Ireland – at the time. You'll never amount to anything looking like that. For God's sake cut your hair properly. Wear something respectable. Go out and get a bloody job.

The Edge came up with the idea of the unison singing that would hint of army life. Weirdly, the track began to evoke another of the leading lights of the era, Talking Heads, who had drawn on the same well as U2. That was okay. "We knew that we couldn't possibly be as cool as The Clash," Bono adds. "That's proven to be true. But we did think we could get behind a sort of social justice agenda."

Still, over 40 years on, this is where you can reach them now.

This Is Where You Can Reach Me Now Written: U2 • Duration: 5' 06"

The Troubles

It was Brian Burton, aka Danger Mouse, who thought of Lykke Li. The Swedish indie singer-songwriter received a text asking her would she like to sing on a U2 track. She took it as a compliment and said 'Yeah'. Inside her heart was beating just a little bit quicker. Her father would love to hear about this! There was no sign of the band when she got together with Burton in an LA studio and recorded the breathy vocals. It was one of those low-key things that might never have seen the light of day. But when Danger Mouse took the result back to U2, they liked it. The only problem was that the rest of the track didn't seem to be quite adding up. That took a bit of figuring out. It was Bono, who eventually suggested a key change. A short while later Lykke Li got a second call, wondering if she was free to re-do the vocals.

She travelled to London, and this time the singer was there, being his ever-charming self. He chatted between takes and told her rock 'n' roll stories. "Mostly they let me do my own thing," she told *Rolling Stone*, "but we tried different things like to whisper it to someone or to scream it to someone, but it was all about creating intimacy. We turned off all the music and sang only to the drums, so it was really getting to what the core of the song meant."

Anyone who grew up in Ireland in the 1970s will at first have assumed it was a companion piece to 'Raised By Wolves', a song about the long war in Northern Ireland, for which the euphemism 'The Troubles' had been invented along the way. As a title, it has the feel of a deliberate mistake. But the song is ambiguous in a way that separates it from the rest of the album. It is probably best understood in the light of 'Lucifer's Hands', the track that follows it. Lykke Li's sensuous vocals capture the seductive aspect of the destructive nihilism to which so many teenagers are drawn. *"Somebody stepped inside your soul/Somebody stepped inside your soul/Little by little they robbed and stole/Till somebody else was in control."* Not for long, they weren't. The devil was in the detail.

The Troubles Written: U2 • Length: 4' 46"

Lucifer's Hands

A moment of spiritual awakening was vital to U2, and what they would become. *"The spirit's moving through a seaside town,"* Bono sings. *"I'm born again to the latest sound."* The lyrics of 'Lucifer's Hands' are cleverly constructed so that the meaning might be ambiguous if you didn't know. The song recalls the influence of the *NME* and how U2 went beyond it. It recalls the intense immersion of some of the band in charismatic Christianity. And it turns the theme of 'Rejoice', from *October*, on its head. Back then, Bono declared: *"I can't change the world/ But I can change the world in me."* Now, he recalls the sense of mission, which U2 felt, that they could – and that they might indeed – be able to wield a wider influence. *"Yes, I can change the world,"* he repeats twice, leading on to a different conclusion: *"But I can't change the world in me."* That, he seems to be saying, he had already done...

Lucifer's Hands Written: U2 • Duration: 3' 55"

The Crystal Ballroom

McGonagle's was just off Grafton Street, in the heart of Dublin. One of the venues where U2 learned their chops, it was a rock 'n' roll haven of sorts, that played host to the Jingle Balls series of gigs the band did in 1979. But in a previous life, the same building had been known as The Crystal Ballroom. It was one of the top dancehalls in Dublin at the time and Bono's father, Bob, and his mother Iris, used to go there when they were courting. That subterranean connection was the springboard for a song of loss and loneliness which, unconsciously perhaps, plays on the idea celebrated by Paul Auster in *The Music of Chance*.

Remembering the McGonagles that he knew, with its tacky plastered walls, grubby carpets and dated chandelier in the centre, Bono made the imaginative leap of placing himself back on that stage – and of looking down and seeing his mother and father together in the crowd. Larry supplied a rackety one-two on the side of the snare at the opening and it felt like a moment. *"We're the ghosts of love and we haunt this place,"* Bono sings, thinking of the mysterious events that bring people together, that spark our essential belief in the idea of love – and in the absence of which any of us must recognise: I would not be here but for that accident. But 'The Crystal Ballroom' is a lament nonetheless. *"Everyone's here with me tonight,"* the singer croons. And he throws in a keening falsetto before he concludes: *"Everyone but you."* Iris' loss looms as large as ever.

The Crystal Ballroom Written: U2 • Duration: 4' 40"

SONGS OF EXPERIENCE

If the release method of *Songs of Innocence* was a surprise, so was the fact that U2 had a second new album ready to go – and a new digital music format in the pipeline.

The Music of Chance is right. Bono called the U2 way 'songwriting by accident', but this wasn't exactly what he had in mind. What if that bike smash hadn't happened in Central Park? That was November 2014, just two months after the release of *Songs of Innocence*. It felt worse than weird lying there in a heap on the road, with a smashed face and multiple bones broken. All too human after all. That scuppered the tour, pushed everything back by nearly a year. Left too much time for thinking dark thoughts.

One thing after another. What if Donald Trump hadn't been elected President of the United States of America in November 2016? Without that disastrous swerve to the right, taking *The Joshua Tree* out on a 30th Anniversary tour might have seemed like too much of a concession to nostalgia. Now that all bets were off, the tour was on. It'd make sense to be out there cooking up an incendiary noise and howling at the moon.

Besides, that twist of fate, and the lunacy of Brexit alongside it, put the nascent *Songs of Experience* in a different perspective. Whatever doubts might have niggled about substance were suddenly intensified. The companion to *Songs of Innocence* needed more production clarity. It also required fresh muscle. It'd have to reflect the new, invasive sense of peril. Time to speak up.

Bam. Another explosion, only this time it was personal. Wake up dead man. Think about it in retrospect, though: what if that brush with mortality had waited to strike another day? Would that sage advice offered by Brendan Kennelly have come to the fore in the same way? The great Irish poet, from Ballylongford in Co. Kerry, had influenced 'Until The End of the World' with his rumination on where we might be without Judas. Now, like a new-fangled John the Baptist to Bono's Macpisto, he was back. "Write as if you are dead," he had advised. That was how to go beyond ego, to get to the dark heart of the matter. Which was where Bono wanted to be.

All of this stuff was going around in the singer's head. Early in the morning. Late at night. When he couldn't sleep. All the what-ifs spinning back to when he was a kid. And then the latest one. What if you did drop dead tomorrow? Write as if you are already dead seemed like a new way in. Send love letters to the ones that matter most to you. It'd be a chance to say the things that you really wouldn't want not to have said when you were alive. He was determined: there'd be no surrendering to melancholy. He'd fight his way back if he had to.

How to finally piece all of the elements together. The old U2 songwriting conundrum. The clock was ticking. It had to be done. A hammer, chain, furnace and anvil might be required, to turn the ark around and make it fly. That'd be some trick if you could do it. It was, U2 decided, worth a try.

Love Is All We Have Left

Andy Barlow of Lamb was about to go onstage at a gig in Russia when he got a call from the manager of his band. Fuck! When the phone rings at an inopportune moment a chill runs down the spine. Has somebody died? Barlow immediately knew it had to be important. He answered. "I'm going to tell you something but you can't tell anyone," the voice at the other end of the line said. "WTF?", Barlow thought, shifting his location to guarantee privacy.

"I've just spoken to U2's manager," the voice confided, "and they wondered if you would like to do a two-week tryout?" To say that Barlow was relieved would be misleading. He felt a surge of exhilaration that had an element of the uncanny to it. "When I was 19," he later explained to *Billboard* magazine, "I had the premonition that one day I was going to produce a U2 album. And the even weirder thing is that, 24 hours before I got the call, my best friend said to me 'What do you want to do next?' And I said 'I'd love to do a U2 album. Wouldn't that be something.'" Wouldn't it just! A week later, he flew to France for two weeks... Later again, he spent six weeks with the band in Vancouver.

Opening lines haven't always been Bono's strongest suit. He often quotes the beginning of 'Where The Streets Have No Name' as one that merits a 'must try harder' note. This one is different. "*Nothing to stop this being the best day ever*," his younger self declares, innocence talking boldly to experience. It is a key to the dynamic which drives the album, this sense that the 'we' of now might well be judged harshly by our younger selves. It is worth bearing in mind, if we want to avoid the trap of settling into an acceptance of less. Meanwhile, Bono's fabled brush with immortality feeds quietly into the lyric. "*Now you're at the other end of the telescope*," he sings, "*Seven billion stars in her eyes/ So many stars so many ways of seeing/ Hey, this is no time not to be alive.*"

How to deliver a song is always a challenge. There are times when a singer has to imagine him – or her – self as someone else, to really get to the heart of the emotion of a lyric. Recording 'Love Is All We Have Left', Bono – not for the first time – imagined himself as Frank Sinatra.

Crowd pleasers: The Songs of Innocence tour was planned over two legs, North America and then Europe.

Release date: December 2017
Producer: Jacknife Lee, Ryan Tedder, Steve Lillywhite, Andy Barlow, Jolyon Thomas, Brent Kutzle, Paul Epworth, Danger Mouse, Declan Gaffney
Track listing: Love Is All We Have Left, Lights of Home, You're the Best Thing About Me, Get Out of Your Own Way, American Soul, Summer of Love, Red Flag Day, The Showman (Little More Better), The Little Things That Give You Away, Landlady, The Blackout, Live is Bigger Than Anything in its Way, 13 (There is a Light)
Book of Your Heart (Deluxe Edition)
Highest Chart position: No. 5 (UK), 1 (US)

Only this time, he pretended he was singing on the moon! It has a faint whiff of 'The Wanderer' about it, only different, a kind of sci-fi love song in which innocence admonishes experience. Which beats it being the other way around. The last thing you want is to sound like your old man.

Love Is All We Have Left Written: U2 • Duration: 2' 41"

Lights of Home

Bono on his back, staring at the ceiling. The fear had crept in to his very bones. It colonized his thoughts. He felt it in the pit of his stomach. For a long time, he'd lain there, wondering where the immortality he had always assumed was his to own had gone. Or maybe not quite immortality: he always knew he would die. Eventually. But that was all a long way off, into the far distant future. Longevity. That was the word. He was going to stick around for a long time. Or so he'd imagined. He certainly hadn't ever pictured anything like this. Struck down before he had a chance to make a good record even. That was worth a smile. Gradually, the sense that this might just be the end subsided. He was in good hands. That much he could say for certain. It was an advantage of the life he had chosen to lead, part of the pact he had made with U2 fans. He gave them his art, his heart and his life. They paid his medical bills, no matter how extravagant. His mind was whirring. There was a song in this. There'd have to be to justify the time out. And it'd have to be a good one.

It started out as 'The Lights In Front of Me', with a riff lifted from a bass breakdown in Haim's 'My Song 5'. "I said to Edge, 'Well, sample stuff if you want'," Bono told *Q* magazine. "Sampling stuff is great freedom. Freedom to have fun. To make it a playground again, where you have access to a wider palette of colours." The band loved the basic cut and feel of the song, but it had a retro spirit that they knew wouldn't sit right on the album they were crafting. Sometimes, it's a question of persevering. Of pushing and pulling a track, this way or that, until a breakthrough moment materialises. Jacknife Lee, who was at the heart of the production on this one, did a stripped-down version, searching for the essence of the song. No one knew quite yet where to go with it. Larry Mullen provided the answer, when he added a new drum part. The Edge saw the implications straight away: what he later described as a beautifully played human drum part had been added to a very disciplined contemporary R'n'B-tinged production. This was precisely the kind of synergy that the band had been digging for. "Those small clues make you go: 'Wow! That's the synthesis we're trying to achieve here," Edge explained.

It matched where Bono's head was at. The front-man had hit on another good opening line. *"I shouldn't be here cause I should be dead,"* he confessed, before describing the experience that so many people talk about when they first go knocking on heaven's door: *"I can see the lights in front of me."* That brush with the beyond was the secret at the heart of *Songs of Experience*, and in particular the fact that it had been delayed for so long. But the song needed another dimension to make it the cornerstone track that the band felt it should be.

That the alarm had gone off around Christmas might have lent a crueler twist to Bono's predicament. It was like an insult to his beliefs. Far from compromising Bono's faith, however, this skirmish with mortality served to strengthen it. "Belief is preposterous," he told the *Sunday Times*, "but I have it, and I thought, 'I'm experiencing fear!' It was new, and I realised I don't want to die. I want to spend more time with my kids. There are songs I want to write, stuff I can be useful for. Then, when I admitted I was afraid, my faith returned."

It didn't require a huge leap to turn the song into a prayer. *"In your eyes I see it,"* the lyrics run, *"In your eyes alone/ I see the lights of home."* The only thing we can really say with absolute conviction is that this is where we are all going in the long run. The question then is: where might that final destination truly be? No one knows. We believe what we want to believe. As it was in the beginning...

Lights of Home Written: U2/Haim/Ariel Rechtshaid • Duration: 4' 16"

You're The Best Thing About Me

Any regrets? It was a question asked of The Edge. The guitar wizard didn't flinch. The Edge seldom does. "Yeah," he said. "We didn't get disco." U2 weren't alone of course, back in the day. The conventional wisdom among rock bands, and their fans too, was that disco sucked. In the early days of *Hot Press*, in the era of *Saturday Night Fever* and 'Staying Alive', we put John Travolta on the front cover and it was seen as a form of sacrilege. A sell-out. But for anyone who had come through the 60s, and been inspired by the extraordinary outpouring of genius pop music from Berry Gordy's Tamla Motown label, the connection between irresistible hooks, great rhythms and the sheer joy of being alive was made forever. U2 may have come to that realization comparatively late, but once they'd twigged it, there was no stopping them. From the early 90s onwards, at least some of the time, they just wanted to make people dance.

What someone described as the holy conjunction of rhythm and joy: that was where 'You're The Best Thing About Me' started. But if you could combine that ambition with lyrics that actually said something, well, that'd be even better. In the first serious incarnation of the song, a mellow opening led into a musical structure that eventually started to feel as if it was, what? Too complicated maybe. No one was sure that the arrangement would work live, and so The Edge went digging for fresh inspiration. He uncovered an earlier demo that was more guitar-driven, and which stuck to what the guitarist himself describes as the 'primary colours' of U2's music: guitar, bass and drums. The Motown element subsided: Bono would later characterise the resulting track as punk-Motown and wax lyrical about The Supremes' 'Stop! In The Name of Love'. The idea of writing a great love song, however, remained the kernel of the band's ambition here.

Sometimes having a sense of humour makes all the difference. The band's former biographer Eamon Dunphy had slagged Bono in an

Rock the mic: Bono's voice has considerably matured over the years. Thin and overly dramatic in the early days, it now sounds richer and has a more nuanced timbre.

interview, making the cutting observation that the best thing about the U2 singer is his wife Ali. The neatest way of turning the tables, Bono decided, would be to appropriate the line and make a song of it. In the wake of his health scare, he had wanted to write a love letter to Ali anyway. This would be it: 'You're The Best Thing About Me'. He couldn't resist smiling at the idea.

Still it was a struggle, one that he wasn't sure he could win. Then, he woke up in a freak sweat one night, surfacing like he'd just escaped a drowning incident, after a bad dream in which he had been dogged by the thought that he had destroyed the thing that was most important to him. Out of the fug he knew that it was his relationship with Ali that seemed to be on the line.

Bono was aware that the exercise might be perceived as self-indulgent. "You're putting out a song about your girlfriend when the world is on fire?" he quipped, anticipating the brickbats. But he had no doubt. Faced with intimations of his own mortality there were things he had to say. And besides, when the world seems to be falling apart, letting our loved ones know how we feel is an antidote that works. The expression of joy becomes an act of defiance. It is, The Edge says, the best response in the face of those who want to suck the joy out of everything.

Bono put it differently, but the essential message was the same. "We must resist surrendering to melancholy," he reflected. And how better to do that than by singing about the joys of love? Not that 'You're The Best Thing About Me' takes anything for granted. "I never wanted to do Ali the disservice of a sentimental song," Bono confessed to the *Sunday Times*. "So I wrote a mid-life crisis one instead. It is the portrait of an idiot."

As a not-so-young man...

You're The Best Thing About Me Written: U2 • Duration: 3' 45"

Get Out of Your Own Way

U2 have always understood that making the right friends is the smart thing to do, especially if there is a fellow spirit out there who might just sprinkle a bit of magic dust on a record. So when they listened to Kendrick Lamar, it felt like a light bulb going on. While so many others in the hip hop world were all about bling and money and violence and pussy, Lamar had started out as a worried young man, for whom philosophy was more important than drugs. For Kendrick, religion wasn't just a social occasion around which a congregation gathered. He was serious about wanting to understand what role Christianity – or spirituality – might yet have to play in people's lives and thoughts. Just like U2 had been almost forty years earlier. The fact that he happened to be widely acclaimed as the hottest new name in hip-hop added to the potential intrigue: it was worth making a phone call at least. For it to work, however, there'd have to be more than mere whimsy involved.

Bono sent a track to Kendrick. He seemed to be impressed. Once he'd added some of his own ideas to it, he decided to pilfer it – or bits of it at least – for his own *DAMN* album. That was okay with Bono. He could have the chorus. 'XXX' was a good track. Another song out there, earning royalties – and there'd be a bit of caché in it to boot. What's not to like? They agreed that they'd do something else together later – and kept their phones open. The moment would come, they knew that. And it did.

Bono had been working on a different track with Jolyon Thomas; Ryan Tedder had a hand in it too. "That was the very first one I worked on," Thomas remembers. "Bono and I did a demo of it. The opening, I made on my iPad. It's all just my voice that I sampled. I made this sort of euphoric, reverb sound. I'm also credited with playing guitar on the track, because that melody in the chorus was something that Bono and I came up with quite early on. The track has gone through a few different versions, but that really stuck."

Lyrically it was one of Bono's 'love letters'. There is a hint, in the first half of 'Get Out Of Your Own Way', of a parent admonishing a daughter. *"Love hurts,"* the verse opens, *"Now you're the girl who's left with no words/ Your hearts a balloon but then it bursts/ It doesn't take a cannon just a pin/ Your skins no covering."*

The song offers a different take on the idea that sometimes we are our own worst enemies. But if that is the starting point, 'Get Out of Your Own Way' becomes something else entirely, morphing into a protest song, in which the irony is laid on hard, a way of reflecting the growing anger on the streets in the land of Trump. In a sense, while one of Bono's daughters was undoubtedly in the original idea, it became a different kind of love letter, written to America, with an eye to the damage being done to the ideal represented by the Statue of Liberty, post-Obama. *"Fight back,"* the singer urges, *"Don't take it lying down/ You've got to bite back/ The face of liberty is starting to crack."*

Maybe Bono had been reading George Sanders' *Lincoln In The Bardo*. There is a reference to the founding father's ghost urging people to "Get out of your own way."

The song done, more or less, Bono came up with the idea of a psychedelic preacher, who'd rap a modern take on the Beatitudes – eight blessings for the downtrodden that are preached by Jesus in Matthew's version of the gospel. He did a demo of how it might sound. The Edge again: "We thought, 'Wow, Kendrick could do that!' It was really last minute – we're talking like the last couple of weeks before the record was done. He said he would do it. He phoned it in, literally on his phone."

"There's a righteous anger that is hard to argue with," Bono says of Kendrick's contribution. "I asked him would he rap about where America is at; his reply was to rap about where America isn't at."

"Blessed are the arrogant," Kendrick asserts, getting into the flow, *"For theirs is the kingdom of their own company/ Blessed are the superstars/ For the magnificence in their light/ We understand better our own insignificance/ Blessed are the filthy rich/ For you can only truly own what you give away/ Like your pain..."*

"Protesting works," Bono said before one performance of the song. "It gets things done, slowly and surely. This song is like a protest song against yourelf, really, because it turns out (that) one of the biggest obstacles we encounter on the way to a better world is often ourselves."

You've gotta free youself, to be yourself. He'd said it already, in a different way, in 'Iris'.

Get Out Of Your Own Way Written: U2/Kendrick Lamar • Duration: 3' 58"

Top hat: Performing in character during the iNNOCENCE & eXPERIENCE tour at the Capital One Arena in Washington, DC. June 17, 2018.

American Soul

Bono couldn't let the idea he had given to Kendrick go, not completely. Instinctively, he felt that U2 would get a song out of it too. And in the modern era, when nothing is ever truly finished, and bits of so many of us are posted out there at different angles and in related forms across disparate media, what would be wrong with taking the raw material which had come together in 'XXX' and giving it a different spin – a defiantly U2 twist? And so the thought crystallized of splitting the Kendrick rap in two. 'American Soul' takes up where 'Get Out Of Your Own Way' left off. "*Blessed are the bullies*," Kendrick raps, "*for one day they will have to stand up to themselves*." It is like a warning: Donald Trump will finally face his day of reckoning.

"I think we share a lot of values with Kendrick," The Edge says. "We are fans of his. We reached out and initially asked him to guest on our album, and then we sent him a tune. He got back in touch with us asking if he can put it on his record. We were like, okay, yeah that's great! So one of the tracks from our album kinda debuted in part on his record."

The Edge is riffing about 'American Soul', which touches on the crisis of identity which the US is undergoing, with Donald Trump as President.

"I think we felt that, to ignore what was happening in America would just be weird," the guitarist explains. "Knowing that these are the things that we care deeply about, I think people would expect us to step forward to a degree. Obviously democracy sometimes throws up surprise results and you gotta respect the result, whether it goes for you or against you. But in terms of values and ideals, we're so fundamentally different from what President Trump is putting forward. And the sentiments that he's putting out there, and who he's looking to get support from – it's fear politics of the most cynical type."

"*Put your hands in the air* ," Bono sings by way of answer, "*Hold up the sky/ Could be too late but we still gotta try/ There's a moment in a life where a soul can die/ In a person, in a country when you believe the lie*."

Believing the lie has never been U2's style. Bono had the feeling that the rise of the so called alt-right was predictable. But there was something even more sinister afoot. "To see the Ku Klux Klan marching the streets of Charlottesville without the silly costumes and the pointy hats – that was a new level of absurdity and danger. Why do they feel so emboldened?"

It was a good question. "We don't necessarily want to get wrapped

Eyes on the prize: The band performed remotely for the 60th GRAMMY Awards show on January 28, 2018 in New York.

up in the 'resistance' to his presidency as such," The Edge adds. "What we want to do is keep moving forward with the issues that we care about and keep the agenda alive, that we believe we will all be getting back to. We've been inspired by what some of the governors and mayors in the USA have done in response to him. They just don't care what the President says or thinks – they're moving forward. That's positive. We feel okay about taking him on, on certain levels, but we're really just gonna keep on ploughing forward with what we really believe in."

"Let it be unity," the song runs, *"Let it be community/ For refugees like you and me/ A country to receive us/ Will you be my sanctuary/ Refujesus."*

It is a message that resonates widely: we are all refugees. A song that at once speaks of U2's fascination with America and recalls the idealistic ambitions of the Conspiracy of Hope tour of the 1980s, with its appeal for mutual togetherness and support, 'American Soul' strikes all of the notes that Donald Trump misses. Sing it loud: *"You are rock 'n' roll/ We came here looking for American soul"*...

American Soul Written: U2/Kendrick Lamar • Duration: 4' 21"

Summer of Love

We all know the image. A close up, taken by Marc Riboud, of a then-17 year-old Jan Rose Kasmir confronting the US National Guard outside the Pentagon, during a peace march opposing the Vietnam war, in October 1967. Kasmir is caught by the camera, staring down the barrells of bayoneted guns, holding a single chrysanthemum in front of her face. A flower to say that she has come in peace. A flower to give the cosmic finger to the militarists, the securicrats and the war-mongers. A flower as the best possible natural antidote to the evil glint of the bloody hardware of war.

1967. That was the year during which 100,000 young people descended on Haight Ashbury, San Francisco, to create the Summer of Love. *"If you're going to San Francisco,"* Scott McKenzie sang at the time, *"be sure to wear/ Some flowers in your hair."* The hippie dream of peace and love and – as Joni Mitchell put it in 'Woodstock' – getting back to the Garden, may ultimately have died with the loss of life at the Rolling Stones infamous gig at Altamont, but the memory and the myth lives on. Besides, the anti-war movement of that era really did achieve remarkable things, by turning the widespread opposition to the excesses of the US war in Vietnam into a movement, with music at the heart of what was , in many ways, a defining political moment.

Is it entirely implausible that the spirit of '67 might be re-energised 50 years on, in the land of Donald Trump? That's the question which is implicit in 'Summer of Love', released a half-century after the original phenomenon became immortalized – and described by Bono himself as "achingly beautiful." The context is different. Trump was elected as President of the USA on a ticket of non-involvement in foreign conflicts. Perversely, it was this policy which gave a free hand to Russia to pursue its own interests in Syria and the surrounding region, by supporting the murderous regime of the Syrian President, Bashar al-Assad. But, of course, Trump went further than advocating non-involvement in the Arab world, blithely stirring up hatred of, and hostility towards, muslims in America. And he put a number of Arabic countries, including war-torn Syria, on a blacklist: no refugees welcome in the home of the free.

"I've been thinking about the West Coast," Bono sings, echoing the One Republic song that would provide the hook for 'Summer Of Love'. *"Not the one that everyone knows/ In the rubble of Aleppo/ Flowers blooming in the shadows/ For a summer of love."*

"One of the jumping off points for 'Summer of Love' was a CNN story about the gardener of Aleppo," The Edge reflects. In the UK, Channel 4 took up the story of Abu Ward, who created a small oasis of colour and natural life inside the area controlled by rebels, in what was then – and as of the summer of 2018 still remains – one of the world's worst hell-holes of war, violence and brutality.

"He maintained a garden that he kept going through the war," The Edge adds. "It was a political statement to the entire world, that he did that. It was an act of defiance to grow flowers in the middle of Aleppo. Bono was really inspired by that."

This remarkable, true story has a tragic end. A barrel bomb landed near the garden Abu Ward had cultivated with such passion and courage: he was killed by the blast. His son, Ibrahim, had left school to help him plant the flowers; now, feeling that there was no alternative, he shut down the garden.

"We've one more chance before the light goes/For a summer of love," Bono sings, struggling to find hope amid the devastation. Is it possible to believe that, anymore? Not, you might say, unless things can be changed radically. Which, in the end, is surely the purpose of a song like 'Summer of Love': with the audible assistance of Lady Gaga, to at least try to nudge things in that direction. Hope springs eternal, they say. U2 at least have not given up on it entirely.

Summer of Love Written: U2 • Duration: 2' 24"

Red Flag Day

There's always a pile of songs that don't make it onto a U2 album. Some, like Paul McCartney's symbolic 'Blackbird' breaking into song, are just waiting for their moment to arrive. Others might never see the light of dawn. 'Red Flag Day' had slipped down the rankings and seemed destined to be shunted into the also-rans. Then, the shifting sands of political life – including the rise of anti-immigrant sentiment across Europe, and the moate-building implicit in Brexit and the election of Donald Trump alike – pushed it back into contention for *Songs of Experience*. "We made it a priority," The Edge says. "There was something very powerful in it."

There is indeed. The original idea had taken root in the South of France, where both Bono and Edge have holiday homes. The village they live in overlooks the Mediterranean Sea, which stretches from the south-east of France, to surround Italy – and extends from there across to North Africa and on to the west coast of benighted Syria. For Bono, looking down at the ocean, it was impossible not to think of the battered ships and boats – many of them unseaworthy and dangerously over-crowded – regularly leaving North Africa, or the Middle East, to transport people to Europe, in the hope of finding a better world and a safer life. Some hope. On that perilous journey many lives have been lost as ships went down. Hundreds had to be rescued, and were brought ashore – battered and bedraggled but still alive – onto the Greek islands, and along the east coast of Italy.

"We watched nurses and teachers, and people who looked a lot like us," Bono reflects, "tying themselves to almost nothing. To a hope, to a dream of another shore. Human wreckage washing up in Turkey or Italy or who knows where.

"Just knowing that where you're having your vacation, on the same sea people are fighting for their lives, attaching themselves to bits of wood and rubber tyres – that puts things into perspective," he adds.

There is a reference back to 'Every Breaking Wave' on *Songs of Innocence* (*"I'll take you where the waves are breaking"*). But ultimately 'Red Flag Day' is a song about privilege, and the dread of what the nearby crisis might ultimately bring. There is the personal: *"Baby, it's a red flag day/ Baby let's get in the water/ Taken out by a wave/ Where we've never been before."* And the political: *"Not even news today/ So many lost in the sea last night/ One word that the sea can't say/ Is no, no, no, no..."*

A great rock tune replete with a stonking Adam Clayton bassline, it makes a devastating companion to 'Summer of Love', the two songs providing a powerful centre-piece in what is surely U2's most politically engaged record since the 1980s.

Red Flag Day Written: U2 • Duration: 3' 19"

The Showman (Little More Better)

No one can accuse U2 of not being able to laugh at themselves. One of Bono's great distancing stratagems was the invention of alter egos for *Achtung Baby* and the Zoo TV tour, chief among them The Fly and MacPhisto. It gave him a licence to say – and do – things which, until then, U2 couldn't possibly have contemplated. 'The Showman' offers more anarchy in the same vein. "It's not about me," Bono told one interviewer. "It's about me," he told another. Both statements were probably half true.

It was conceived, at least in part, as a letter to U2's audience, on the theme of the, ahem, ego of performers. This, of course, is Bono poking fun at himself – and at others like him, who have the temerity to believe that they have what it takes to entertain the masses. The intentions of these vaudevillians, the song implies, are not always wholly admirable.

U2 have been here before, with Bono singing about the treachery that is often at the heart of great art in 'The Fly'. *"Every artist is a cannibal, every poet is a thief,"* he mused back then, *"All kill their inspiration and sing about the grief."* 'The Showman' offers a variation on that theme, only this time he has the guy who enjoys hogging the limelight, by jumping on the table at eight o'clock every night, and howling, in his sights.

During the 1970s, there was an Irish showband singer called Magic – real name Kevin Walsh. He was the frontman of a showband, that traded under the epic name Magic and his Magic Band. If memory serves, the singer was about 5ft 2ins tall and dressed like a 1970s, bogman's David Bowie – a frightening thought for sure. But he could sing. The quest for his minders and mentors should have been: let's talk about Kevin, and decide how we can get people to take him seriously as an artist. Instead, they tried to answer a different teaser: how can we get the shaggin' crowds excited and turn little Kevin into a feckin' supertar? With that in mind, they decked Magic out in a silver suit, bedecked with battery-operated fairy lights that lit up as he performed. Magic wasn't – or isn't – the word to describe the ensuing pocket rocket! It's as if that mordant spectre from his teenage years had lodged itself somewhere deep in Bono's mind. *"Walk through the room like a birthday cake,"* he sings, *"When I am all lit up I can't make a mistake/ And there's a level of shallow that you just can't fake/ But you know that I know/ Oh you don't care/ But you know I'm there..."*

Of course, the U2 singer is really having a laugh at his own expense. "It is kind of about performers and how you shouldn't trust them too much," he elaborated to *Rolling Stone*. "There's a funny line – well, I think it's funny anyway: *'I lie for a living/ I love to let on/ But you make it true/ When you sing along'*."

This has been a consistent U2 trope: it is those moments when the crowd takes over that make it all worthwhile. Elsewhere, discussing the song, Bono doubled back to the same theme. "We give birth to these songs," he said, "but it is our audience who give life and meaning to them." This, of course, is true – up to a point. But – while it was kicked into fulness for U2 when Larry sat behind his kit and in one session added a whole new dimension to the tune – 'The Showman' is one of those songs that would have had heft and meaning no matter who was singing it. It is studded with great lines.

"It is what it is, but it's not what it seems/ This screwed up stuff is the stuff of dreams," he admits, before the real confession begins. *"I got just enough low self esteem/ To get me where I want to go."* Magic.

The Showman (Little More Better) Written: U2 • Duration: 3' 23"

The Little Things That Give You Away

U2 have been here before. *"And you give yourself away,"* Bono sang in 'With Or Without You'. It's a line to which a number of different meanings can be ascribed. It's an inevitable part of being the lead singer in a rock 'n' roll band that you have to give pieces of yourself to your audience. No matter how well disguised, they are there in the songs. They are there too, when you go on stage, stand in front of the crowd and perform. Every slip-up, every false note can be judged. Ever since Bono first went onstage, he had been giving bits of himself, again and again, never knowing for sure that it was going to be enough, even when it was.

But there was another meaning to that line too. A writer may intend to say one thing – but the language unintentionally reveals something completely different. It is what is called a give-away. We are revealed in our true light. People see through us: *"And you give yourself away."* There is a sense in which, at some point, every artist feels like a fraud. Sometimes the audience too sees the man behind the mask.

These oppositional ideas are intrinsic to the way Bono works. In 'The Little Things That Give You Away', however, the focus of the ambiguity has shifted. Here, he is writing a letter to himself – or to a different version of himself, another alter ego. The problem, as U2 were making the album, was how to capture the magic that the band saw in the core idea.

It became a personal mission for producer Andy Barlow: he had to master it. He had to get it right. "Although a few of us worked on it," he

Despite everything, the honest truth is that I wish we were a better band, I wish we were a more talented band. We go through excruciating humility these days when songwriting." Bono

recalled, talking to *Billboard*, "Jolyon Thomas and myself really shaped that track. It's got that Lamb kind of shape to it. The way it goes up the gears and explodes at the end."

Meanwhile, Bono was still getting metaphysical about it. "The best songs, for me, are often arguments with yourself or arguments with some other version of yourself," he explained. "Even singing our song 'One,' which was half fiction, I've had this ongoing fight. In 'Little Things,' innocence challenges experience: *'I saw you on the stairs/ You didn't notice I was there/ That's cause you were busy talking at me, not to me/ You were high above the storm, a hurricane being born/ But this freedom just might cost you your liberty*.'"

As indeed, in certain respects, it has. There, laid bare, is the irony. But this is a song too about mortality - and the imminence of death. "*Sometimes/ Full of anger and grieving/ So far away from believing/ That any sun will reappear/ Sometimes/ The end is not coming/ It's not coming/ The end is here*."

"At the end of the song," Bono added, "experience breaks down and admits his deepest fears, having been called out on it by his younger, braver, bolder self."

Having debuted it in Vancouver at the start of the tour, the band played the song as the final encore in their The Joshua Tree 30th aniversary tour gig in Croke Park, Dublin, a few months before the release of *Songs of Experience*. "We played 'Little Things' for ourselves really," Bono explained, "just to prove we could write some new songs that can go the distance with the best of our old songs. Rough spot to put one in, though, that's for sure..." The end may be nigh - but it has been that way for a long time.

The Little Things That Give You Away Written: U2 • Duration: 4' 55"

Landlady

On occasion, you have to go way back to understand. Making a living from working in a rock 'n'roll band isn't easy. There were times when U2 went out on the road and came back with nothing. In those early days, as often as not, their tours actually cost them money. At the tail end of the 70s and the beginning of the 80s, the band used to do ads for their gigs in *Hot Press* - but by the time they had bought petrol and hired gear and paid for the van, and all the rest of the shit that a band needs just to stay on the road, there was nothing left in the kitty. We'd call the band's manager Paul McGuinness to see if we could arrange to collect a cheque. They always paid eventually, of course. But in the meantime, they were furiously scraping the bottom of the barrel to make ends meet. And so when Bono and Ali moved out to Howth to live together, there was really no likelihood that he'd earn enough money to meet his share of the rent payments. Ali was working in an insurance company at the time. It was a living, with a regular income. So when Bono had nothing to show for his labours, Ali paid the bills. It wasn't an occasional, isolated incident. For a long time, she really was the breadwinner.

"The question I couldn't get out of my head was 'Could I write Ali a song, a love song?,'Bono said, reflecting on the genesis of *Songs of Experience*. He wanted to write what he called songs of exaltation. "Without inducing the projectile vomit that is sentimentality," he added. "Maybe humanity, if I could remember what that was, might help."

'Landlady' was one of those love songs. It started out in Ryan Tedder's ken and he had a hand in the melody. Garret "Jacknife" Lee took it over and delivered the final product, adding rock 'n' roll muscle. It is a companion song to 'You're The Best Thing About Me' - but this one probably has the better lines.

"*I'll never know*," Bono confides, "*Never know what starving poets meant/ 'Cause when I was broke/ It was you that always paid the rent*." It might not seem like the most romantic thought ever, but that is the point. Love can be a practical thing too.

Landlady Written: U2 • Duration: 4' 01"

The Blackout

Where are we heading? They say that the only certainty in life is death, and that thought was very much on Bono's mind. Yes, he'd had a brush with mortality, staring the grim reaper in the eye, before the cavalry arrived. That's the way it happens sometimes: here today, gone tomorrow. But the U2 singer lived - not to tell the tale, so much as to draw some conclusions on the wall. Let's face it: if someone hits you with a hammer and you survive, you are likely to be that much more aware of the fragile hold we have on life, even at the best of times. You think of the people you love, and that you hope love you.

Paranoia rears its ugly mug. Maybe they don't! Perhaps there're things you need to tell them, events you need to explain, advice you need to offer. The whole of *Songs of Experience* thus became imbued with a fresh sense of urgency it might not otherwise have had. It was as if Bono had wakened up one morning in a terrible lather. 'Quick, nurse! There's lots I have to say and do before I die. Let me out of here!'

'The Blackout' started as one of those self-reflections, about what it's like to be a rock star in your middle years. "*Dinosaur, wonders why it still walks the earth/ A meteor promises it's not going to hurt*," the song goes. "That would have been a funny line about an ageing rock star," Bono ruminated later. But the Trump curveball had shunted the thought process onto a different track. "It is a little less funny when we're talking about democracy and old certainties – like truth."

Now, 'The Blackout' had taken on a different sheen. It was the first track U2 shared from *Songs of Experience* and the move made sense. It has a poppy chorus, made for singing along to: Ryan Tedder had a hand in that. But it also wears its political disquiet openly. "*Statues fall*," Bono sings, again recalling 'The Fly', "*democracy is flat on its back, Jack/ We had it all and what we had is not coming back, Zac/ A big mouth says the people they don't want to be free for free/ The blackout, is this an extinction event we see?*"

This is U2 – with a sly nod to Blake's anti-child labour poem 'The Chimney Sweep' – harking back to the glory days of the '80s, with Adam and Larry pitching in enthusiastically, to give the song its shape and its clout. With the aid of Jacknife Lee in the final stages, they conjured up a rough and ready sonic storm to match the lyric. It was a statement of intent: U2 were not planning to stumble quietly into premature obsolesence.

"It's a letter to the moment we're in," Bono said, "where both the personal and political apocalypse combine. Not just the rock behemoth, slaughtered by time, but the dinosaur democracy, facing extinction. Sounds like melodrama, but that's what we want from opera, isn't it? Big melodies. Big emotions."

Another cautionary note springs to mind and it's this: be careful what you wish for. There were those who railed against the elite and helped to deliver Trump. Bad bargain. "Democracy," Bono reflected, "is a mere blip in history." The singer's own 'brush with mortality' proved not to be terminal. We can only hope that the same proves true for universal suffrage. Otherwise, the lights really will go out.

The Blackout Written: U2 • Duration: 4' 45"

Love Is Bigger Than Anything In Its Way

It is a long title for a song (does it need a bracket?). And it started out as something else. As far back as 2014, Bono had been working on the idea: write a song in which you ask your younger self for help. Underlying this startling jumping off point is clearly a sense of frustration: how come it has all dwindled down to this? An awareness that the dreams of youth have in some way solidified into what might be thought of as middle-aged complacency; and a feeling of disappointment that somehow the idealism that got you into music in the first place might have been compromised by what was always one of the project's key objectives: the kind of soaring success which means that you are the biggest band in the world, and therefore in a position to speak to the largest possible audience. U2 have always been attuned to the contradictions implicit in all of this. But how to resolve them can seem more and more tenaciously obscure. That's where a song idea called 'The Morning After Innocence' started: like there was a kind of hangover involved. But the title of the song was destined to change.

"I came up with the phrase 'Love Is Bigger Than Anything In Its Way', Bono explained to Xirius FM, and it was the key line in a note posted on Instagram, on 14 November 2015, in the immediate wake of the murderous terrorist attacks on Paris which killed 130 victims, including 89 at the Bataclan Theatre, where Eagles of Death Metal had been playing. The note was signed by all four members of U2. "And I mean it," he added. And that is not an airy-fairy, flowers in the hair version of love. I mean that most of the songs on the album are details of emotional landscapes. I mean, the thing that experience has taught me, above all else, is the primacy of fun and frolics and devilment and mischief and joy as a defiant act against our mortality. And that brings us back to rock 'n' roll. That's where U2 came from."

It is a wonderfully anthemic song, made for live performance, that looks beyond heartache in search of something more joyous. It is as if the young Bono can see his later self crushing those shells on Killiney Beach. "*The door is open to go through*," he admonishes, "*If I could I would come too/ But the path is made by you/ As you're walking start singing and stop talking*." It is a great line for the band's live shows. It is also a rare moment in rock 'n' roll of inter-generational reassurance: it is up to us to forge our own path. But if we do, we have the opportunity to realize our dreams.

U2 commissioned the photographer David Mushegain to make a video for the track. What he produced was something gorgeous and lyrical, featuring members of the colourful young tribes that represent the new Ireland, many of them from the LBGTQ community. That is a statement, in itself, of the open-ness with which U2 have embraced things that they might once have barely understood.

"*If the moonlight caught you crying on Killiney Bay*," the younger Bono sings to his older self, "*Oh sing your song/ Let your song be sung/ If you listen you can hear the silence say/ Love is bigger than anything in its way*."

We can only hope that he is right.

Love Is Bigger Than Anything In Its Way Written: U2 • Duration: 4' 00"

13 (There Is A Light)

In '40' U2 took the psalm of the corresponding number and turned it into a song. "*I waited patiently for the Lord*," it begins, "*He inclined and heard me cry*." '13' harks back to that early defining moment. It is the lullaby with which U2 have consistently chosen to end their records. It is the light at the end of the tunnel, the moment in which faith is restored. But it is a different kind of lullaby, almost a show tune with Bono looking into his heart and realising that 'Song For Someone' might indeed have been a case of looking in the mirror.

On '13', the transition from doubt to faith is more difficult to make. That is because, on this occasion, the doubt feels more deeply personal. "*And if the terrors of the night/ Come creeeping into your days*," Bono speculates, like a man who knows what he is talking about, "*and the world comes stealing children from your room/ Guard your innocence*

from hallucination/ And know that darkness always gathers around the light." Psalm 13 too begins in despair. *"How long, Lord,"* it opens, reminding us of the source of the final section of '40', *"Will you forget me forever?/ How long will you hide your face from me?"*

"You start with emptiness," Bono had said of his modus operandi fashioning lyrics for *Songs of Experience*. "You start with nothing. You start with the void." It was as if he was thinking about Psalm 13 from the start. But it is what comes after, that makes all the difference.

"Look on me and answer, Lord my God," the Psalm pleads. "Give light to my eyes or I sleep in death."

And then comes the coup de grace.

"But I trust in your unfailing love. My heart rejoices in your salvation. I will sing the Lord's praise for he has been good to me." Of course, there are many who couldn't ever say that. There are many for whom it just isn't true.

In '13', the initial doubts lead into a reprise of 'Song for Someone', only this time with a difference. It is as if, having stared into the abyss, Bono is now ready to acknowledge the slim hold that we all have on what it is - or we think it is - all about. In many ways, he has been fortunate and he knows it: the whole album recognises that simple truth. And, as an integral part of his mission as a rock star, he has tried to spread the love. In the end, however, maybe it really is only on his own behalf that he can speak. The message remains the same: we should never let the light of love go out. But there is a hint of loneliness, intended or otherwise, in the downbeat denouement: *"This is a song for someone/ Like me."*

"There are a lot of songs about light in the U2 repertoire," Adam Clayton says. "It's an image of faith and obviously people having near-death experiences describe seeing a bright light. So these are themes that are being spoken about."

Glasto glory: Having had to cancel their Glastonbury 2010 appearance due to Bono recovering from back surgery, the band finally made it to the esteemed festival the following year.

Book Of Your Heart

(Deluxe Edition)

It isn't always evident, but David Bowie was a big influence on U2. You can hear it here, in a song that reflects a much more intimate side to the band than the rest of *Songs of Experience*. The rushed ending suggests that there is an element of unfinished business about the track, which might explain why it isn't on the album, but was instead included as a bonus cut.

Sonically, it feels like it could have slotted neatly onto the *Passengers* album; there is a bit of *No Line On The Horizon* to it too; and, in spirit, it harks back to 'Ultraviolet' (*"Your love was like a lightbulb/ Hanging over my bed"*) and 'The Ground Beneath Her Feet'. It is Bono looking back, in a sonorous voice, on his relationship with Ali. *"You can change your name or even who you are,"* he reflects and the line might as easily be directed at himself, as his wife. *"That's the beauty of the scar/ That's the contract of the heart."*

The conclusion, when we get there, is a powerful one. *"Baby I don't belong to you/ Love is what we choose to do/ Baby you don't belong to me/ It's not that easy..."*

Love, after all, is blindness.

THE EDGE

BY BRIAN BOYD

A remarkable guitarist who has had his own style since Day One, The Edge is the creative driving force behind the group's music. And the least likely U2 member to start an argument.

David Howell Evans was born in London to Welsh parents on 8 August 1961. When he was a year old the family relocated to Dublin due to his father, an engineer, receiving a promotion. He was given the nickname "The Edge" by friends of Bono when he was a teenager. Depending on who you talk to, he got his nickname either from his sharp, edge-like facial features or because his shyness meant he used to stay in the background – on the edge of what was happening around him.

He and his older brother Richard (Dik) were both interested in the guitar. They had bought a second-hand acoustic guitar at a jumble sale for £1 while in their early teens and learnt basic chord structures from plonking away on it.

When Larry Mullen's now famous notice went up on the board at Mount Temple School, both Edge and Dik went to the first audition and both were accepted into the band. Dik Evans played only a few shows with the band (when they were still known as the Hype), but there was always a feeling that the musical unit would work better as a four-piece so Dik was "phased out" – as the band put it. The Edge still remembers the heartbreak of telling his brother the news.

Even on the band's first album, *Boy*, it was immediately clear that this was no ordinary guitar player. The Edge's playing style was the very opposite to what a lead guitarist usually plays. He favoured a minimalist style, which allowed him to explore different textures. He never played that many notes but did use delay effects which created a more ambient sound. So out of synch with then prevailing guitar playing styles was his approach that you could immediately recognize a U2 song just from his guitar parts.

While his playing style is minimal, his use of effects and pedals really fills out his sound. His short and sharp approach was very much of the New Wave era of music influenced by bands such as the Skids. He cites guitarists Tom Verlaine (from the band Television) and Irish blues guitarist Rory Gallagher as his main inspirations. He also has impressive keyboard skills.

The Edge: During the October tour, the guitarist struggled with his religious beliefs.
Guitar god: Performing in Toronto for 2009's 360° tour.

A fine singer in his own right, he is the band's backing vocalist – frequently harmonizing to Bono's voice. He sings lead vocals on 'Van Diemen's Land' from *Rattle and Hum* and 'Numb' from *Zooropa*. On later U2 tours he sang lead vocals on 'Sunday Bloody Sunday'.

He released his own solo album in 1986 – a soundtrack album for a film called *Captive*. On the song 'Heroine' from the album, the vocals are supplied by a young Sinead O'Connor.

Now regarded as one of the best popular music guitarists in the world, he played arguably his best work on the *Achtung Baby* album – particularly on 'The Fly' and 'Mysterious Ways'.

He married his school girlfriend Aislinn O'Sullivan in 1983. The couple had three children before separating in 1990. He met the choreographer Morleigh Steinberg when she appeared as a belly dancer on the Zoo TV tour. They have two children and were married in 2002.

> “I’m interested in music. I’m a musician. I’m not a gunslinger. That’s the difference between me and guitar heroes.” The Edge

He appeared in the music documentary film *It Might Get Loud* (2009), which explored his guitar life as well as those of Jimmy Page and Jack White.

Following the 2005 Hurricane Katrina cyclone, he helped set up Music Rising – a charity that helped to provide replacement musical instruments for musicians in the New Orleans area who had lost everything. Following one of his daughters successfully battling against cancer, he became very involved with the Angiogenesis Foundation – a research organization that looks at new scientific techniques to treat cancer and other serious illnesses. He is one of the directors of the foundation.

While hiking with his wife in the Malibu area of California shortly after they were married, the couple fell in love with a particular area of land which they bought. For the last eight years The Edge has been in talks with the Coastal Commission of California about his plans to build five houses on the land.

Known for his placid manner, all three of his bandmates cite him as the real key to the band’s success.

Homecoming: Slane Castle was the backdrop for a homecoming gig in September 2001.
Weapon of choice: In Toronto, one of the band’s favourite cities, for the Joshua Tree tour.
Cap doff: Exclusive! The Edge without his hat – an early shot of the virtuoso guitarist.

B-SIDES AND EXTRA-CURRICULAR ACTIVITIES

They could have done a straight concert film and a live double-album. "And made a lot of money for very little work," Bono argued. "That's what big rock bands do. They take the money and run." Instead, U2's restless desire to keep moving got the better of them. Part documentary, part travelogue, part concert film, *Rattle and Hum*, the movie, is big, loud, sketchy, humorous, gauche, powerful, revealing. *Rattle and Hum*, the album, is sprawling, eclectic, eccentric, throwaway, inspiring, magnificent. Hammered in the press, it sold 14 million copies. The myth wasn't going to be easily deflated.

RATTLE AND HUM

Release date: October 1988 • Catalogue number: U27 • Producer: Jimmy Iovine • Track listing: Helter Skelter/Van Diemen's Land/Desire/ Hawkmoon 269/All Along the Watchtower/ I Still Haven't Found What I'm Looking For/Freedom for My People/Silver and Gold/Pride (In the Name of Love/Angel of Harlem/Love Rescue Me/When Love Comes to Town/ Heartland/God Part II/The Star Spangled Banner/Bullet the Blue Sky/All I Want Is You. • Highest Chart position: No. 1 (UK and US)

Helter Skelter

There were people who ridiculed the choice of 'Helter Skelter' as the opening track on *Rattle and Hum*. In fact, it would be hard to pick anything more appropriate. *The Joshua Tree* had catapulted the band into the front line, right up there as contenders for the title that no one really wants: the biggest rock 'n' roll band on planet Earth. On a tour that was scheduled to run over 264 days and through 15 countries, they would do 110 shows at 72 venues in front of a paying audience of 3,160,998 fans. In addition, there was the San Francisco Save The Yuppie free concert, with an audience of at least another 20,000 people. And, meanwhile, chunks of all this mayhem were being filmed for a major rock 'n' roll film. It was a roller coaster ride all right, in which everything was capable of being turned upside down.

In one obvious sense, U2 were on top of the world. In another, they had been plunged into the vortex, where every aspect of their operation was under scrutiny, and every element of their increasingly hydra-headed organisation under severe strain. None more so than the band themselves. "'Helter Skelter' was exactly what we were going through on The Joshua Tree tour," Bono said. "It was one of the worst times of our musical life. First a falling light cut me up, and I had to have stitches in my chin. My voice failed for the first week because of dry heat – the press came to the opening show and I couldn't sing. We were on the run the whole time and I busted up my shoulder and was in a lot of pain. And I found that I was drinking a lot just to stop the pain."

Recorded at the McNichols Arena in Denver on 8 November, 1987, it featured in the black and white footage of the film *Rattle and Hum*. "The line about Charles Manson was just an off-thecuff remark on the night," Bono recalls. "If I got up people's noses, that's fine. But I still think it was relevant. We were travelling around the United States and I had a few incidents coming up against the hard-core spontaneous combustion of violence that seems to happen there. I've always been fascinated with that and still am." Look no further than the sign marked 'Exit'.

Helter Skelter Written: Lennon/McCartney • Duration: 3' 07"

Van Dieman's Land

In 1845, Ireland lost its potato crop. It was the signal for an economic and social catastrophe of ghastly proportions. Yet the worst ravages of what became known as the Great Famine could have been averted.

Enough food was being produced within the 32 counties of Ireland to feed the population. But the dictates of the market prevailed. Throughout 1845, '46 and what became known as Black '47, the food that was being produced in Irish fields on the back of Irish labour was being exported. Meanwhile, as successive potato crops failed as a result of blight, the death toll mounted. In the long run, two million were to die and as many emigrated to the USA in what became known as the coffin ships. Hundreds of thousands died en route, of starvation, typhoid and other diseases associated with malnutrition.

In Ireland, meanwhile, experience of the famine dovetailed with the nationalist sentiment burgeoning throughout Europe. In 1848, an uprising was planned but it petered out miserably and the leaders were arrested. Among them was a Fenian poet, John Boyle O'Reilly, who was deported to Australia for his role in orchestrating the rebellion. In Irish folk culture, the name given to Tasmania – where citizens who had fallen foul of the Crown and the courts were frequently transported – was Van Diemen's Land; it was already the title of a familiar rebel ballad. But U2's 'Van Diemen's Land' – like 'Sunday Bloody Sunday' – is not a rebel song. Written and sung by The Edge against the sparse backdrop of his own plucked electric guitar, it is a sad and moving reflection on the continuity of suffering, injustice and violence, with the scarlet coats of the Fenians now being replaced by the black berets of the IRA.

"It's an emigrant's song – or an immigrant's song," Bono comments. "That's what justifies its place on the album. But I have to be very focused in a record, and for me that record was set in only one place."

As it happens, The Edge's plaintive appeal for justice without violence, recorded in The Point Theatre where U2 were rehearsing, provides one of the most beautiful and striking moments in the film, with Phil Joanou's cameras sweeping kinetically down the River Liffey that runs through the heart of the city and out into Dublin Bay, a place from which at least some of the emigrants of the 19th century embarked.

John Boyle O'Reilly had been bound for Australia. U2 were travelling deep into the heart of the USA . All of us, to one degree or another, are on the run. Driven – but by what?

Van Diemen's Land Written: U2. • Duration: 3' 05"

Movie stars: Poster for the release of the *Rattle and Hum* documentary movie, released shortly after the album in October 1988.

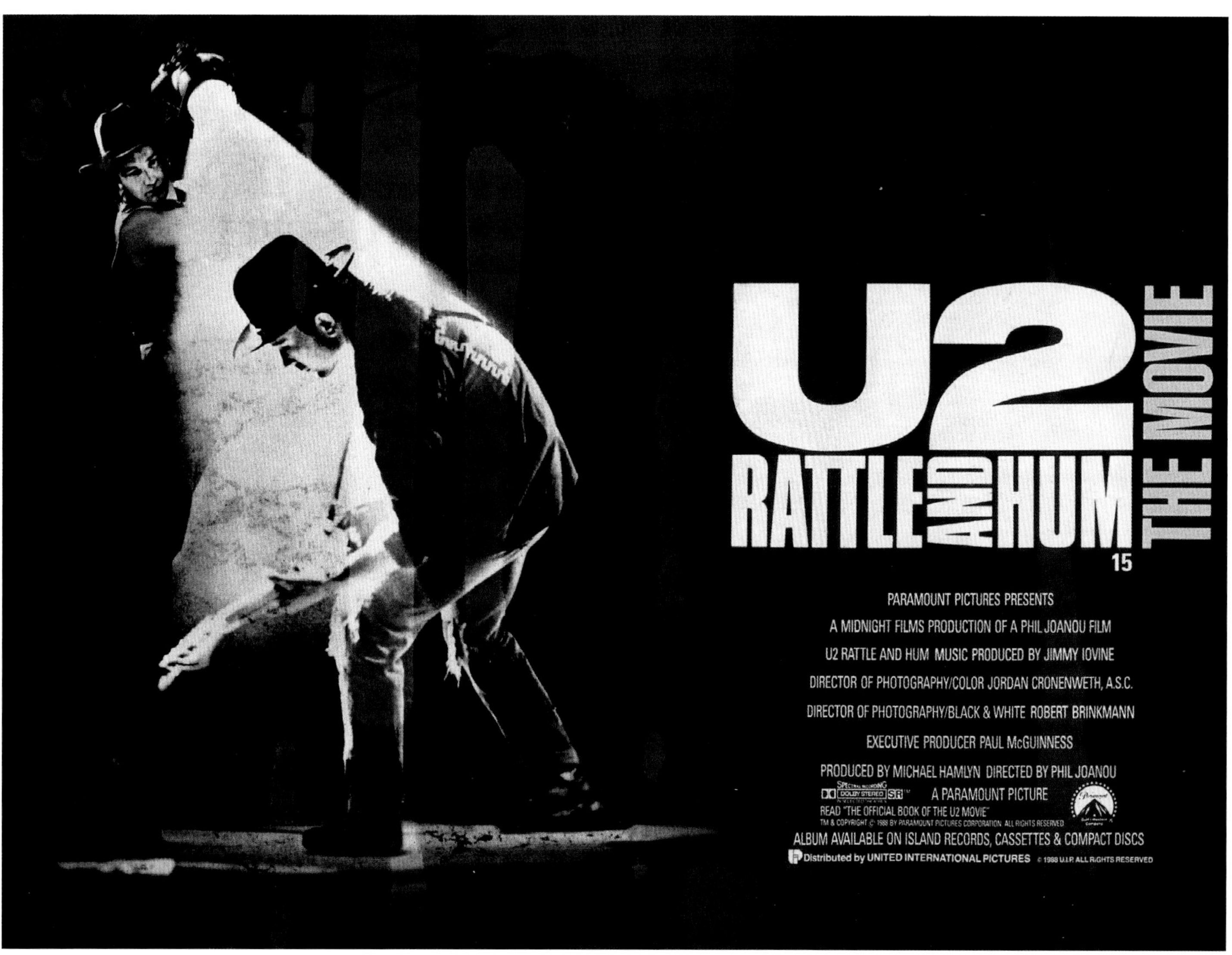

Desire

The first single off *Rattle and Hum*, 'Desire' confounded expectations. If anything on *The Joshua Tree* half-pointed in this direction it was 'Trip Through Your Wires' but that was sprawling and indulgent. By comparison, 'Desire' was loaded, cocked and ready to go off in the listener's hand. The Edge claimed that they'd been listening to Iggy Pop's coruscating '1969', which may indeed have been the case, but this rhythm was sired by Bo Diddley and made its first global impact on the charts via the Rolling Stones, out of Buddy Holly's 'Not Fade Away'. On its release, 'Desire' went straight to No. 1 in the UK, and U2 were understandably pleased.

"We were going back to rhythm and blues as part of our wanting to understand America," Bono explains. "We'd been reading the beats and various travel writers. Then we started to get into the music. Travelling through America, you're listening to different radio stations, rhythm and blues, country, soul, jazz, and you realize that rhythm is the sex of the music. So I think we got into dealing with those subjects, including desire, when we were making that jump musically."

The Edge had never been an R'n'B fan. Now he'd begun to see the great emotional strength of the music. "At the time, I think I had begun to realise that music had become too scientific. Too often, listening to modern records, you'd hear a producer rather than musicians interacting. I liked about 'Desire' the fact that it was totally not what people were listening to. It was a rock 'n' roll record, not a pop song."

For Bono, however, it was also a reflection on the condition of being a rock star. "I wanted to admit to the religiosity of rock 'n' roll concerts and the fact that you get paid for them. On one level, I'm starting to criticise these lunatic fringe preachers, 'stealing hearts at a travelling show' – but I'm also starting to realize that there's a real parallel there between what I'm doing and what they are."

'Desire' was the beginning of a process. Increasingly, Bono would consciously begin to own up to the contradictions in his own and the band's position. It was a reflection of the fact that U2 had come of age that they could produce with such enormous relish something that, on the surface at least, was so utterly basic.

Desire Written: U2 • Duration: 2' 59" • UK singles chart position: 1 • US singles chart position: 3

Hawkmoon 269

The road can be a good place to write. The stimuli are all around – new sights, sounds, experiences that provide the base metal from which songs can be wrought. The Edge had the Walkman doing overtime during The Joshua Tree tour.

'Hawkmoon 269' was one of the structures he sketched on acoustic guitar, onto a cassette. "Hawkmoon is a place in Rapid City, Dakota," he says. "We passed by it on the Amnesty Conspiracy of Hope tour and Bono, ever a man with a notebook handy, thought 'That sounds good'."

Bono remembers a crushing hangover that heightened the sense of dislocation that frequently infects musicians on the road, and the refrain comes straight out of that particular black pit: "*When the night has no end/ and the day yet to begin/As the room spins around you/I need your love.*" Maybe it was symptomatic that it became such a demon to record. Bob Dylan came along to play on the track and contributed a kind of inebriated hurdy gurdy effect. The band piled in but the battle to put a final shape on it continued. "It was mixed 269 times," Joe O'Herlihy laughs. "That's where the title came from." Bono looks unhappy even discussing it now. "That was my favourite song on the record," he says, "but we actually physically wore down the tape doing that number of mixes."

Not that anyone outside the camp would notice. Beginning as a love song, it transforms into a howl of lust, a molten volcano of a piece that climaxes in an intense gospel chant: "*Meet all your love in the heartland*", the backing trio of Edna Wright, Carolyn Willis and Billie Barnum repeat. "I'm sure there was enormous sexual frustration in the performance of that song," Bono admits. "I don't know how long we'd been away but at this point we were fully grown men of 26, 27, 28. We were recording in Sunset Sound. Sunset Strip. Hookers. Every neon sign advertising sex in some way. You could feel all that coming through in 'Hawkmoon'."

It's there in the rhythms, in Larry Bunker's thunderous timpani explosions and Larry Mullen's crashing cymbals. It's there in Bono's tortured metaphors and his yowling vocals. It's there in The Edge's blistering, dirty guitar. It's there in Adam's palpitating bass.

'Hawkmoon 269' may feel less than perfect to the band but perfection is hardly what it's about. Robert Palmer may have sung about being addicted to love but this was the real thing. Even better than the real thing.

Hawkmoon 269 Written: U2 • Duration: 6' 22"

All Along The Watchtower

It is 11 November, 1987. In between dates, the band decide to do a free gig on the back of a truck in an open space in San Francisco city centre, by the Embarcadero. Their own equipment is already on its way to Vancouver for the band's next show, so they borrow a sound system from – who else? – The Grateful Dead. Given the proximity of the location to the city's financial district – and in honour of the stock market crash of the week before – Bono dubs it the "Save the Yuppie" benefit.

The opening number they perform is a rough, improvised version of Bob Dylan's 'All Along the Watchtower'. In contrast to his first attempt at a Dylan cover, when Bono joined the maestro on stage at Slane for 'Blowin' in the Wind', on this occasion he clearly knows the words. Not that he's unduly constrained by that small detail.

The red guitar, on fire in 'Desire', reappears here, as Bono improvises: "*All I've got is a red guitar/three chords and the truth/All I've got is a red guitar/the rest is up to you.*"

The band don't seem to know the chords quite as well as Bono does the lyrics, however, and there are some startlingly odd moments of musical disjointedness. The first 30 seconds of the guitar intro are missed by the recording engineer and The Edge has to dub it in later. "Otherwise, everything else is as it was performed live," The Edge confirms.

As it happens, the occasion becomes more memorable for its off-stage antics. Aware of the fact that the mayor of San Francisco, Diane Feinstein, has offered $500 as a bounty for bringing any of the city's numerous graffiti artists into custody, Bono climbs to the top of the adjacent fountain sculpture and sprays "Stop the traffic – rock 'n' roll" on it.

A warrant is issued for his arrest but, the graffiti having been cleaned off by the following day, the attempt to bring the singer to justice eventually peters out. In the long run, Bono puts it all down to mid-tour madness, but there's no mistaking the satisfaction U2 feel when Diane Feinstein is replaced as mayor soon after the gig and her successor, Art Agnos, abolishes the bounty and, instead, sets up a fund to sponsor the work of graffiti artists in the city.

All Along The Watchtower Written: Dylan • Duration: 4' 24"

I Still Haven't Found What I'm Looking For

One criticism levelled at U2 during the squalls that surrounded their Self-Aid performance in Dublin was that, in the USA, they were still playing to predominantly white audiences. The implication was that they had failed to cross the class and racial divide, despite their overt celebration of Martin Luther King in 'Pride (In the Name of Love)' and 'MLK'.

My own impression at the time was that Bono had been stung by these accusations, angered at the suggestion that any artist or band could somehow be held accountable for the audience that chose – or chose not – to acknowledge them.

It may, however, have been a critical catalyst, inspiring the band to begin their odyssey in search of the roots of rock 'n' roll in black music, and in particular through rhythm and blues, gospel and soul. It must have felt like a remarkable vindication, then, when they first got wind of the fact that 'I Still Haven't Found What I'm Looking For' was being covered by a gospel group, trading under the name of The New Voices of Freedom, in Harlem.

The choir had sent a tape of their version of the song to Island Records, who passed it on to U2. Bono, Adam, Larry, The Edge and Gavin Friday went to check out the choir in their Harlem church and were impressed. As The Joshua Tree tour wound up to hit New York, a collaboration seemed like an attractive option.

The band suggested some rehearsals, to see if the different versions of the song could be integrated. The result provides one of the outstanding moments in the movie *Rattle and Hum*, a gloriously exuberant, thrilling musical encounter in which the common spirituality of the different participants is celebrated, tentatively at first and then with a rare and infectious abandon. Later, the choir joined the band for their date at Madison Square Garden and, although more formal, the performance is hardly less compelling. Bono's vocals are superb, as he trades licks with the two soloists George Pendergrass and Dorothy Tennell, creating the atmosphere of a Pentecostalist gospel service at its most transcendent.

The New Voices of Freedom's own version of 'I Still Haven't Found What I'm Looking For' was released as a single on the New Jersey label Doc Records. The song was later recorded by the Chimes, who had a hit with it in the USA and the UK. You could say that it's on its way to becoming a standard.

I Still Haven't Found What I'm Looking For Written: U2. • Duration: 5' 53"

Voice of a generation: Bono performs on stage at The Point December 26, 1989 as part of the Lovetown Tour.

A night to remember: Bono celebrates on stage at The Point during the filming of *Rattle and Hum*.

Freedom For My People

In the film, it was the kind of moment that inspired scepticism. U2 go for a stroll in downtown Harlem, to meet The New Voices of Harlem, followed by the cameras. There, they happen on a busker, one Mr Sterling Magee, with his harmonica sidekick, Adam Gussow, performing 'Freedom For My People'. The band hang about and observe, under the watchful artificial eye of the camera.

It's easy to see the point that's being made: a bunch of rock 'n' roll superstars still have something to learn from a rough 'n' ready street performer. In *Rattle and Hum*, U2 undertook their musical odyssey as both fans and pupils. But the presence of the camera made the value of that gesture a little harder to take at face intent: inevitably, it introduced an element of self-consciousness that a cinema audience would find it difficult to overcome. On record, however, 'Freedom For My People' – written by Sterling Magee, Bobby Robinson and Macie Mabins – drifts in and out, a found piece of street noise that acts as an appropriate prelude to what follows. Rock 'n' roll superstar or a bluesman? A bit of both of course.

Freedom For My People Written: Magee/Mabins/Robinson • Duration: 0' 38"

Silver And Gold

It was backstage at Slane, interviewing Bob Dylan for *Hot Press*, that Bono was given his first lesson in the importance of tradition. Dylan, who was almost as familiar with Irish ballads as he was with the work of Woody Guthrie, Leadbelly and Robert Johnson, mentioned the McPeakes from the north of Ireland. Bono looked at him blankly. "There's no particular musical roots or heritage for us," he explained about U2. "In Ireland there is a tradition, but we've never plugged into it."

"Well," Dylan insisted, "you have to reach back into the music." Bono was struck by an inadequacy at the core of U2's schtick, and he resolved to go about rectifying it. Part of the answer was to begin to move in different musical circles. Taking a break in New York late in 1989, he hooked up with Peter Wolf of the J. Geils Band. They visited a Rolling Stones session and became involved in a jam. With Keith Richards playing the piano, Wolf and Jagger traded vocals and harmonica licks. Bono was forced merely to watch – he didn't know any of the R'n'B standards that they were familiar with. They listened to some John Lee Hooker and Bono was hooked on the raw power of the voice, the rhythm and the stinging guitar.

To some extent the experience was humiliating, but Bono was spurred into action. Back in his hotel room, in a fever he wrote his own take on the blues. He had just been in Ethiopia with Ali. He had seen first-hand the impact of Western economic policies on the African continent and his sense of outrage is palpable in 'Silver and Gold', a song about imperialism, greed, exploitation and repression.

Bono borrowed the line "I am someone" from black civil rights leader Jesse Jackson. And he plundered the Irish literary landscape for a couplet deriving from Brendan Behan: "*I have seen the coming and going/The captains and the kings.*" But in writing the song from the perspective of a black political prisoner, he made a crucial leap of the imagination. The original acoustic version was recorded with Keith Richards and Ronnie Wood for the Sun City album. On *Rattle and Hum*, the whole band are on board and the result is inevitably heavier, Bono entering into the spirit of the performance with an improvised anti-apartheid rap, ending in a preemptive strike against the inevitable accusations of political posturing. "Am I buggin' you?" he asked sardonically. "Don't mean to bug you." Curiously the throwaway line "OK Edge, play the blues", introducing the guitar break, generated the most flak. But the solo is quintessential Edge, and underlines just how far from the blues he'd been reared.

Silver And Gold Written: U2 • Duration: 5' 49"

Angel Of Harlem

The improvisations that had kick-started so many U2 songs weren't coming quite so easily. The Edge realized that they needed new ways of writing, and his response was characteristically sensible. He decided that he would learn. He had come up with the basis for 'Desire' and 'Hawkmoon 269' on the acoustic guitar. Now add to that list 'Angel of Harlem'. From a musical perspective, something curious happened.

Because he was at the centre of things on acoustic, The Edge found it more difficult to identify a space for himself on electric lead guitar. He was going to have to master some Steve Cropper-style licks to slot in and around the Stax-like horns on a sweet soul ballad of this kind.

Bono had been thinking about Billie Holiday. A friend of his, a girl called Alexis whom he'd met in San Francisco when she was 15 or 16, had moved to London and kept in touch. She'd given him a biography of the singer they called Lady Day. His fascination had been primed, and as U2 travelled around the States, picking up on gospel, jazz and R'n'B stations, it was intensified. 'Angel of Harlem' was written on the road but it's got the pulse of New York in its veins, with John Coltrane, Charlie Parker and Miles Davis making cameo appearances alongside the star of the scenario.

The lyrics have a strong visual, cinematic feel, but it was the Memphis Horns that completed the picture. Anyone familiar with Southside Johnny and the Asbury Jukes will know where this one is coming from. "Funny, I can hear Dylan in it more than Stax," Bono smiles now, and the reference makes sense. What's important, however, is the sheer mastery of it all.

On their musical odyssey through the American heartland, the band had decided to swing by Sun Studios in Memphis and to line up a session there. With the Memphis Horns in attendance and Cowboy Jack Clement at the desk, they recorded what became a tribute not just to Billie Holiday but to the vast legacy of great music that America had bequeathed to the world. Upful and celebratory, it remains one of U2's finest moments.

"It's a jukebox song," Bono says. "We don't have many jukebox songs, maybe six or seven, but that's one that people play in bars." And anywhere else they need to get that rush.

Angel Of Harlem Written: U2 • Duration: 3' 49" • UK singles chart psition: 9 • US singles chart position: 14

Love Rescue Me

The Joshua Tree tour was half-done. The idea for *Rattle and Hum* had been worked out, and it was clear that the band were going to have to do some serious recording. Rather than de-camping, returning to Dublin – where it was winter – and attempting to re-focus there, someone suggested heading for the West Coast and working in LA. If the album was going to be about America, then it made sense to hang out there.

The Edge took a house out in Beverly Hills with his wife Aislinn and their kids. It was the house where the Menendez brothers later murdered their parents. "We were the last guys there before them," Bono says. "I was staying in the mews and that was where I wrote 'Love Rescue Me'." If "wrote" is the right word. After a night of debauchery, Bono was sleeping fitfully and had a bizarre dream about Bob Dylan. He woke up and, under the cloud of a massive hangover, began to write the lyrics of the song he thought he remembered Dylan singing in his dream, about a man people keep turning to as a saviour, but whose own life is increasingly shattered, and who could do with a shot of salvation himself.

Shortly afterwards, Bono got a call, asking him if he wanted to pay a visit to Dylan – and thus, with a weird synchronicity, he ended up finishing the song later that day with the man in his dream. "I thought it was a Dylan song," Bono recalls. "So when I met him I said, 'Is this one of yours?' and he said, 'No, but maybe it could be'. So we worked on it together."

How much of the finished product is Bono and how much Dylan remains unclear. "Listen, I'd polish his shoes, I really would," Bono says. "A lot of people want their heroes to not let them down. I think it's a duty of heroes to let you down in some ways." Dylan recorded a lead vocal for the track but it was withdrawn, apparently at Dylan's request, because of a potential clash with his Traveling Wilbury commitments.

The lyric is powerful, poetic and unremitting in its harsh, tormented glare. *"In the cold mirror of a glass/I see my reflection pass/I see the dark shades of what I used to be/I see the purple of her eyes/The scarlet of my lies/Love rescue me."* Beginning as a country ballad, the song is transformed by the entry of the Memphis Horns, lifting it into the realms of country-soul à la Otis Redding. "I don't think I fully pull it off in the singing stakes," Bono admits. "At that point, I was still allowing black influences into my voice, whereas now I am fully content to be white. Pink even [laughs]. I like it as a musical influence but in the voice it's dangerous for me."

Love Rescue Me Written: U2/Dylan • Duration: 6' 24"

The King: The legendary B.B. King joins U2 on stage to sing 'When Love Comes to Town'.

When Love Comes To Town

Early in 1986, B.B. King landed in Ireland. After his Dublin date, he hooked up with U2. B.B. asked for a song and Bono came up with the basis of it pretty quickly. "Writing songs for other people can be so easy," Bono reflects. "You're out of your own head and into someone else's." The challenge is to finish the job – typically, Bono completed the lyric in his hotel room just before he was due to present it to B.B.

It seems Bono had always envisaged sharing the vocals in the context of *Rattle and Hum*. Legend has it that when King met Bono after reading the lyrics he asked, "How old are you? They're heavy lyrics. Heavy lyrics." The album version was recorded in Sun Studios, where so much seminal rock 'n' roll had been produced by its original owner, Sam Phillips.

"You go into the Sun room, and it's a modest room," Adam recalled later. "It's got the old acoustic titles on the wall and the pictures of Elvis and Roy Orbison and Jerry Lee and Carl Perkins – it's just history."

'When Love Comes To Town' brilliantly fuses gospel and blues influences. With the redemptive power of love as its theme, it goes back even further for its clinching biblical metaphor as the two singers trade verses: "I was there when they crucified my Lord," B.B. sings, "*I held the scabbard when the soldier drew his sword/I threw the dice when they pierced his side/But I've seen love conquer the great divide.*"

Bono is freewheeling. "It's like that line from Brendan Kennelly's Book of Judas: 'The best way to serve the age is to betray it'," he says.

When Love Comes To Town Written: U2 • Duration: 4' 15" • UK singles chart position: 6 • US singles chart position: 68

Heartland

"We don't write many straight love songs," Bono says. But U2 do write about love all the time. In fact love in its many facets and guises is the terrain their music most frequently occupies. 'Heartland' is a love song. It was written during 1986 for *The Joshua Tree* and was one of the five or six tracks that remained unfinished from those marathon sessions. When it came to the cut, the band went for 'Trip Through Your Wires' in preference; it was a question of flow and balance.

It gelled with the theme of *Rattle and Hum* perfectly. If *The Joshua Tree* had attacked the duplicity and deceit at the heart of US political machinations, its follow-up was a much more affectionate document, in its new songs celebrating popular culture and the country that had provided the breeding ground for the blues and rock 'n' roll. 'Heartland' emerges as a love song to the nation. Ireland had frequently been characterised as a woman by poets like James Clarence Mangan in 'My Dark Rosaleen' and William Butler Yeats, who cast the country as Caitlín Ní Houliháin in a variety of works. Now Bono was applying for the same kind of poetic licence. He passed the test with honours.

"America both fascinates and frightens me," Bono said. "I can't get it out of my system. Wim Wenders has said that America has colonised our unconscious. He's right. You don't have to go there – it comes to you. No matter where we live it's pumped into our homes in *Dallas*, *Dynasty* and *Hill Street Blues*. It's Hollywood, it's Coca-Cola, it's Levis. There's good and bad in all of these, but either way you've got to deal with it."

Heartland Written: U2 • Duration: 5' 03"

God Part II

You're trying to make sense of the madness around you. Album sales are going through the roof. The tour is like a military operation. There are hundreds of people on board now and they all want a piece of you. The record company wants a piece of you. The media wants a piece of you. The fans want a piece of you. And your family – they're entitled to a piece of you that you can't give them.

And on top of all that – the usual mayhem, only worse – someone had the bright idea of making a fucking film of the tour. Something inside keeps telling you that it could be a catastrophe.

There's so much money at stake and so little control you can exert. They get in the way, shove cameras up your nose, follow you around – as if you didn't feel that you were in a goldfish bowl already. You remember Washington DC. Falling on the stage. Dislocating your shoulder. Being wheeled into an ambulance. Looking up and seeing Phil Joanou – you'd nicknamed him ET – and his cameras. You said: "ET", you said, "what the fuck are you doing in my ambulance?" And he said: "Hey, you wanted me to make a documentary!" Madness. Complete fucking madness.

And if you whinge about this kind of thing, if you complain – it's like, "You ungrateful bastard, you. You've got money, success, hit records, hot and cold running groupies, stretch limos, champagne on ice everywhere you go – and you're complaining?" As if that was what it was all about. It makes you think about what it must have been like for Elvis. Why he hid himself away in Graceland and ate a mountain of cheeseburgers. It makes you think about what it must have been like for the Beatles, for John Lennon.

That was why you decided to open the set with 'Helter Skelter'. Now the word was out that Albert Goldman was about to do a hatchet job on Lennon. Goldman. His Elvis book stank. Made Presley out to be a rock 'n' roll idiot. Now the same asshole was going to do John Lennon over, and portray him as a rock 'n' roll fool. As a bully. As a reptile. Albert Goldman. What the fuck would he know?

There's a song in all this. Make it a tribute to Lennon. Jimmy Iovine knew him. Worked with the Plastic Ono Band. 'God Part II ', you could call it. Send up all that Hollywood sequel stuff. That's a new twist. Give Goldman a going over himself. Get some of that pent-up bile out of your system. Say some things about Lennon. Own up to some things about yourself. Have some fun doing the whole thing in the Plastic Ono mould. Only re-vamped. Upgraded. Look for a new dynamic. A good excuse to check out how this grunge thing feels. Nice and quiet and then WHAM! IN YOUR FACE! Keep it tight, restrained and then USE the SLEDGEHAMMER. Bam! Jimmy should be able to handle that.

'God Part II ', you call it. It's hard alright, a sort of a half-way house between *The Joshua Tree* and the future. It's got Lennon written all over it. It's got drum loops for Larry to kick against, which is interesting. It's got you being all nice and reasonable and then WAH! Throwing a bit of a tantrum. You get a chance to quote Bruce Cockburn: a good line of his, that one about kicking the darkness till it bleeds daylight. You use the opportunity to show your own darker side. To be a bit irresponsible. To reveal your anger. And to do a Lennon yourself, trying to wrap up the truth in a single phrase. "*I believe in love.*" Because it's true. You do. Not that it cut much ice with Yoko. "That was a nice cover version you did of John's song," she'd said when you met her. Cover version! At least she didn't look for royalties.

Looking back on it later, with a bit of distance and detachment, it's not a track you'll make a passionate case for. The thing that stops it coming off is the singing: it does sound like a bit of a tantrum. You can laugh at that now yourself, but there's not a lot of humour in the song or on the record. Vitriol is at its best with wit.

What the hell. 'God Part II ' may not be the best thing you've done by a long shot but it was necessary. It helped. Sometimes that's the point. Whatever gets you through the night, it's alright. It's alright.

God Part II Written: U2 • Duration: 3' 1

All I Want Is You

One of U2's writing strategies was for Bono and The Edge to head off into the country somewhere, to isolate themselves, the better to let the muse speak through them. When The Joshua Tree tour finished, they took a short break, and then began the process of writing new material for *Rattle and Hum*. They retreated to a house in Connemara owned by John Heather. The Edge was working on the basics of 'Desire' – the Bo Diddley rhythm, the main riff. He also had this beautiful chord sequence and melody that Bono immediately saw potential in. "It became a meditation on commitment and what that means," Bono says. It became 'All I Want Is You'.

If *Rattle and Hum* had begun with the Beatles via 'Helter Skelter', it would end with them too, in a string coda that was reminiscent of 'A Day in the Life'. Ironically, it was the wayward genius Van Dyke Parks who contributed an arrangement that leaned back in the direction of Europe, bringing the whole album to a haunting, ethereal finale.

'All I Want Is You' is a love song and Bono doesn't usually talk about these things – but on this occasion he does. "That's clearly about a younger version of myself and my relationship with Ali," he reflects. "It takes a huge generosity of spirit to be around somebody who's in the position I'm in, and who can expose you. If you're a very private person, as she is, that's something you have to be very careful about.

"That's a song about commitment, really. I don't think being married to someone is so easy. But I'm interested in the idea of marriage. I think it's madness but it's a grand madness. If people think it's normal, they're out of their minds. I think that's why a lot of people fall apart, because they're not prepared for what it is. Once they've made that commitment, they think that's the end of it, now they can rest easy.

"I'm very restless. I am not the kind of guy who would normally settle down with a family and one person. I'm a tinker. I like to travel. The only reason I'm here is because I met someone so extraordinary that I just couldn't let that go. So a lot of the sense you get from the work is that some of the characters want to run, to get to the airport and just fly away. And other characters could never be away from this."

All I Want Is You Written: U2 • Duration: 6' 30" • UK singles chart position: 4 • US singles chart position: 83

Rattle and strum: U2 performing on the balcony of the Gresham Hotel in Dublin at the premier of *Rattle and Hum* in 1988.

EXTRA-CURRICULAR ACTIVITIES

PASSENGERS

Released in November 1995, *Passengers: Original Soundtracks 1* was a one-album side-project for U2, recorded by the band as the Passengers, together with Brian Eno, as a tribute to their favourite cinema soundtracks. The loose idea was that Eno would call the creative shots and U2 would obey...

United Colours of Plutonium

U2 recorded this track thinking of the bullet train in Japan. "We wanted that sense of speed," says Bono. "We wanted it to sound like being aboard the bullet train." Originally U2 and Eno recorded an extended improvisation piece. It was cut down to seven minutes, then Howie B played around with it and it was snipped down to fiveand- a-half. "It's a helluva sound as an opening track," says Bono. "But probably still a bit too long."

Slug

'Slug' was an attempt to paint a picture of the lights coming on in a city like Tokyo. "It's like a Christmas tree," explains Bono of the sweet musical tinkling that opens the track. It was originally called 'Seibu', after a Japanese department store. "It's a portrait, like '...Arms Around The World', of somebody a little the worse for wear," says Bono, "which we all were in Tokyo, because it was the end of the tour."

Your Blue Room

Musically, on this track, U2 were thinking of Serge Gainsbourg, yet Bono's voice has the deep, reassuring quality adopted by Leonard Cohen on his songs of seduction. "It's my favourite song on the record," says Bono. "If we weren't keeping a low profile – we have to, because people get sick of us if we're always putting stuff out – we'd have really pushed it." It also features Adam Clayton's first lead vocal as the bassist's voice comes in at the end, quietly chatting in the background as if in a late-night conversation post-sex.

Always Forever Now

While U2 were recording as Passengers, somebody scrawled a slogan on a blackboard in their new Dublin studio: MAKE THE MUSIC OF THE FUTURE YOU WANT TO LIVE IN. The album was to reflect a positive vision of where Earth was heading, and 'Always Forever Now' fits the bill. The title was based on a picture by artist Damien Hirst. "It's just an affirmation," says Bono. "The words are self-explanatory."

A Different Kind of Blue

Some reviewers claimed U2 were nowhere to be heard on 'A Different Kind of Blue'. At best, they were only partially right. Bono came up with the title and the beginnings of a jazz song to go with it, Edge did a version of it and then Eno sneaked into the studio overnight. "In a sense, it's a hybrid," says Bono. "I'd say the perfect hour to listen to the record is either at dawn or in the half-hour of twilight, when the sun is going down. What it suggests to me – 'Twilight breaking through' – is getting up out of bed for the night."

Beach Sequence

"That was me playing one-finger piano," says Bono. "In fact, it was called 'One Finger Piano' at one point." Which only goes to show that it doesn't really take an instrumental genius to produce beautiful notes. Like 'Your Blue Room', 'Beach Sequence' was used in the Michelangelo Antonioni and Wim Wenders collaboration Par-Dela Les Nuages (Beyond The Clouds).

Miss Sarajevo

After MacPhisto phoned Pavarotti live from the stage in Bologna during the Italian leg of the Zooropa tour, Pavarotti began phoning U2 demanding to record a song together. Bono became obsessed with the idea of finding the right track and U2 came up with a track that ended up on the Passengers album. "We came up with the libretto by impersonating my father singing in the bath, impersonating Pavarotti," admits Bono. The song was about the Serbian siege of Bosnians in Sarajevo, a city that U2 had made a satellite connection to on the night they also phoned Pavarotti. Bono was to finance and produce a film on the underground resistance in the city. The song was premiered at the annual Pavarotti and Friends concert in Modena, Italy on September 12, 1995. It was released as a single in aid of the War Child charity two months later and only prevented from being a UK Christmas No.1 by Michael Jackson's 'Earth Song'.

Ito Okashi

Brian Eno contacted a Japanese singer, Holi, who had moved to London. She met U2 in the studio with nothing planned, but Bono was impressed nonetheless: "She kept using this phrase over and over – ito okashi." The term means 'something beautiful' and Holi used that simple idea to create a short, evocative, almost haiku-style lyric in Japanese in a reflective piece evoking the sun rising in the East.

One Minute Warning

U2 often played along to Japanese animation movies being shown on a studio TV as they recorded Original Soundtracks 1. They were greatly influenced by Jean Luc Godard's Alphaville and then got a request to produce a piece for Ghost in the Shell, an animation feature directed by Mamoru Oshia. The improvisations inspired by Alphaville seemed to fit – and then Howie B got to work on it. "When Howie came in, he left out huge elements that we had thought were very important," says Edge. "Suddenly that was very refreshing."

Corpse

'Corpse' saw U2 twist a blues lyrical convention to have the song's protagonist moan that the chains binding him were too long. The Edge adopted the persona of a character on Death Row and sang it as a dirge-like acknowledgement of what can happen to someone who doesn't recognise any limits to human behaviour. It is, you could say, a different kind of blues.

Elvis Ate America

This song began life as 'Elvis: American David', a beat poem written by Bono as the preface to an art exhibition book named 2 x Immortal: Elvis + Marilyn. "It's just like a list," explains Bono. "Some people don't get that concept but the American David idea is interesting. I've always conceived of David in the Bible as the first blues singer." The list became a rap and Howie B made it into a song. "He's the guy who's chanting 'Elvis' throughout it," confirms Bono.

Plot 180

In A Year With Swollen Appendices, his diary of 1995, Brian Eno unveiled some of the rationale behind the *Original Soundtracks 1* concept – namely, that an awareness that music is being composed for a film stimulates the imagination to think pictorially and scenically. It also opened up opportunities for humour, and 'Plot 180' sounded like a send-up of some standard stereotypical piece of Hollywood flim-flam.

Theme from The Swan

Eno would go into the studio before anyone else and find a loop to operate as the basis of a track. The band would then come in and build on top of it. Eno's signature was supposed to be clearly discernable and it was on 'Theme from The Swan', a slow, haunting piece where he plays the cello. There were times when U2 had sounded like Talking Heads – and there is, of course, a lot of Brian Eno in Talking Heads. "He'd always talked about doing an experimental record with us, along the lines of Bush of Ghosts that he'd done with David Byrne," says Edge. With that in mind, this impressive African-influenced rhythm piece was a fitting wrap-up for *Passengers*.

THE MILLION DOLLAR HOTEL

U2 and Daniel Lanois contributed five songs to the soundtrack of this 2000 Wim Wenders movie based on a drama story by Bono and Nicholas Klein and starring Milla Jovovich and Mel Gibson. Bono was inspired to sketch out the movie's storyline when the band did a photo shoot at LA's Million Dollar Hotel in 1987. "I think it is sad," laughs Bono, "but I know a lot about hotels."

The Ground Beneath Her Feet

Featuring Daniel Lanois on pedal steel, the spookily melancholic ballad 'The Ground Beneath Her Feet' was the first song featured on the *Million Dollar Hotel* soundtrack. Bono took the lyrics almost verbatim from a passage in Salman Rushdie's novel of the same name (meaning that Rushdie got a 50% share in the songwriting credit). The band wanted to release it as a single, but Interscope refused, fearing it would confuse fans before the release of 2000 comeback album *All That You Can't Leave Behind* – though it was released as a bonus track on UK, Australian and Japanese releases of that album. Rushdie said that it had "some of the most beautiful melodies [Bono] had ever come up with." U2 played the song several times on their 2001 world tour.

Stateless

'Stateless' came out of a soundcheck jam before a U2 show in Australia which they returned to during the recording of *All That You Can't Leave Behind.* "It's mostly Bono," says Daniel Lanois. "He picked up Edge's guitar, with those huge sounds, and came up with this on the spot." "It's like a Robert Johnson blues," avers Bono. "Kind of a sci-fi blues."

Dancin' Shoes

Producer Daniel Lanois confirms that Bono being involved in *The Million Dollar Hotel* at the same time as the recording of *All That You Can't Leave Behind* was not regarded as good timing. "Bono asked me to do the soundtrack with him and I largely did it so we could finish the U2 record," he says. The pair created 'Dancin' Shoes' from a chord sequence that Lanois had lying around.' Before he wrote his *The Ground Beneath Her Feet* novel, author Salman Rushdie – then lying low after being the victim of a religious fatwa following the publication of The Satanic Verses – stayed at Bono's place in Killiney. Rushdie wrote lyrics for a song of the same name, which Bono shaped a song around. The singer put it forward for *All That You Can't Leave Behind* but found the band unenthusiastic and so used it on *The Million Dollar Hotel.* Wim Wenders described it as "... the song that defines the spirit of the film."

Falling At Your Feet

This beautiful Bob Dylan-like litany song found Bono back in familiar terrain, echoing the adoration – abasement, even – of 'Mysterious Ways'. Written for the movie, it was constructed around a chord sequence that Lanois had already sketched out. "I like love songs that are bittersweet," explains Bono. "I don't want to hear a song that reddens my face when I hear it on the radio."

Never Let Me Go

Trumpeter John Hassell got a writing credit on 'Never Let Me Go', a song that began with a jam over which Bono improvised a lyric that was later refined. "This is the first U2 song that sounds specifically influenced by Gavin Friday," said *Hot Press* writer Peter Murphy. "I wouldn't rule it out," says Bono. "He's influenced pretty much everything else. He certainly lent me the big shoes."

SINGLES, B-SIDES AND BONUS TRACKS

Boy-Girl

The third track on U23, the band's legendary Ireland-only debut recording, 'Boy-Girl' was born when U2 and the Virgin Prunes took the title and wrote two separate songs. "Ours was dealing with bisexuality," recalls Gavin Friday. "They were talking about a more conventional form of love, with quite a strong boyhood-to-manhood theme going down."

Another Day

'Another day' was recorded at the same time as U23 and released in February 1980. The theme was one of adolescent angst, with Bono struggling to be optimistic, despite waking up to 'the toll of another dull day'.

11 O' Clock Tick Tock

Late one evening, a teenage Gavin Friday stuck a note on his friend Bono's bedroom door: "11 o'clock, tick tock. Gav called." Ever the magpie, Bono stole the phrase for a song that criticised the style self-consciousness that dominated the UK's music scene at the end of the 1970s. "I've no time for cynicism with no direction," commented Bono at the time. "I've no time for casual rebels." Produced by Martin Hamnett, '11 O'Clock Tick Tock' became U2's second single.

Touch

Originally called 'Trevor', possibly after the Virgin Prunes' Trevor Strongman, the Martin Hamnett produced 'Touch' was the b-side of '11 O'Clock Tick Tock'.

Things To Make And Do

This whimsical instrumental appeared on the B-side of 'A Day Without Me' in August 1980. "No one else was in town and we needed a B-side," recalls Edge. "So I just did it on the 4-track cassette – just me in the rehearsal room."

J. Swallow

U2 needed a song for the b-side of 'Fire'. "It was done in a mad panic," says Edge. "It was a case of two hours to go, let's do it. Johnny Swallow was one of our mates, called Reggie Manuel."

A Celebration

Recorded as a single between *October* and *War*, 'A Celebration' was intended to fill a gap caused by the relative lack of singles on the former. Like much of *October*, it reflected U2's Christian commitment, although the Dublin references to Christ Church and Mountjoy give the hint of a social context. Bono remembers the video. "We had itinerant boys as the four horsemen of the Apocalypse and me in ridiculous red pants in Kilmainham jail. I think I had a badger on my head, as well. Some pieces of music are obscured by the haircuts, I think it's fair to say."

Trash Trampoline And The Party Girl

Written, according to one rumour, about the Edge's wife-to-be, Aislinn O'Sullivan, this B-side to 'A Celebration' was trashy, throwaway and fun. But who was Trash Trampoline? The smart money was on Adam Clayton, who played the field in a way the rest of U2 never did.

Treasure (Whatever Happened To Pete The Chop)?

Written about Pete the Chop, a friend of early U2 management associate Andrew Whiteway, 'Pete The Chop' was so poppy that Paul McGuinness wanted to release it as a single. "It was very melodic," says The Edge, "but not really very good." It eventually surfaced as 'Treasure', the B-side of 'New Year's Day'.

Endless Deep

Adam Clayton focussed on the business side of U2 in the early days but by *War* he was coming into his own as a bass player. This was evident on this track, the B-side of 'Two Hearts Beat As One'.

Boomerang I and Boomerang II

U2 had always liked Talking Heads so it was almost inevitable that the influence would show when they began to work with the band's producer, Brian Eno. 'Boomerang' came in two mixes, which accompanied different releases of 'Pride (In The Name Of Love)' as a single. "I think African influences were important there," says The Edge. "That was when the first wave of African music was hitting the West: Fela Kuti, King Sunny Ade and all those people."

The Three Sunrises

U2, Eno and Lanois concluded that 'The Three Sunrises' would not have worked on *The Unforgettable Fire* but its Beatles-style pop harmonies and stabbing, almost hard-rock guitar made it an interesting departure. Neil McCormick of *Hot Press* called it "One of U2's finest out-takes."

Love Comes Tumbling

This was relatively unfamiliar company for U2 – a simple, gentle, rhythmic love song with a distinctly romantic feel. It was released first with the 'The Unforgettable Fire' single, with the 'Pride (In The Name Of Love)' double 7" pack and on *Wide Awake In America*.

Bass Trap

Produced by Eno and Lanois, 'Bass Trap' was a bonus track on the 12" single of 'The Unforgettable Fire'. "Brian [Eno] used a really cheap electronic device to trap a bass figure that Adam had played," says Edge. "It was sort of like what Philip Glass does with his work."

Sixty Seconds In Kingdom Come

This was an extra track on the double 7" single of 'The Unforgettable Fire' but – despite its great title – Edge dismisses it as a piece of music that never went anywhere.

Luminous Times (Hold Onto Love)

The piano-driven 'Luminous Times' didn't make the cut for *The Joshua Tree* but surfaced on the 'With Or Without You' single. It sounds improvised but has a quality of emotional honesty running through it that is hugely impressive as Bono struggles to come to terms with love's contradictions and complexities.

Walk To The Water

This also didn't make *The Joshua Tree* but Philip Lynott's influence is discernable in the gentle evocation of some past, more romantic Dublin – and might Bono have been trying to describe the courtship between his own father and mother on Dublin's north side? Either way, it was an impressive first flirtation with rap.

Spanish Eyes

'Spanish Eyes', released as a B-side to 'I Still Haven't Found What I'm Looking For', ranked alongside 'Desire' and 'Hawkmoon 269' as a statement of intense, primal lust. "I think it is Ali, to be honest," says Edge. "I think that's what Bono was on about."

Deep In The Heart

With love and sex not heavily represented on *The Joshua Tree*, it was left to B-sides and bonus tracks such as this to carry the torch. Like 'Spanish Eyes', 'Deep In The Heart' does so powerfully, depicting a Lolita-style scene with an almost disquieting sense of detachment.

Sweetest Thing

Bono was not totally convinced about 'Sweetest Thing'. It would have made a powerful, radio-friendly single – but might it have tilted the perception of the band in a way that might ultimately prove unhelpful? It was consequently omitted from *The Joshua Tree* and turned up on the B-side of 'Where The Streets Have No Name', where Adam supplied a massive, rumbling bass attack to give musical root to Bono's intense, besotted ode to Ali. Realising that a hit had been missed, in October 1998, U2 re-recorded it for *The Best of 1980-1990*, released the following month. The lyrics had been written by Bono as an apology to Ali for having worked in the studio on her birthday. The playful video, made by Kevin Godley, capture Bono in mock in-the-dog-house mode as he takes Ali on a carriage ride from Fitzwilliam Place down to Merrion Square, on the south side of Dublin. It features a cast of Irish celebrities, including members of Boyzone and boxer Steve Collins, as well as the band. Released as a single, it went to No. 1 in Ireland and Canada, No. 2 in Italy and Spain, and No. 3 in the UK and is considered one of U2's big pop songs

Race Against Time

Like 'Sweetest Thing', 'Race Against Time' – which also appeared on the 'Where The Streets Have No Name' 12" – is interesting as an indicator of the album U2 might have made instead of *The Joshua Tree*. "It was a kind of Afro-centric piece I put together," says Edge. "We realised it wasn't going to make the album so left it to one side."

Hallelujah (Here She Comes)

The B-side to 'Desire', this was a piece of upful gospel rock that was written by Edge and Bono in John Heather's house in Connemara.

A Room At The Heartbreak Hotel

This song saw Bono explore his fascination with Elvis Presley to reflect on the themes of love, lust, fidelity and betrayal without achieving the condensed poetic power that Achtung Baby was to reveal. The Edge calls it "Gospel meets Suicide" and it appeared on the 12" of 'Angel of Harlem'.

Alex Descends Into Hell For A Bottle Of Milk

Director Ron Daniels approached U2 to write an original score for the Royal Shakespeare Company's theatrical production of Anthony Burgess's *A Clockwork Orange* in 1990. "He wanted a hit musical," says Edge. "We warned him we weren't very good at hits." Burgess was reportedly disdainful towards U2's efforts but, says Edge, "I've a feeling it was just a reaction against the fact that it wasn't Beethoven, so I'm not too upset." A few of the snatches of music U2 prepared were combined for this track, a B-side to 'The Fly'.

Lady With The Spinning Head

The original demo backing track that spawned both 'The Fly' and 'Light My Way' on Achtung Baby, 'Lady With The Spinning Head' had a good groove courtesy of Larry's carefree drum part. U2 tracks that aren't laboured over tend to sound like someone else and Primal Scream and Happy Mondays lurked in the shadows here.

Where Did It All Go Wrong?

When George Best was at the height of his powers and fame, he was staying in a suite at the Dorchester Hotel. As the famous – and possibly apocryphal – story goes, as a grizzled old porter from his home town of Belfast brought the footballer up yet more champagne, he looked at Best lying on the bed, surrounded by beautiful women and wads of cash, and asked: "George, where did it all go wrong?" "It's a great story," says Edge. "We just wrote the song around that quote."

Salome

This was recorded at STS Studios in Dublin, which played a pivotal role in U2's development. It had a dual existence: a blistering R&B version on the cassette single of 'Even Better Than The Real Thing' and a Zooromancer dance remix on the 'Who's Gonna Ride Your Wild Horses?' single.

Slow Dancing

Bono wrote 'Slow Dancing' for Willie Nelson, sent it off and heard nothing. Assuming the country star was not interested, U2 recorded it and put it on the 'Stay (Faraway So Close)' single only for Nelson to make contact with the band next time he played Dublin. Nelson recorded a vocal and this appeared as an additional track on the 'If God Will Send His Angels' single.

Bottoms

"This was one of Brian [Eno]'s crazy mixes of 'Zoo Station'," explains Edge. "He did different prototype mixes which helped us to get to our final version." 'Bottoms' appeared as an extra track on the Japanese version of *Original Soundtracks 1*.

Hold Me, Thrill Me, Kiss Me, Kill Me

Bono was initially dismissive of the idea of U2 contributing a song to the *Batman Forever* soundtrack but Edge was keener: "I figured it'd be good for us to be involved in something that's basically throwaway and light-hearted." The band revisited a piece they had been unable to finish for Zooropa and the cartoon video that accompanied it was nominated for Best Video from a Film at the MTV Awards, losing out to Seal.

Mission Impossible

Strictly speaking, this theme from *Mission Impossible* isn't a U2 track but Adam Clayton and Larry Mullen Jnr, underlining something that is too often ignored: they make a great rhythm section, and one which has been absolutely central to U2's success.

North and South of the River

Written with Christy Moore in 1995, U2's version appeared on the CD single of 'Staring At The Sun'. At heart it's a political song about the difficulties of reconciling Nationalist and Unionist traditions in Northern Ireland and is a companion piece to U2's other songs about the national question, from 'Sunday Bloody Sunday' to 'Please' and 'Peace On Earth'.

Two Shots of Happy One Shot of Sad

Bono was proud of this song, which in his head was being sung by Frank Sinatra. He tried to get Old Blue Eyes to sing it but Sinatra didn't bite, which is a shame, as it captures his persona superbly, peppered with sparkling nuggets that temper the braggadocio of 'My Way'. Produced by Nellee Hooper, it was released on the 'If God Will Send His Angels' single.

I'm Not Your Baby

'I'm Not Your Baby', an instrumental piece that would not be out of place on Passengers, was U2 gone trip-hop. Produced by Howie B and Flood, it's engaging in its combination of sonics and rhythm but is essentially background music.

Summer Rain

Written at Larry's place in the south of France, 'Summer Rain', a B-side to 'Beautiful Day', is a gentle acoustic track in a minor key that resonates of the 1960s. Bono muses on how he lost himself to the summer rain: you can almost see the clouds rolling in over Provence. "I love that tune," says Edge. "It just didn't quite measure up against other tunes on the record [*All That You Can't Leave Behind*]."

Big Girls Are Best

From the Pop sessions, this didn't surface until the release of the 'Stuck In A Moment' single. The melody owes more than a bit to John Lennon, as does the sentiment of homage to a departed mother. The title is hardly politically correct, but Edge says: "I think when Bono talks about big girls, he means large girls - not big-breasted. He's talking about women who aren't stick insects. It's pretty tongue-in-cheek and throwaway."

Always

'Always' is the original band jam that gave birth to 'Beautiful Day'. "It really wasn't that unique or special," says Edge. "So when we finished 'Beautiful Day', we went back and said, 'That's a B-side.' It doesn't really stand up."

Conversation on a Barstool

As the title suggests, 'Conversation on a Barstool' is a meandering, whiskey-soaked piece. Written by Bono and Edge for Robert Altman's 1993 movie *Short Cuts* (based on the short stories of American writer Raymond Carver), the lyrics are bruised and bittersweet: *"But I won't be sorry if you won't be/ And I don't want your pity or sympathy/ But for forty five dollars I can make it/ You wait and see."* The song was performed by legendary British-American jazz singer Annie Ross, who also appeared in the film. It slotted neaty onto a soundtrack that also included songs by the likes of Elvis Costello, Iggy Pop and Michael Stipe.

In The Name of the Father

In 1993, Bono teamed up with his old Cedarwood Rwoad mate Gavin Friday and pianist Maurice Seezer on a number of songs for the soundtrack of Jim Sheridan's Oscar-nominated *In The Name of the Father*, starring Daniel Day Lewis, about the wrongly convicted 'Guildford Four', imprisoned for an IRA pub bombing in the UK in the 1970s. *"In the name of United and the BBC/ In the name of Georgie Best and LSD/ In the name of the father/ And his wife the spirit/ You said you did not/ They said you did it."* The tension builds steadily, before exploding into a chaotically tribal, industrial-sounding and impassioned climax. The trio also wrote the ballad 'You Made Me The Thief of Your Heart' for the film's soundtrack. It was the perfect vehicle for Sinead O'Connor's extraordinary vocal talents.

Billy Boola

A funky workout with a big beat and horns aplenty, 'Billy Boola' was co-written and performed by Bono and Gavin Friday, also for the Oscar-winning Jim Sheridan film, *In the Name of the Father*. Originally recorded in STS Studios in Dublin, it played over a scene in which Gerry Conlan and the boys rummage through a prostitute's flat . An overtly sexual song - *"Baby's a big flirt/ Nipples in a tee-shirt/ Took a boat across the drunken sea/ I'm still afloat, you're going down on me"* - it also featured on Gavin's 1995 single, 'You and Me and World War Three'.

Goldeneye

Asked about the most important source of inspiration, the great songwriter Sam Kahn, who won four Academy Awards, including for 'All The Way' and 'Call Me Irresponsible', answered cryptically: "The phonecall." That was how Bono and The Edge were asked to write the theme song to 1995's James Bond movie *Goldeneye* - which starred Irishman Pierce Brosnan as Bond for the first time. Produced by Nellee Hooper and featuring synthy beats, staccato string plucking, canned horn blasts and a bossa nova shuffle, it worked. Written with Tina Turner in mind, she did a fine job on the vocals, building up from a vaguely sinister lower register to a truly spine tingling finish, *"Revenge is a kiss/ this time I won't miss/ Now I've got you in my sight."* Reeased as a single, and included in Turner's *Wildest Dreams* album, the song has been widely remixed, sampled and covered, including by Nicole Scherzinger for the Goldeneye 007 video game.

Holy Joe

In February 1997 U2 announced details of their upcoming PopMart Tour at a press conference in the rather unlikely environs of the lingerie department of a downtown Manhattan Kmart. They played just one song - the B-side of the 'Discotheque' single, 'Holy Joe'. A melodic, guitar-heavy number featuring a catchy chorus of, *"Come on, come on, come on, come on/ Be good to me,"* it was described by the *New York Times* as sounding "like U2 imitating Oasis imitating the British invasion bands of the '60s." They haven't played the song live since.

The Hands That Built America

U2 received their first Oscar nomination for 'The Hands That Built America' which featured on the 2002 Martin Scorsese epic *Gangs of New York*. The song's title was inspired by Horslips' title track to their album *The Man Who Built America*, and was used with the full blessing of that band's singer/bassist Barry Devlin, who has produced a number of U2 videos. The song is about the experiences of 19th century Irish migrants arriving in New York and their contribution to building America: *"Oh my love/ It's a long way we've come/ From the freckled hills/ To the steel and glass canyons."* The soundtrack mix of the song featured Andrea Corr on tin whistle and Sharon Corr of The Corrs on violin. In the Oscars, U2 lost out to Eminem's 'Lose Yourself'.

Electrical Storm

'Electrical Storm' was a 2002 single released to promote the compilation *The Best of 1990-2000*. Equating a lovers' tiff with an upcoming storm, Bono's vocals have rarely sounded so yearning. *"You're in my mind all of the time/ I know that's not enough."* The Anton Corbjin-directed video was shot on location in Eze, France, and depicted Larry Mullen encountering a mermaid, played by English actress Samantha Morton. 'Electrical Storm' reached No. 77 on the US *Billboard* Hot 100; topped the charts in Canada, Spain and Italy; and went Top 10 in most other countries, peaking at No 5 in the UK.

Xanax and Wine

You won't find the line "how to dismantle an atomic bomb" anywhere on 2004's *How To Dismantle an Atomic Bomb*, but it does feature on electro-influenced 'Xanax and Wine', written in a typical U2 frenzy on the second-last night of the recording (*"I'm going nowhere/ Where I am, it is a lot of fun/ There in the desert/ to dismantle an atomic bomb"*). "Bono wanted to get that lyric back onto the record and we didn't have much time so the idea came to start from scratch, replay it with a sparse arrangement and adapt melodies and lyrics to fit the new format," Adam later recalled. "It turned into 'Fast Cars'. It really ended those sessions on a high note." The original song was released as part of a demo set, included with digital box set *The Complete U2*.

Mercy

Originally set to appear on *How to Dismantle an Atomic Bomb*, the anthemic 'Mercy' was dropped at the last moment. However, a bootlegged copy made it onto the Internet in late 2004 and lots of fans fell in love with the song. Some described it as "one of the most U2-ish songs ever written" (*"I was drinking some wine and it turned to blood/ What's the use of religion if you're any good?"*). It took six years for the band to agree, and they finally began playing a revised version in concert in 2010. Recorded live in Brussels, it was included on their limited edition 2010 EP *Wide Awake in Europe*.

The Ballad of Ronnie Drew

'The Ballad of Ronnie Drew', co-written by Bono, The Edge, Simon Carmody and Robert Hunter of Grateful Dead, was a 2008 charity single by U2, Kila and A Band of Bowsies, celebrating the life and work of The Dubliners' legend Ronnie Drew, who was dying of cancer at the time (all proceeds went to the Irish Cancer

Society). U2 teamed up with a veritable Who's Who of Irish musical talent to record the song at Windmill Lane Studios, in Ringsend, on January 14/15, 2008. It was produced by John Reynolds and filmed by John Carney, director of the Academy Award winning *Once*, and the 'Bowsies' present included Mary Black, Mundy, Christy Moore, Sinéad O'Connor, Moya Brennan, Christy Dignam, Gavin Friday, Bob Geldof, Ronan Keating, Damien Dempsey, Shane MacGowan, Mary Coughlan and honorary Irishman Joe Elliot of Def Lepperd (amongst others). Glen Hansard's vocal contribution was recorded over the phone, as he was attending the Academy Awards at the time. Ronnie Drew passed away just a few months after the single's release in August 2008.

Winter

Produced by Eno and Lanois, 'Winter' is a ballad about a soldier in an unspecified war zone written for the closing credits of Jim Sheridan's 2009 thriller *Brothers* – starring Tobey Maguire, Jack Gyllenhaal and Natalie Portman. U2 wanted to include the track on *No Line on the Horizon*, but it was ultimately dropped . The Edge later noted that "though it's a beautiful tune, it doesn't quite fit on our record thematically." A rockier version of 'Winter' was used in the Anton Corbjin film *Linear* that same year. The slower, piano-led *Brothers* version was nominated for a Golden Globe for Best Original Song in 2009, losing out to Ryan Bingham's 'The Weary Kind' (from *Crazy Heart*).

Return of the Stingray Guitar

Featuring a monster guitar riff but no properly finished vocals, 'Return of the Stingray Guitar' was originally written during the sessions for *The Unforgettable Fire* in 1984. Twenty-six years later, the band dusted it off, reworked it, and played it live as the opening track when their 360° Tour hit Europe and South America in 2010. 'Lucifer's Hands', a bonus track on the vinyl release of *Songs of Innocence*, is a re-worked version of it. The opening verse describes an early Lypton Village gathering: "*Punk rock party in a suburban home/ Everybody's famous here but nobody's known/ We got no music 'cause the speaker's blown/ Apart.*" (see also *Songs of Innocence*).

Glastonbury

'Glastonbury' made its live debut in Frankfurt's Commerzbank Arena in August 2010. "This is a new song we're trying out," Bono announced. "It's kind of a rocking 1970s thing. It's called 'Glastonbury'." The band had been scheduled to play the UK's biggest music festival that summer, but the singer's back problems ultimately delayed the show for a year. Curiously, they didn't actually play the song when they finally played Glastonbury in July 2011. Bono didn't enjoy that particular show: "There were a couple of things," he said afterwards. "There was a DJ under the stage, playing music in between sets, and he bumped into our keyboard computer. So we lost all the keyboards... I walked out and realized that the stage was like an ice rink and I was wearing the wrong shoes. I couldn't move – I was stuck on the spot. We were a bit freaked out."

Ordinary Love

It was the (now discredited) Hollywood movie mogul Harvey Weinstein who invited U2 to write a song for the soundtrack of the Nelson Mandela biopic, *Mandela: Long Walk to Freedom*. Having been friends with the South African leader for several years, the band had no hesitation. After seeing a rough cut of the film, they recorded 'Ordinary Love' in New York's Electric Lady Studios. "Writing for films, we try to find a tangent," Bono explained. "It's a complicated love story. We wrote a kind of complicated love song in honour of that." The song was given a limited 10" vinyl release on Record Store Day, November 29, 2013, less than a week before Mandela died. U2 won the 2014 Golden Globe for Best Original Song. The song was also nominated for an Oscar, but lost out to 'Let It Go' from *Frozen*. "It took a while," Edge said, "as all our songs do. We're very proud of it." A new version, titled the 'Extraordinary Mix', was included on the deluxe edition of *Songs of Experience*.

Invisible

"*I'm more than you know/I'm more than you see here/More than you let me be.*" An electro-tinged rock anthem which was first unveiled in a Super Bowl television advertisement, 'Invisible' was released as a free iTunes digital download in February 2014, with Bank of America donating $1 per download to (RED) – the charity co-founded by Bono to fight AIDS. In an interview with BBC Radio 1's Zane Lowe, the singer explained that the song is about him "leaving home with just enough rage to see it through and this feeling of arriving in London, sleeping in the station and coming out into the punk rock explosion that was happening." It was a potent precursor to *Songs of Innocence*. "They were really wild, extraordinary people," he said of the London punks, who made him feel "deeply not extraordinary. You feel invisible and you're screaming to be seen and you've got your band and this is your whole life. It's that feeling of getting out of town." 'Invisible' was then included as a hidden track on the deluxe edition of *Songs of Innocence*.

PICTURE CREDITS

The publishers would like to thank the following sources for their kind permission to reproduce the pictures in this book.

Key: t = Top, b = Bottom, c = Centre, l = Left, r = Right

4. Evan Agostini/Invision/AP/REX/Shutterstock, 7. Simone Cecchetti/Corbis via Getty Images, 8-11. © Patrick Brocklebank, 12. Martyn Goddard/REX/Shutterstock, 13. David Corio/Redferns/Getty Images, 14-15. Photoshot/Paul Slattery/Retna Ltd, 16. David Corio/Redferns/Getty Images, 19 & 20. David Corio/Michael Ochs Archives/Getty Images, 23. Private Collection, 25. Clayton Call/Redferns/Getty Images, 26-27. Clayton Call/Redferns/Getty Images, 29. Rob Verhorst/Redferns/Getty Images, 30-31. Andre Csillag/REX/Shutterstock, 34-35. ITV/REX/Shutterstock, 36. Private Collection, 38. Stephen Wright/Redferns/Getty Images, 39l. Debra Trebitz/Corbis/VCG via Getty Images, 39r. Neal Preston, 40. Mirrorpix, 41 & 42-43. Private Collection, 44. Richard E. Aaron/Redferns/Getty Images, 45. Ebet Roberts/Redferns/Getty Images, 46. Photoshot/Retna, 48. David Corio/Redferns/Getty Images, 49. David Pearson/REX/Shutterstock, 50. Henry Ruggeri, 51. Alamy/DPA Picture Alliance Archive, 52-53. Neal Preston, 54 & 55. Private Collection, 57. Rob Verhorst/Redferns/Getty Images, 58-59. Sipa Press/REX/Shutterstock, 60-61. Peter Carrette Archive/Getty Images, 64-65. Lex van Rossen/MAI/Redferns, 66. Private Collection, 68. Peter Still/Redferns/Getty Images, 70. Neal Preston, 71. Private Collection 73. Neal Preston, 74. Mirrorpix, 75t. Dave Hogan/Hulton Archive/Getty Images, b. Private Collection, 77. Michel Linssen/Redferns/Getty Images, 78-79. Rob Verhorst/Redferns/Getty Images, 81. Michel Linssen/Redferns/Getty Images, 82. Brian Brainerd/The Denver Post via Getty Images, 84. Kevin Cummins/Getty Images, 86. Alamy/A.F. Archive, 87. David Atlas/Retna Ltd., 88. Neal Preston, 89. Peter Noble/Redferns/Getty Images, 90. Philip Grey/Lebrecht Music & Arts, 91t. Neal Preston, b. Aaron Harris, Retna Ltd. 93. Peter Stone/REX/Shutterstock, 94. Private Collection, 96. Paul Bergen/Redferns/Getty Images, 97-99. Private Collection, 100-101. Bob King/Redferns/Getty Images, 102. Mirrorpix, 103t. Neal Preston, b. In Pictures Ltd./Corbis via Getty Images, 105. Rob Verhorst/Redferns/Getty Images, 106-107. Andrew Murray/Sygma, 108. Private Collection, 109. Jon Levy/AFP/Getty Images, 110-111. Tim Mosenfelder/Getty Images, 112-113. Private Collection, 115. Paul Bergen/Redferns/Getty Images, 116-117. Andy Paradise/The Independent/REX/Shutterstock, 118. Kevin Mazur/WireImage, 121. Private Collection, 124. Press Association Images, 126. David Corio/Redferns/Getty Images, 126-127. Robb D Cohen/Retna Ltd., 128. Neal Preston, 129. Photoshot/LFI, 130-131. Insight-Visual UK/Rex/Shutterstock, 132. Private Collection, 135. Press Association Images,138. Bryan Bedder/Getty Images, 140. Press Association Images, 142-143. Simone Cecchetti/Corbis via Getty Images, 144. Alamy/Brooke Ismach/ZUMA Press, 147. Alamy/DPA Picture Alliance Archive, 148-149. Simone Cecchetti/Corbis via Getty Images, 151. Lluis Gene/AFP/Getty Images, 153. Lloyd Bishop/NBC/NBCU Photo Bank, 154, Press Association Images, 156. Justin Sullivan/Getty Images, 160-161. Press Asssocation, 165. Brad Loper/Dallas Morning News, 166. Startraks Photo/REX/Shutterstock, 169. Paul Morigi/Getty Images,170. Eugene Gologursky/Getty Images for NARAS, 175. Brian Rasic/Getty Images, 176. Photoshot/LFI, 177. Canadian Press/REX/Shutterstock, 178. Henry Ruggeri, 179l. Peter Anderson, r. Peter Noble/Getty Images, 181. Private Collection, 183, 185 & 187. Independent News and Media/Getty Images.

Every effort has been made to acknowledge correctly and contact the source and/or copyright holder of each picture and Carlton Books Limited apologises for any unintentional errors or omissions, which will be corrected in future editions of this book.

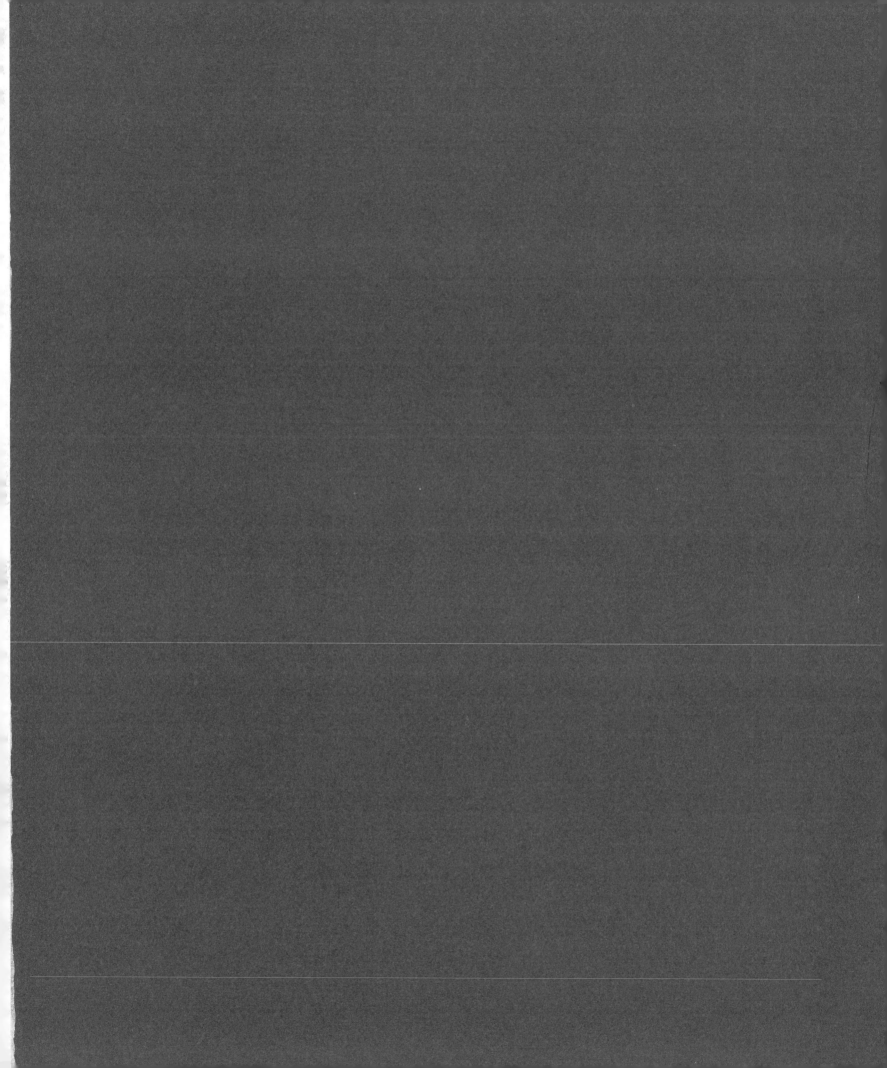